Solution-Focused Brief Therapy with Clients Managing Trauma

Solution-Focused Brief Therapy with Clients Managing Trauma

EDITED BY

Adam S. Froerer
Jacqui von Cziffra-Bergs
Johnny S. Kim
Elliott E. Connie

OXFORD
UNIVERSITY PRESS

OXFORD
UNIVERSITY PRESS

Oxford University Press is a department of the University of Oxford. It furthers
the University's objective of excellence in research, scholarship, and education
by publishing worldwide. Oxford is a registered trade mark of Oxford University
Press in the UK and certain other countries.

Published in the United States of America by Oxford University Press
198 Madison Avenue, New York, NY 10016, United States of America.

Library of Congress Cataloging-in-Publication Data
Names: Froerer, Adam S., editor. | Cziffra-Bergs, Jacqui von, editor. |
Kim, Johnny S., editor. | Connie, Elliott E., editor.
Title: Solution-focused brief therapy with clients managing trauma /
Adam S. Froerer, Jacqui von Cziffra-Bergs, Johnny S. Kim, Elliott E. Connie.
Description: New York, NY : Oxford University Press, [2018] |
Includes bibliographical references and index.
Identifiers: LCCN 2018003374 (print) | LCCN 2018004372 (ebook) |
ISBN 9780190678791 (updf) | ISBN 9780190678807 (epub) |
ISBN 9780190678814 (Online Component) |
ISBN 9780190678784 (preprinted case cover : alk. paper)
Subjects: | MESH: Psychotherapy, Brief—methods |
Stress Disorders, Traumatic—therapy
Classification: LCC RC489.S65 (ebook) | LCC RC489.S65 (print) |
NLM WM 420.5.P5 | DDC 616.89/147—dc23
LC record available at https://lccn.loc.gov/2018003374

9 8 7 6 5 4

Printed by Sheridan Books, Inc., United States of America

■ **Adam S. Froerer:** *To my wonderful wife, Becca, who fills my life with hope. To my kids, Rachel, Toby, and Julia, who have taught me the value of letting hope grow!*

■ **Jacqui von Cziffra-Bergs:** *I would like to dedicate this book to the three people that give me hope and inspire me to teach hope. Geza, Mateo, and Luc—thank you for keeping me real, for making me laugh, and for showing me the extraordinary. Also, I would especially like to thank and honor the late Professor Coley Lamprecht for always believing in me even at times when I did not believe in myself. His incredible support and unconditional trust and belief in my ability has fueled my ambitions and allowed me to soar.*

■ **Johnny S. Kim:** *To my children, Bridget and Shamus, thank you for giving my life so much love, joy, and laughter.*

■ **Elliott E. Connie:** *This book is dedicated to all of the clients who have trusted me with their hearts during their toughest times. I only hope my words help and that the words in this book continue to help.*

■ CONTENTS

■ ACKNOWLEDGMENTS

This book is only possible because of the clients who trusted us with their care and healing. We want to express appreciation for the courage, strength, and hope they shared with us. We would also like to thank our publisher, Dana Bliss, for his support and encouragement throughout this process. Many thanks are due to the contributing authors who contributed significant chapters to this book and were willing to share their work with us and the world. We would like to express appreciation to the reviewers and those around us who provided valuable feedback. Finally, we would like to thank those meaningful people in our personal lives who surround us and fan our hope, not just through this project but also in all aspects of our lives.

■ CONTRIBUTORS

Christopher K. Belous
Mercer University, School of
  Medicine

Kristin Bolton
School of Social Work, University of
  North Carolina, Wilmington

Elliott E. Connie
The Solution Focused University,
  BRIEF International, Private
  Practice

Dawn Crosswhite
University of Denver, Graduate
  School of Social Work, and Private
  Practice

Calyn Crow
Rocky Mountain Solutions, PLLC

Heather Fiske
Private Practice, College of
  Psychologists of Ontario

Cynthia Franklin
Steve Hicks School of Social Work at
  the University of Texas at Austin

Adam S. Froerer
Mercer University, School of
  Medicine, BRIEF International

Johnny S. Kim
University of Denver, Graduate
  School of Social Work

Stephen M. Langer
Director, Northwest Brief Therapy
  Training Center, Olympia,
  Washington, USA

Swathi M. Reddy
Steve Hicks School of Social Work at
  the University of Texas at Austin

Carla P. Smith
Mercer University, School of
  Medicine

Karla Gonzalez Suitt
Pontifical Catholic University of
  Chile, School of Social Work

Jacqui von Cziffra-Bergs
Solution Focused Institute of
  South Africa

Cecil R. Walker
Mercer University, School of
  Medicine

Stacey Anne Williams
University of Denver
Graduate School of Social Work -
  (Animal-Assisted Social Work)
Josef Korbel School of International
  Studies (MA)
Aurora Police Department Victim
  Services Unit - Victim Advocate

1 Introduction

■ ELLIOTT E. CONNIE

Hope. Having been given the privilege of writing the opening chapter for this book, I wondered about how to begin. Then it hit me: this is actually a book about *optimism*. Or perhaps even more accurately, this is a book about courage. So I cannot think of a better word to open this book than the word *hope*. I don't mean this as a euphemism. In fact, I mean that quite literally; this really is a book about hope, especially since hope is the key ingredient to helping people overcome challenging events in their lives. So although this book will feature content and treatment suggestions for managing trauma, it is just a stage on which to demonstrate the power of hope.

In this book we (the editors and authors) will be discussing people that have been faced with overwhelming traumas in their lives; we will be explaining how to use this approach in various settings with survivors of traumatic experiences. However, before we get into that I want to make sure you understand a few things about this approach because it will help you make sense of the content that comes later in this book.

As I mentioned above, hope is powerful, and hope is a crucial component of solution-focused brief therapy (SFBT). In fact, I would even take this statement a step further; I argue that any effective psychotherapy must contain an element of hope. This means that if the professional does not believe in the client's ability to change, then client-change is less likely to occur. This is a radical statement that places some onus for change on the therapist and what the therapist does during psychotherapy sessions. In SFBT, hope is overt and is a clear part of the conversation, which means that hope should also be a clear and overt component of this book.

It is not lost on the editors of this book that this may be a different way for readers to view the topic of trauma. Many books written for helping professionals are focused on educating the reader on the problem itself. It is not uncommon for several chapters of professional books to focus on diagnostic symptoms, possible implications of a given diagnosis, and/or potential historical factors that might contribute to the client/patient becoming more vulnerable to troublesome situations. In this context, a book like this one about trauma is focused on increasing the reader's knowledge about trauma. You would typically read something about the potential causes of trauma, the many diagnostic features that distinguish various types of trauma, and the devastating impact of experiencing or witnessing a trauma on potential clients. While I believe that sort of learning is important, I have often wondered if this is the best way to go about truly mastering the skill of psychotherapy and help clients managing trauma experience more and more hope. I am excited that this book is one that will shift the focus from the problems associated with trauma to the client, their strength, their capacity for change, and of course to *hope*.

This shift toward hope is both significant and necessary in truly understanding the essence of the solution-focused approach. This hopeful shift is also necessary in the development and mastery of the language and psychotherapy skills that allow professionals to use this approach with any client, regardless of their presenting problem, even trauma. I know that may seem like a hyperbolic statement, but with this approach it is true. In the following chapters we will supplement hopeful case examples with supporting research evidence about the efficacy of this approach. But before we get to this important material I would like to share a foundational example of hope.

Before I was introduced to the solution-focused approach I was in a job that required me to use cognitive-behavioral therapy (CBT). It is certainly not my intention to say anything negative about CBT; however, it wasn't the best fit for my personality and was not the way I wanted to work with clients. At that time, I did not know there were other ways of working with people, so I just assumed it was up to me to figure out a way to make this approach work. In my attempt to become proficient with CBT I spent countless hours in training (usually mandated by my employer) and read many CBT books. By the time I was introduced to SFBT I believed the idea that understanding the details of the problem was requisite for effective therapy. In fact, I believed in this idea so completely that although I listened to the lecture that introduced me to solution-focused brief therapy, I spent more time doubting what I was hearing than I did actually listening to the content of the lecture itself.

Looking back, the one thing that stuck with me from that lecture, despite my criticisms of the approach, was the idea that a psychotherapist could help clients overcome problems without "focusing" on them. This idea did seem to make sense on some level to me because I had experienced improvements in my own life without directly confronting or investigating the "root cause" of my experiences; I just hadn't thought about it like this before; besides, my clinical training hadn't focused on this.

Despite my initial skepticism, I kept thinking about the ideas presented during that lecture. Through the years this idea of helping without "focusing" on the problem has continued to influence me. Perhaps an additional analogy will help explain why this is important. Imagine I am someone with a significant goal—let's use weight loss as an example. In my efforts to lose weight, would it be more helpful to focus on how I gained weight or to sort out the path to being healthy? If I talk about all of the unhealthy food I ate over the years and all the healthy foods I should have eaten but didn't, and if I talk about the exercise that I should have done but didn't, does any of that help me lose a single pound? No, focusing on the problem doesn't help me move toward a helpful solution.

On the other hand, if I begin following an exercise program, if I eat healthy foods in appropriate quantities, and if I gather supporters around me, I am likely to begin losing weight. I can reach my goals without focusing on what caused me to gain weight.

When the question is posed about weight loss, how we traditionally think about this concept begins to make sense. However, it is also worth asking a similar question in the context of psychotherapy: Do we need to focus on what caused the problem in order move in a helpful direction? If someone has had a difficult (or even a traumatic) experience in their life and they have a goal they would like to achieve that is being impacted by their life experience, would it be more helpful to focus on all of the details surrounding that troubling life event— or would it be more helpful to focus on the path to accomplishing their goal in spite of the troubling event from the past? We proposed that focusing on the path to achieving change is more helpful. It was in this way that the solution-focused approach made some sense to me during that first lecture, even though I was having a hard time fully accepting what I was hearing.

Ironically it was a book about another approach that drove home the point about the power of hope and impacted my belief in the solution-focused approach. In his book *Man's Search for Meaning*, Viktor Frankl (1959) explains the role of hope in his ability to deal with the atrocities of one of the most dreadful events in human history: the Holocaust, which took place during World War II in an attempt to exterminate European Jews. Frankl (1959) shared several stories in which even the smallest hints of hope carried him through some of the traumas he experienced while imprisoned in a concentration camp. Perhaps the story that illustrated the power of hope most tangibly comes from what Frankl shared about what would occur as the prisoners were served their meals. In one of his examples, when it was time to eat, the prisoners would line up and have soup ladled into their bowls. Given the nature of these camps, the soup they were served didn't have much in the way of substantial ingredients such as meat and potatoes. In fact, much of what the prisoners were served was merely the broth of the soup. However, occasionally the person serving the meal would accidently drop the ladle into the soup, causing it to sink to the bottom where the few pieces of meat and potatoes rested. In these cases, the person to receive the next serving of soup was quite lucky, as their bowl would surely contain a bit more sustenance than usual. What were the chances that he would be the prisoner to receive this little bonus? But this was the type of thing that Frankl would hope for as he coped with the horrors of his environment.

According to Frankl, a trained psychiatrist, he noticed that he could predict the impending deaths of his fellow prisoners in the concentration camp when he noticed they lost hope: the hope of seeing loved ones after the war, the hope of surviving the war, the hope that life could get better, and so on. When people lost these hopes they would perish within days. In response to this, Frankl began to develop habits to ensure that he would be able to maintain his hope. In similar ways, we can help our clients to begin looking for reasons to hope.

In reading this story, as well as the others contained in Frankl's book, I could not help but reminisce about the role hope played in my own life. I thought about the difficult situations I had to overcome, the lofty goals I pursued, and how the presence of even an inkling of hope helped me along the way. I also had another thought that would impact my work as a psychotherapist and shape my thinking about the solution-focused approach going forward. If hope is as powerful as it seemed to be, then we should be working on ways to make hope more overt and the center of therapy.

This single thought caused me to look at the solution-focused approach, as well as trauma, through a different lens. Instead of thinking that people needed to have an understanding of the origins of their pain, or an acceptance of their traumatic experiences (as some approaches emphasized), I began thinking that perhaps having more hope for a new future would be more helpful. Perhaps thinking about a future wherein the client is the person they aspire to be, as opposed to the person who is overwhelmed by a traumatic event, would be a more efficient way to benefit from psychotherapy. The only approach that seemed to be in line with these thoughts was solution-focused brief therapy.

■ THE HISTORY OF THE SOLUTION-FOCUSED APPROACH

Since the following chapter of this book contains a detailed description of SFBT, I would just like to point out a couple of aspects about the origins of this approach and allow the subsequent chapters to further elaborate on this topic. The reason for needing to understand the beginnings of this approach are quite simple and pragmatic: it provides the context for why we are doing the things we are doing now in our work from this approach.

The first thing you must understand is that from its inception SFBT has been an evolving approach, and this remains true into the 21st century. So, as you read this text about how we use this approach to work with people who have experienced a trauma, understand that this information is not static. This may seem like a bit of a paradox, as this is both a book about how to use SFBT with clients managing trauma and a book that expresses the idea that SFBT is used the same way with all clients regardless of the issue that brought them into therapy, including trauma. But this approach in its current guise may change as we continue to learn more and more about what helps people. This approach was founded on the process of observing what works and putting that approach into practice. By stating what we do to help clients managing trauma now, we don't want to lose the value of believing that we might still come up with increasingly effective ways. We'll keep watching for these improvements, and we hope you will too.

This belief in continued evolution has been the case within SFBT from the beginnings of Steve de Shazer's work at the Mental Research Institute (MRI) under the tutelage of John Weakland. As the solution-focused approach evolved and de Shazer moved to Milwaukee, Wisconsin with Insoo Kim Berg, an analysis of the problem was eventually dropped all together; they began, instead, to only look at the client's preferred future. Because of this evolution and move away from problem analysis, a SFBT professional now conducts a SFBT session with someone who has experienced a trauma and may not ever be aware of the client's traumatic past. A professional taking this approach should not be thought of as neglectful but, in fact, respectful of the client. This distinction gets back to precisely the importance of hope that I mentioned above. The emphasis of the approach is on the future—not just any future but the future that the client most hopes for. Thus, a professional using this approach should be compelled to focus the conversation on the client's hoped-for future. Imagine the difference a client will feel when they get to talk about the future they hope for rather than the past they would like to forget. This future focus is not compromised by the knowledge of a traumatic experience in the client's past; if anything, it makes the presence of a hoped-for future even more critical for the process of change. Throughout this book you will see many examples of clients who have experienced various traumas; however, do not get sucked into the trauma story to the point that you lose sight of the client's strength. Do not immerse yourself in the trauma story to the extent that you no longer believe that the client can experience a change simply from describing their hoped-for future as a result of answering solution-focused questions. Do not get so taken in by the traumas being described that you forget to the see the hope that is being expressed in each of the situations. More than anything else, this is the message I would like to leave you with as you read this book: be more interested in your client's capacity to change than you are in following their trauma narrative. Trauma narratives are not where hope lies, and they are not the best way to inspire change.

The SFBT approach has been described as a future-focused approach ever since it was developed by the team of clinicians at the Brief Family Therapy Center in Milwaukee, Wisconsin, led by Steve de Shazer and Insoo Kim Berg. After observing hundreds of hours of therapy over the course of several years, the team developed major tenets that have guided this approach. It is important to note that SFBT is not "theory-based" but was pragmatically developed by the team in Milwaukee with many professionals contributing to these ideas from simply observing what worked in the therapy room.

It is difficult to recite the history of the SFBT approach in a single chapter and do it, as well as all of the people who contributed to the development of this approach, justice. So I will only focus on a few key parts that are relevant to this chapter.

First, the story of the SFBT approach starts with John Weakland becoming friends with Steve de Shazer while he was living in Palo Alto, California. It was also John Weakland who introduced de Shazer to Insoo Kim Berg in the hopes they would get along, since their professional ideas seemed similar. This not only led to Steve and Insoo becoming lifelong professional partners but also resulted in a marriage that would last until Steve's death in 2005. The couple eventually moved to Milwaukee from California and began working with a team to create solution-focused brief therapy. According to de Shazer, when they moved to Milwaukee their work still looked very much like the work of the MRI. They continued to be interested in problem patterns and giving clients tasks that would lead to change, which would in turn impact the presence of the problem (Ratner, George, & Iveson, 2012).

Eventually, according to Ratner et al. (2012), their work evolved to become more focused on exceptions, with a keen interest on what the client wanted instead of what the client did not want (or even what they wanted less of). This shift began while the team was working with a family that was reported as having exactly 23 problems they wanted to solve. The team, not knowing which problem to start with, asked the family to focus on the things they wanted to keep the same so they could describe those things to the team when they returned to therapy. To the team's surprise, when the family returned they reported that many of the problems they initially complained about had been solved. The family had made so much progress that they soon decided that they no longer needed the therapy. The Milwaukee team was so affected by this progress that they began asking other clients to notice things in their lives they wanted to stay the same. The results were consistent: clients continued to improve without even focusing on the problem, and the team became more and more impressed. They set up an experiment where they gave this assignment to every client, referring to this as the first session formula task (FSFT), and the outcomes continued to be remarkable (Ratner et al., 2012).

This was the beginning of the solution-focused departure from interventions that are linked to the client-specific problem presentation. Even in the 21st century, this is a groundbreaking idea, but in the early 1980s it was nothing short of earth shattering. The team could not ignore the results of their research; this generic intervention was being given to clients, regardless of their presenting problems, and time and time again positive outcomes were achieved. Clients were reporting positive outcomes without spending any time focused on what originally brought them to therapy, instead focusing on what they wanted the future to look like. De Shazer later said that it was out of this experiment that the SFBT approach was born.

In reading the subsequent chapters of this book there will be the temptation to think of how to use the SFBT to help clients overcome the different types of trauma highlighted throughout these chapters. You might feel overwhelmed, as the Milwaukee team did, by the presence of significant effects. You might feel tempted to do what you have always done. But I urge you to fight the temptation to think of this approach in that way. Be willing to see something new, like the Milwaukee team did. Instead of succumbing to the temptation to fix your clients' trauma-related problems, allow these chapters to convince you that clients can overcome the kinds of traumas included in this book and many more. Allow these chapters to convince you that you can believe in your clients. Allow the chapters to convince you that clients can have hope in themselves. That hope that clients can feel and reexperience is the curative element that brings lasting change for clients. This hope is the element that will truly help clients manage their traumatic experiences. People are amazing. You need to be able to hold on to the belief that people are amazing as you engage in these SFBT conversations with clients, especially with clients who are managing trauma. Holding on to this view is important for any psychotherapist, but it is especially true for professionals using this approach. Because this is a questions-based approach, and these questions must be based in the client's hope, clinicians using this approach must ask their questions from a place of hope. If the professional loses hope in the client, the questions they ask will also inherently change. If clinicians lose hope in their clients' abilities and strength, they may stop asking their clients hopeful questions altogether.

Let me use an example to highlight the importance of this hopeful idea that was stumbled upon in those early days. I met with a client early in my practice who taught me this lesson. The client was a woman in her mid-twenties that I'll refer to as Kimberly. When Kimberly arrived for her session, I could quickly tell that she had been really struggling with something. The was evident because she was crying while she was waiting for me in my waiting room. I escorted her to my therapy office, and we began to work. From the opening question the SFBT approach is different from other more problem-focused therapies. While other professionals may have reacted to her tears—with "Are you OK?" or "What's troubling you today?" or even "What brings you to therapy?"—SFBT does not begin therapy in this problem-focused way. In doing solution-focused work my initial task was to first identify her desired outcome from the therapy; this was done by asking, "What are your best hopes from our work together?" The client's response was somewhat surprising given what I later learned about her.

She wiped away her tears and stated, "All I want is to be happy." In hindsight, this answer should not have been that surprising. Regardless of what a person has been through, or what traumas they have experienced or witnessed, the pursuit of happiness is a reasonable desire and makes a wonderful focus of therapy. As a consequence of asking this best-hopes question instead of a problem-focused question (even though there was a temptation to ask if she was okay), the conversation immediately shifted toward what her life would need to look like to help her accomplish her happiness. We got to have a "happiness" conversation as opposed to a conversation that was dominated with the details of her problems, and we got to have a conversation that was not overrun with the very apparent absence of hope. If I had stopped to conduct a trauma assessment or other problem-focused task, I would have missed the opportunity to engage in creating change by talking about what she wanted rather than where she had come from. In that first session, the client worked hard to answer my questions. The whole session I was aware that this client was in a tough spot in life, but I pressed on asking SFBT questions. I did this because doing so conveys complete trust and hope in my client. Compared to my original training in problem-focused approaches, this conversation was very different. In spite of the difficult circumstances that were clearly present in her life, we talked about something that was just as present in her life but perhaps a bit less obvious: her hoped-for future. Believing that our clients hope for something different and better is the key to asking questions, even when it is hard, that encourages them to reflect on this innate hope.

In short, SFBT is a conversation about the details of the client's hoped-for future. This is always a truth in this approach, regardless of the client's referral problem(s). In working with Kimberly, when we arrived at the end of the session, I hadn't learned that much about her problem, but that did not matter. What did matter, and what she learned a tremendous amount about, was her own happiness. In describing the details of her hoped-for future she made discoveries about how to attain happiness. For example, she described the importance of holding her husband in the same way that she hugs her children. When asked how that would be different, Kimberly responded by explaining that she did not like to be touched; as a consequence, she did not usually hug her husband. This was a significant discovery for Kimberly on multiple levels. Firstly, prior to this moment she would have described herself as someone who did not like hugs, but in her responses she realized she does, in fact, enjoy hugging (or at least can hug others and feel okay) as she proved in her actions as a mother towards her children. She hugs them, and in doing so, can no longer describe herself as a person incapable of hugging. Secondly, and perhaps most significantly, she realized that she was capable of changing the way she treated her husband—something that she wondered if she would ever be able to do. I want to note that at no point did I ask what was blocking her ability to hug her husband. That sort of question would have distracted from the work the client was doing in the session, and it would have interfered with her ability to make discoveries related to her particular desired outcome.

When Kimberly arrived for her follow-up session two weeks later it was clear from the moment I saw her in my lobby that things were different. In this session the client explained that there had been a number of changes in her life that were significant. The most profound were the changes that had taken place in her marriage that helped her to have hope that she was overcoming her previous traumatic experiences. She explained that after the session she decided to hug her husband every morning. This evolved into a hug and kiss; then it was a hug, kiss, and longer embrace. She remarked that she and her husband had never been happier. She was surprised by what she achieved after only one session and mentioned she had been in therapy most of her life after being violently raped in her late teens. Since that event, she did not like being touched and as a result had created a relationship where there was little or no touching. However, when she started thinking about the pursuit of her happiness, as opposed to the trauma event, her actions and capabilities immediately changed. Hope increased, and therefore change occurred, without ever talking about the traumatic events.

This kind of hope and lasting change is what this book is about, how to shift client focus from the problem to their desired outcome using language and questions. Even though the title of this book includes the word "trauma" and even gives the impression that this is a book about trauma, it is actually a book about the human ability to overcome even the most difficult circumstances. This is a book about managing trauma with hope, optimism, and courage. This is a book about using the solution-focused approach to honor this pursuit toward hope. And just as the team in Milwaukee discovered, it is never really about the problem.

Enjoy the book!

■ REFERENCES

Frankl, V. (1959). *Man's search for meaning*. New York: Washington Square.

Ratner, H., George, E., & Iveson, C. (2012). *Solution focused brief therapy: 100 key points & techniques*. Hove, U.K.: Routledge.

2 Intersection of SFBT and Trauma

■ JOHNNY S. KIM AND ADAM S. FROERER

■ OVERVIEW OF TRAUMA

Clinicians from varying disciplines and across many treatment settings are recognizing the role trauma has played in their clients' lives. Studies have found that more than two-thirds of the general population will experience a traumatic event at some point in their lives. In the United States, one in five will experience a significant traumatic event in any given year (Galea, Nandi, & Vlahov, 2005). There is a great emphasis in the helping profession to provide trauma-informed care and to understand how exposure to various traumas pose short-term and long-term risks for the clients (Hanson & Lang, 2016). Despite the recent focus on trauma, the history of trauma can be seen in the work of Sigmund Freud, who theorized and wrote about trauma in the late 19th century (Jones & Cureton, 2014). For example, Freud theorized that childhood trauma, especially incest, caused hysteria. While Freud later abandoned this theory, Freud continued to study trauma and looked at symptoms experienced by World War I veterans. He proposed a model of trauma where people struggle with unbearable situations such as war and where people also wrestle with unacceptable impulses such as in the case of incest (Smyth, 2013). Those studying trauma began focusing on the experiences of male soldiers in various wars and conflicts and their reactions to the various horrors they experienced. Focus then shifted to finding interventions for the traumatic stress soldiers experienced during World War II and the Vietnam War in an effort to rehabilitate them so they could be redeployed (Jones & Cureton, 2014). During the mid- and late-1900s, trauma expanded to focus on various natural disasters and the mental impact on those involved. Mental health practitioners and researchers studied the traumatic effects of the 1942 Cocoanut Grove nightclub fire in Boston and the 1972 Buffalo Creek flood in West Virginia (Smyth, 2013). In the 1990s, aspects of trauma were being applied to victims of sexual abuse, domestic violence, and child abuse (Jones & Cureton, 2014). More recently, terrorist attacks in the United States (as well as abroad) such as the 9/11 attack on New York City have helped draw more attention to trauma. Clinicians and mental health researchers studying trauma began to educate the public on how the harmful and public health costs associated with this problem can affect all individuals as a result of violence, neglect, loss, wars, and disasters (SAMHSA, 2014).

Trauma was introduced as a mental health problem in 1980 with the diagnosis of posttraumatic stress disorder (PTSD) in the third edition of the *Diagnostic Statistical Manual* (*DSM-III*; APA, 1980). The *DSM-III* described trauma as an unusual event that a person experiences and something outside of the range of normal experience. The idea behind this concept of traumatic events was to distinguish common painful experiences, such as divorce or serious illness, with unusual human experiences such as the Nazi genocide on the Jews during World War II, or torture experienced during war (Friedman, n.d.). This initial definition and understanding of trauma and PTSD would evolve as more research led to better understanding of the various aspects of trauma.

In the mid-1990s and 2000s, the *DSM-IV* and *DSM-IV-TR* were introduced as updates that further changed the definition of trauma and PTSD. In the *DSM-IV* and revised *DSM-IV-TR*, PTSD was listed as an anxiety disorder and emphasized a fear-based characteristic in making this diagnosis (Friedman, n.d.). The revised definitions also expanded what were considered traumatic experiences to include events such as car accidents, torture, physical abuse, rape, assaults, death of a loved one, difficult divorces, and natural disasters (Jones & Cureton, 2014; Smyth, 2013).

The *DSM-5* is the latest update and was released in 2013. Part of the long separation between updates was due to major changes to the DSM, in particular to how trauma was defined and core criteria to PTSD diagnosis. One of the first major differences is in the reclassification of PTSD away from anxiety disorder and as a separate category. Thus PTSD is listed as a new category called trauma and stressor-related disorders (TSRD), which all have the common characteristic of exposure to a traumatic event or otherwise adverse environmental event. Other changes include the expansion of the exposure to traumatic event criteria to include learning events that happened to a close friend or family, repeated or extreme exposure to details of the event (vicarious trauma), and exposure to sexual violence. Lastly, the new PTSD criteria also has separate criteria for preschool age children (six years and younger) as a new subtype (Friedman, n.d.). These latest revisions in the *DSM-5* demonstrate the evolved changes to our understanding of trauma and PTSD. While social constructionist SFBT practitioners may likely not approve of classifying trauma and PTSD in this diagnostic manner, the implications of the changes to the *DSM-5* does impact whether clients can receive services for mental health treatment that is covered by insurance.

Given the varying changes and understanding of trauma, we will conceptualize the concept based on the broad definition proposed by the Substance Abuse and Mental Health Services Administration (SAMHSA). This U.S. federal agency was one of the earliest proponents of studying trauma and its negative impact on individuals in order to develop more trauma-informed care. SAMHSA weighed into the trauma discussion in 1994 when it convened the Dare to Vision Conference on trauma, which was the first national conference in the United States where women trauma survivors talked about their experiences. In 2001, SAMHSA also funded the National Child Traumatic Stress Initiative, which aimed to promote attention and understanding of child trauma and develop effective treatment interventions (SAMHSA, 2014). Furthermore, SAMHSA worked to develop a definition of the concept of trauma that practitioners, researchers, and clients could share. Consequently, according to the Substance Abuse and Mental Health Services Administration (SAMHSA, 2014), "Individual trauma results from an event, series of events, or set of circumstances that is experienced by an individual as physically or emotionally harmful or life threatening and that has lasting adverse effects on the individual's functioning and mental, physical, social, emotional, or spiritual being" (p. 7). This current definition of trauma is broad enough to encompass the many forms of trauma this book hopes to address and a nice working definition for us to use when talking about SFBT techniques.

■ VARIOUS ASPECTS OF TRAUMA

Despite the great interest in trauma, the study of trauma in its current form has really only been around since the 1980s (Smyth, 2013). The broad definition of trauma proposed by SAMHSA (2014) is useful because it incorporates three important elements (the three E's), when conceptualizing trauma. The first is an *event* or *multiple events* where there is an actual threat of bodily or psychological harm, or neglect for a child that jeopardizes healthy development. This component is a key criteria used by the *DSM-5* when defining trauma and PTSD and necessary to meet the clinical criteria under their new category of "Trauma and Stressor-Related Disorders." Examples of events could be commercial airline crashes, tornados, wars, mass shootings, fires, terrorist attacks, sexual assaults, interpersonal violence, death, and serious physical injuries (Kilpatrick et al., 2013).

The second element is how a person *experiences* these events and is important when determining whether an event is traumatic or not. For example, there are many soldiers who fight in multiple wars who are not adversely affected by those experiences while others are severely impacted psychologically and emotionally. Research on trauma recognizes that an individual's experience and interpretation is another key factor in determining whether a problem is trauma-related one. This is also in evidence when a natural disaster impacts a large number of people. There are many who react differently to the life-threatening event, with some able to cope and move on, while many others experience anxiety and fear and are unable to move on with their lives. It is how the person experiences these events—specifically how they label and assign meaning to their experiences—that influences their reactions to the events. Many risk and protective factors, such as cultural beliefs, social supports, maturity, socioeconomic status, and mental health, also contribute to how people interpret these events and contribute to whether a person experiences trauma-related problems.

The third E involves the lasting adverse *effects* of the event. This component of the definition recognizes that individuals experience negative effects from the events such as memory problems, lack of attention, inability to control emotions or behaviors, trust issues in relationships, and inability to cope with daily life stresses caused by an event or series of events. The deleterious effects may be short lived or long lasting and may occur right away after the event or occur after a delay (SAMHSA, 2014). The consequences of historical trauma on several generations of disadvantaged or oppressed groups is also being incorporated into the concept of trauma. Examples include the oppression of African Americans and Native Americans as well as survivors of the Holocaust and Japanese American internment camps (Smyth, 2013).

■ TYPES OF TRAUMA AND COMORBIDITY

Many people will experience some traumatic event in their lives, yet they will not develop PTSD because of other protective factors that allow them to regain a sense of normalcy (SAMHSA, 2014). A brief overview of some of the major types of trauma commonly encountered in the counseling field will be described in this section. Below is a listing and description of common types of trauma presented by Briere and Scott (2015):

- *Child Abuse.* This wide-ranging category can include sexual abuse (e.g., rape or fondling), physical abuse (beatings and severe spankings), psychological abuse (verbal abuse), and neglect (malnutrition).
- *Mass Interpersonal Violence.* This is a newer category where a high number of injuries or deaths are caused by intentional violence separate from war. Examples include the terrorist attacks on the United States on September 11, 2001, as well as mass human rights abuses in various countries.
- *Natural Disasters.* These consist of large-scale environmental events that usually produce injury or deaths to a substantial number of people. Typical examples include tornadoes, major flooding, and tsunamis.
- *Large-Scale Transportation Accidents.* These major events involve airplanes, buses, automobiles, trains, and boats with large number of people on board where there are multiple injuries and fatalities.
- *Fire and Burns.* House or building fires can cause injury or death to individuals that causes serious emotional, psychological, and physical problems.
- *Rape and Sexual Assault.* This category includes any forced sexual contact that is nonconsensual and arises through the use of threat or physical force.

- *Stranger Physical Assault.* This involves an unknown assailant who acts out violently toward another through muggings, beatings, stabbings, shootings, strangulations, or other aggressive actions.
- *Intimate Partner Violence.* Physical or sexual assaultive behaviors involving adults in a cohabiting relationship. It is often referred to as spousal abuse, domestic violence, or wife battering.
- *Sex Trafficking.* Forced or coerced recruitment, transport, harboring, or receipt of individuals for commercial sexual exploitation. Most women and girls (although boys are also involved occasionally) are forced into activities such as prostitution, pornography, stripping, becoming mail-order brides, and sex tourism.
- *Torture.* Physical or psychological techniques to intentionally inflict pain or suffering in order to obtain information or confession, or to serve as punishment for an act.
- *War.* Difficulties arise out of combat that can involve things such as death and witnessing or experiencing, for example, physical injury and disfigurement.
- *Murder or Suicide.* Witnessing or learning about death or serious injury of another person, typically via murder or suicide, can cause distress for individuals.
- *Life-threatening Medical Conditions.* Individuals may also experience trauma when experiencing or facing major illnesses and invasive medical procedures associated with pain or life-threatening situations. Examples of this category include major surgery, heart attacks, cancer, and HIV/AIDS.

As you can see from the various types of trauma noted above by Briere and Scott (2015), there are many ways people can experience trauma that leaves them anxious and unable to deal with the distressing feelings and thoughts. Much of this book delves into how to use SFBT with the many types of major trauma our clients experience.

A body of research has also shown that many people with substance abuse problems have also experienced trauma in their lives. Theories attempting to explain this connection found a reciprocal pathway where trauma increases the risk of developing substance abuse, and substance abuse increases the risk of experiencing trauma. People who suffer from trauma turn to substances (e.g., alcohol, drugs, prescription medication) as a way to cope with the many intense emotions and traumatic stressors. Conversely, people who abuse substances engage in risky behaviors (e.g., driving under the influence, walking in unsafe neighborhoods, engaging in fights) that increase their chances of experiencing or witnessing significant harm or life-threatening events (NCTSN, 2008). Therefore, it should not be surprising that the lifetime substance use disorder for men with PTSD in the United States is 52% for alcohol use disorder and 35% for drug use disorder. For women with PTSD, the substance use disorder rate is slightly lower with 28% for alcohol use and 27% for drug use disorder (Najavits & Johnson, 2014). Studies have also found that teens who had experienced trauma through physical or sexual abuse were three times more likely to have past or current substance use and that more than 70% of adolescents receiving substance abuse treatment had a history of trauma exposure (NCTSN, 2008).

Similarly, many people with severe mental health disorders have also experienced trauma in their lives. This is especially the case with PTSD, which most often have a comorbid diagnosis with depression, anxiety, or other personality disorders (Friedman, n.d.). Studies have reported that between 30% and 80% of individuals with substance abuse problems also reported experiencing some traumatic event in their lifetime (Blakey & Smith Hatcher, 2013). Breslau and Kessler (2001) reported that almost five out of every six (roughly 80%) of community mental health clinic clients have experienced at least one incident of trauma in their lifetime. Research studies suggest that stress related to trauma not only increases the risk for mental illness but also the symptom severity of mental illness (Smyth, 2013).

■ CURRENT RESEARCH ON TRAUMA AND COMMON EVIDENCE-BASED INTERVENTIONS

Several federal and private registries have been established to identify current practices and psychotherapy approaches that have sufficient evidence demonstrating their effectiveness with various psychotherapy-related problems. Some of these registries that include trauma-related treatments are the *National Registry of Evidence-based Programs and Practices* (NREPP; https://nrepp.samhsa.gov/landing.aspx) maintained by The Substance Abuse and Mental Health Services Administration (SAMHSA), *California Evidence-Based Clearinghouse for Child Welfare* (http://www.cebc4cw.org/), *The Campbell Collaboration* (https://www.campbellcollaboration.org/), and the *What Works Clearinghouse* (https://ies.ed.gov/ncee/wwc/). Although these registries covered more than trauma treatments, they still contain some of the most current lists of effective trauma treatments with various populations of trauma survivors. Other helpful places to locate information about effective trauma treatments are the *National Child Traumatic Stress Network* (www.nctsn.org) and the *National Center for Trauma-Informed Care* (http://www.samsha.gov/nctic).

The following list includes a summary of some of the therapeutic practices that have been considered evidence based for working with trauma survivors according to SAMHSA's NREPP registry (http://nrepp.samhsa.gov/AdvancedSearch.aspx).

- *Accelerated Resolution Therapy* (ART) was developed in 2008 by Kip, Rosenzweig, Hernandez, Shuman, Sullivan, and colleagues (2013). This is an exposure-based treatment that takes place within a two-week period. It incorporates some rapid eye movement and some visualization techniques. ART is a form of cognitive-behavioral therapy.

- *Mind–Body Bridging Substance Abuse Treatment* is an intensive group therapy program that takes place during 20 sessions of intensive group therapy that takes place during two-hour group sessions over a 10-week period. This treatment has foundations in CBT and includes instructor-led psychoeducation sessions using techniques employed to increase the client's personal awareness of physical sensations. It also counterbalances these with efforts to interrupt dysfunctional habits. Emphasis is also given to improving metacognition skills through exposure and skills training (Nakamura, Lipschitz, Kanarowski, McCormick, Sutherland, & Melow-Murchie, 2015).

- *Trauma Recovery and Empowerment Model (TREM)* is a group-based treatment program for women exposed to sexual and physical abuse. This approach is founded on cognitive therapy and incorporates techniques to aid in cognitive restructuring, psychoeducation, and skills training. This approach helps women process their physical, emotional, and psychological symptoms and includes the processing of the trauma with an emphasis on increasing capacity to cope (Fallot, McHugo, Harris, & Xie, 2011).

- *Trauma-Focused CBT (TF-CBT)* combines aspects of cognitive, behavioral, interpersonal, and family therapy to address various forms of trauma. This treatment focuses on creating a therapeutic alliance and providing psychoeducation and skills training and development. The acronym PRACTICE helps to describe the components of this therapy: P—Psychoeducation, R—Relaxation skills, A—Affective expression and modulation skills, C—Cognitive coping and processing skills, T—Trauma narration and processing, I—In vivo mastery of trauma reminders, C—Conjoint child–parent sessions, and E—Enhancing safety and future developmental trajectory. TF-CBT can be conducted in individual or group therapy settings (Jensen et al., 2013).

- *Sensory Motor Arousal Regulation Therapy (SMART)* is predominantly for children and youth ages 2 to 21 who have experienced interpersonal trauma. SMART focuses intervention on a three-pronged approach (1) trauma regulation, (2) trauma processing, and (3) attachment development. The emphasis is on helping children and caregivers to interact in ways that increase the child's sense of security. Physical items such as balls and weighted blankets are used to increase sensory awareness of the child (Warner, Spinazzola, Westcott, Gunn, & Hodgdon, 2014).

Additional treatments shown to be effective with trauma survivors are included on the Veteran Affairs website. Three of the major treatments include:

- *Exposure Therapy.* During exposure therapy, clients are challenged to face their fears and learn to control their reactions to their trauma memories.

Clients start by retelling details and memories of the trauma that are the least troubling and gradually move to telling more and more troubling details and memories (*desensitization process*). Clients are also taught and practice relaxation skills that can be utilized during times of distress. This telling and retelling of trauma memories happens multiple times during exposure therapy sessions.

- *Eye Movement Desensitization and Reprocessing (EMDR)*. During this treatment, clients are encouraged to repeatedly retell their trauma story with as much detail as possible. While retelling the trauma experience, clients focus on other physical aspects such as eye movement, hand tapping, or rhythmic sounds. It is hypothesized that diverting one's attention enables the client to reprocess the trauma in a less distressing environment, thus helping the client to heal. The physical stimuli may also serve as coping strategies during times of distress that occur outside of therapy.
- *Brief Psychodynamic*. The focus on psychodynamic therapy is to reduce the emotional conflict that is caused by traumatic experiences. During brief psychodynamic therapy, the clinician is the expert and guides the client to several key insight points including: (1) identification of trauma triggers that lead to flashbacks and other symptoms, (2) identification of coping strategies to manage stressful feelings related to past experiences, (3) raise awareness of thoughts and feelings that accompany trauma memories, and (4) increase self-esteem.

These treatments have provided many trauma survivors with relief from their trauma symptoms yet may not be suitable for many clients who prefer not to retell their trauma stories. In addition to these treatment options, another strengths-based, future-oriented approach is also available for clinicians and clients. Solution-focused brief therapy provides an alternative approach that is radically different from many of these problem-focused approaches to trauma treatment by focusing the sessions on ways clients have coped and survived and what they look forward to in their lives.

■ SFBT TRAUMA RESEARCH

It is now safe to say that SFBT *is* an evidenced-based practice. There are currently eight systematic reviews and meta-analyses (Carr, Hartnett, Brosnan, & Sharry, 2016; Gong & Hsu, 2015; Gong & Hsu, 2017; Kim, 2008; Kim, Franklin, Zhang, Liu, Qu, & Chen, 2015; Park, 2014, Stams, Dekovic, Buist, de Vreies, 2006; Suitt, Franklin, & Kim, 2016) that evaluate the research base of SFBT from around the world, including countries in Asia, Europe, North America, and South America. In addition to these eight systematic reviews and meta-analyses there are approximately 100 randomized-control trial studies (the gold standard of research evidence) that consistently show SFBT to be as effective as treatment as usual (or more effective) compared to other evidence-based approaches. Additionally, SFBT is currently listed on SAMHSA's NREPP and CEBC national registries in the United States. Although not all of these research studies evaluate the effectiveness of SFBT with trauma survivors, there are several studies that address symptoms of trauma or are focused on populations that may be managing traumatic experiences.

Some SFBT studies that address trauma-related populations, showing that SFBT is effective, focus on the following populations/presenting complaints: patients dealing with orthopedic rehabilitation (Cockburn, Thomas, & Cockburn, 1997), substance abuse (Kim, Brook, & Akin 2016; Smock, Trepper, Wetchler, McCollum, Ray, & Pierce, 2008), depression (Habibi, Ghaderi, Abedini, & Jamshidnejad, 2016), mothers of child abusers (Maqami et al., 2016), burn victims (Wang, Li, Du, & Feng, 2016), and radical hysterectomy patients (Wu, Xie, & Liu, 2015). Given that up to 80% of clients who present for therapy have experienced some form of trauma before attending therapy (Smyth, 2013) it is safe to say that many of the clients who have attended SFBT therapy have experienced trauma. Therefore, although not all of the studies that demonstrate the effectiveness of SFBT are specifically with clients who present as trauma survivors, we can surmise that it is possible (and very likely) that many of these clients also were trauma survivors and showed positive outcomes from SFBT.

■ COMPARISON AND CONTRAST BETWEEN SFBT AND OTHER TRAUMA TREATMENTS

Each of the trauma treatments discussed above have been identified as helpful and are backed by empirical evidence supporting their effectiveness. However, it is important to consider how these treatment options compare to SFBT, especially since we are advocating that SFBT is at least as effective as these other forms of treatment but might actually be more effective in some situations. Kim, Brook, and Akin (2016) lends additional support to this argument. This research study used a randomized controlled trial design to examine the effectiveness of SFBT for child welfare involved parents for trauma-related problems and substance use. The control group used some form of treatment-as-usual that was evidence based, with most control group clinicians using TF-CBT, CBT, reality-based therapy, and MI. Results from the study showed SFBT clients improved on trauma-related problems and substance use from pretest to posttest. The control group also showed improvements that were not completely surprising since counselors were using evidence-based treatments. While there were no statistical differences between the SFBT and control groups, the between group effect sizes favored SFBT groups and were small to medium. The lack of statistical significance could be due to the small sample size and low statistical power to detect small differences. What we can infer is that the SFBT group improved and did as well as these other evidence-based treatments.

Predominantly the treatments that are considered evidence based are rooted in CBT (with the exception of brief psychodynamic). Jordan, Froerer, and Bavelas (2013) provided a comprehensive outline of the similarities and difference between CBT and SFBT. They mentioned that both CBT and SFBT share the following aspects:

1. Their focus is on cognition and behaviors rather than emotion.
2. Often the duration of therapy is brief and focuses on the presenting problem rather than searching for personality change or understanding of root cause.
3. They share some similar techniques (i.e., assigning homework, scaling questions, and goal setting).

Despite these similarities, SFBT and CBT are different in several significant ways. Jordan, Froerer, and Bavelas (2013) also discuss these important differences. First, CBT is a collection of several specialized orientations and approaches (i.e., mindfulness, cognitive, dialectical behavioral therapy), whereas SFBT consists of a highly disciplined set of communication practices that lead to consistent outcomes.

Second, CBT and SFBT make very different assumptions about their clients: CBT is overtly looking for deficits, unhealthy behaviors, negative core beliefs, and faulty cognitions in their clients. For trauma survivors this translates to looking at the maladaptive symptoms and problematic behaviors that have resulted and are maintained by the trauma experience. This is contrasted by the SFBT view that despite challenges and previous trauma experiences, clients still have resources they can draw on to cope and are inherently resilient. Because of this positive view of clients, SFBT clinicians help their clients to describe their preferred future in great detail rather than focusing on their deficits and unhealthy coping strategies. This also means that clients are not asked to retell or reexperience their trauma by focusing on the terrible events, negative thoughts, and problem behaviors. Change, growth, and healing can take place by being focused on the future and how they will know when they are functioning in optimal ways. This means that exposure, desensitization, and physical stimuli are not needed for healing; rather, the client already has everything they need to manage the trauma in a way that is right for them.

Third, SFBT and CBT differ in their assumption about the importance of language in treatment. CBT views language as useful to changing faulty cognitions and behavior but not necessarily the level at which change takes place. CBT views changing a client's faulty beliefs about an event or situation as the change mechanism (Beck, 2011). SFBT, on the other hand, views language as *the* intervention and the place where change happens. This is likely the most important difference. Because SFBT views language as the essence of the change-model, each word that is chosen and used during the co-constructive process leaves a lasting imprint for the client. This means that if language is used to tell and retell traumatic experiences during therapy, the client is, in a very real sense, being retraumatized over and over with each telling. This is evident in the trauma symptoms that reappear with each telling during CBT treatment. SFBT clinicians understand that language can be used to co-construct a description of when the client will be functioning well, despite the previous traumatic experience. Questions can be used to co-construct new meanings and to introduce possibilities the client is hoping for. SFBT clinicians believe that language shapes the client's life; therefore, each word spoken and emphasized during therapy should be in the direction of healing and coping rather than fear and despair.

The final distinction outlined is that CBT focuses on problem-solving while SFBT focuses on solution-building. It is clear in the description of the CBT approaches that skills training, cognitive tracking, desensitization, and trauma processing are all aimed at reducing symptoms and increasing the client's ability to cope. The direct cause–effect approach highlights that CBT clinicians are interested in only solving the presenting problem. The psychoeducation and skills training teach clients to manage their distress in very specific ways. If clients don't master these techniques, the trauma symptoms are likely to persist. This problem-solving approach is contrasted by SFBT's solution-building methodology. Clients are viewed as agents of change and as the experts of their own lives. This means that clinicians rely on using the client's exact language to discuss hopes and future desires. This also means that clients are trusted to act in a way that is consistent with their best selves, especially when they have co-constructed this version of themselves.

■ CONCLUSION

SFBT provides a unique approach to trauma treatment that respects the client and encourages client to make changes by looking forward rather than by reliving the past, especially the traumatic past. By approaching healing from a SFBT perspective clients not only get better and feel whole again, but they do not have to re-live the worst experiences of their lives on their way to this healing and growth. SFBT provides a positive, hopeful, future-oriented approach to trauma treatment that is respectful and guided by strong, resilient, and competent trauma survivors.

■ REFERENCES

American Psychiatric Assocation. (1980). *Diagnostic and statistical manual of mental disorders* (3rd ed., text rev.). Washington, DC: Author.

Beck, J. (2011). *Cognitive behavior therapy: Basics and beyond* (2d. ed.). New York: Guildford.

Breslau, N., & Kessler, R. C. (2001). The stressor criterion in DSM-IV posttraumatic stress disorder: An empiricial investigation. *Biological Psychiatry, 50*, 699–704. doi: 10.1016/s0006-3223(01)01167-2.

Briere, J. N., & Scott, C. (2015). *Principles of trauma therapy: A guide to symptoms, evaluation, and treatment* (2d ed.). Los Angeles: SAGE.

Blakey, J. M., & Smith Hatcher, S. (2013). Trauma and substance abuse among child welfare involved African American mothers: A case study. *Journal of Public Child Welfare, 7*, 194–216. doi: dx.doi.org/10.1080/15548732.2013.779623.

California Evidence-Based Clearinghouse for Child Welfare. (2017). Retrieved from http://www.cebc4cw.org/.

Campbell Collaboration. (2017). Retrieved from https://www.campbellcollaboration.org/.

Carr, A., Hartnett, D., Brosnan, E., & Sharry. J. (2016). Parents Plus systemic, solution-focused parent training programs: Description, review of the evidence base, and meta-analysis. *Family Process.* doi: 10/1111/famp.12225.

Cockburn, J. T., Thomas, F. N., & Cockburn, O. J. (1997) Solution-focused therapy and psychosocial adjustment to orthopedic rehabilitation in a work hardening program. *Journal of Occupational Rehabilitation, 7*, 97–106.

Fallot, R. D., McHugo, D. J., Harris, M., & Xie, H. (2011). The trauma recovery and empowerment model: A quasi-experimental effectiveness study. *Journal of Dual Diagnosis, 7*(1), 74–89. doi: 10.1080/15504263.2011.566056.

Friedman, M. J. (n.d.). PTSD history and overview. Retrieved from www.ptsd.va.gov/professional/ptsd-overview/ptsd-overview.asp.

Galea, G., Nandi, A., & Vlahov, D. (2005). The epidemiology of post-traumatic stress disorder after disasters. *Epidemiologic Reviews, 27*, 78–91. doi: 10.1093/epirev/mxi003.

Gong, H., & Hsu, W. S. (2015). A meta-analysis on the effectiveness of solution-focused brieftherapy: Evidences from mainland and Taiwan. *Studies of Psychology and Behaviors (CSSCI), 13*(6), 709–803.

Gong, H., & Hsu, W. S. (2017). The effectiveness of solution-focused group therapy in ethnic Chinese school settings: A meta-analysis. *International Journal of Group Psychotherapy, 67*(3), 383–409. Retrieved from http://www.tandfonline.com/doi/full/10.1080/00207284.2016.1240588?needAccess=true

Habibi, M., Ghaderi, K., Abedini, S., & Jamshidnejad, N. (2016). The effectiveness of solution-focused brief therapy on reducing depression in women. *International Journal of Educational and Psychological Researches, 2*(4), 244–249.

Hanson, R. F., & Lang, J. (2016). A critical look at trauma-informed care among agencies and systems serving maltreated youth and their families. *Child Maltreatment, 21*, 95–100. doi: 10.1177/1077559516635274.

Jensen, T. K., Holt, T., Ormhauga, S. M., Egeland, K., Granly, L., Hoaas, L. C., et al. (2013). A randomized effectiveness study comparing trauma-focused cognitive behavioral therapy with therapy as usual for youth. *Journal of Clinical Child & Adolescent Psychology, 43*(3), 356–369. doi: 10.1080/15374416.2013.822307.

Jones, L. K., & Cureton, J. L. (2014). Trauma redefined in the *DSM-5*: Rationale and implications for counseling practice. *The Professional Counselor, 4*, 257–271. doi: 10.15241/lkj.4.3.257.

Jordan, S. S., Froerer, A. S., & Bavelas, J. B. (2013). Microanalysis of positive and negative content in solution-focused brief therapy and cognitive behavioral therapy expert sessions. *Journal of Systemic Therapies, 32*, 46–59.

Kilpatrick, D. G., Resnick, H. S., Milanak, M. E., Miller, M. W., Keyes, K. M., & Friedman, M. J. (2013). National estimates of exposure to traumatic events and PTSD prevalence using *DSM-IV* and *DSM-5* criteria. *Journal of Traumatic Stress, 26*, 537–547. doi: 10.1002/jts.21848.

Kim, J. S. (2008). *Examining the effectiveness of solution-focused brief therapy: A meta-analysis. Research on Social Work Practice, 18*, 107–116.

Kim, J. S., Brook, J., & Akin, B. A. (2016). Solution-focused brief therapy with substance-using individuals a randomized controlled trial study. *Research on Social Work Practice.* doi: 10.1177/1049731516650517.

Kim, J. S., Franklin, C., Zhang, Y., Liu, X., Qu, Y., & Chen, H. (2015). *Solution-focused brief therapy in China: A meta-analysis. Journal of Ethnic & Cultural Diversity in Social Work, 24*(3), 187–201. doi:10.1080/15313204.2014.991983

Kip, K. E., Rosenzweig, L., Hernandez, D. F., Shuman, A., Sullivan, K. L., Long, C. J., et al. (2013). Randomized controlled trial of accelerated therapy (ART) for symptoms of combat-related post-traumatic stress disorder (PTSD). *Military Medicine, 178*(12), 1298–1309.

Maqami, R., Bagajan, K. Q., Yousefi, M. M., & Moradi, S. (2016). The effectiveness of solution-focused group therapy on improving depressed mothers of child abuser families. *International Journal of Social, Behavioral, Educational, Economic, Business and Industrial Engineering, 10*(1), 291–295.

Najavits, L. M., & Johnson, K. M. (2014). Pilot study of creating change, a new past-focused model for PTSD and substance use. *American Journal on Addition, 23*, 415–422.

Nakamura, Y., Lipschitz, D. L., Kanarowski, E., McCormick, T., Sutherland, D., & Melow-Murchie, M. (2015). Investigating impacts of incorporating an adjuvant mind-body intervention method into treatment as usual at a community-based substance abuse treatment facility: A pilot randomized controlled study. *Sage Open*, 1–18. doi: 10.1177/2158244015572489.

National Center for Trauma-Informed Care. (n.d.). Retrieved from https://ies.ed.gov/ncee/wwc/.

National Child Traumatic Stress Network (NCTSN). (2008). Understanding the links between adolescent trauma and substance abuse. Retrieved from www.NCTSN.org.

National Registry of Evidence-Based Programs and Practices. (n.d.). Retrieved from http://nrepp.samhsa.gov/landing.aspx.

Park, J. (2014) *Meta-analysis of the effect of the solution-focused group counseling program for elementary school students. Journal of the Korea Contents Association, 14*(11), 476–485. http://www.dbpia.co.kr/Article/3535871

Smock, S. A., Trepper, T. S., Wetchler, J. L., McCollum, E. E., Ray, R., & Pierce, K. (2008). Solution-focused group therapy for level 1 substance abusers. *Journal of Marital and Family Therapy, 34*(1), 107–120.

Smyth, N. J. (2013). Trauma. In *Encyclopedia of Social Work Online.* doi: 10.1093/acrefore/9780199975839.013.400.

Stams, G. J. J., Dekovic, M., Buist, K., & de Vries, L. (2006). Effectiviteit van oplossingsgerichte korte therapie: een meta-analyse. *Gedragstherapie, 39*(2), 81–95.

Substance Abuse and Mental Health Service Administration (SAMHSA). (2014). SAMHSA's concept of trauma and guidance for a trauma-informed approach (HHS Publication No. SMA14-4884). Rockville, MD: SAMHSA. Retrieved from http://store.samhsa.gov/shin/content//SMA14-4884.pdf.

Suitt, K. G., Franklin, C., & Kim, J. (2016). *Solution-focused brief therapy with Latinos: A systematic review. Journal of Ethnic & Cultural Diversity in Social Work, 25*(1), 50–67. doi: 10.1080/15313204.2015.1131651.

Wang, R., Li, X., Du, Y., & Feng, J. (2016). The effect of solution focused nursing on the self-efficacy of burned patients. *International Journal of Nursing, 35*(15), 1389–1396. doi: 10.1016/j.ijnurstu.2010.05.001.

Warner, E., Spinazzola, J., Westcott, A., Gunn, C., & Hudgdon, H. (2014). The body can change the score: Empirical support for somatic regulation in the treatment of traumatized adolescents. *Journal of Child & Adolescent Trauma, 7*(4), 237–246.

What Works Clearinghouse. (2017). Retrieved from https://ies.ed.gov/ncee/wwc/.

Wu, L., Xie, M., & Liu, P. (2015) Effect of solution focused approach model on negative emotions and quality of life of patients with radical hysterectomy. *Medical Innovation of China, 31,* 81–84. doi:10.3969/j.issn.1674-4985.2015.31.026.

3 Language Creates a New Reality

■ ADAM S. FROERER, CECIL R. WALKER,
JOHNNY S. KIM, ELLIOTT E. CONNIE,
AND JACQUI VON CZIFFRA-BERGS

■ INTRODUCTION

Steve de Shazer suggested that language creates reality rather than describes it. This chapter discusses the current theory of change of SFBT and will look at how using SFBT questions and other language components that elicit a client's best hopes and a description of a preferred future starts creating a new reality for clients who have experienced trauma. It will be proposed that the "truth" of trauma is created by how the client experiences and talks about the traumatic experience and that change can occur through a reconstruction of a new reality through client and clinician language. Ideas connected to neurobiology and neuroplasticity will be discussed in connection with the notion that the more one discusses the details of the positive emotion, coping, resilience, strength, and pride, the more one will build and reinforce neural pathways of a different and more hopeful reality. Finally, the tenets of introducing positive emotion after a trauma situation and expanding the trauma experience with positive emotion will also be discussed.

■ THE CONTINUED EVOLUTION OF SFBT

In chapter one, Elliott Connie outlined the evolution of SFBT. This chapter will describe the theory of SFBT from our current perspective. It is important to note that not all authors in this book will write from this perspective; others may approach therapy from the original Milwaukee approach or from the original BRIEF approach, both of which we believe can be effective with many clients.

■ THE LANGUAGE COMPONENTS
USED IN SFBT

In several of the original works written by Steve de Shazer he laid out clearly the notion that language creates reality. He effectively illustrated through masterfully crafted texts how SFBT clinicians can use language that incorporates the exact words used by clients to help clients create new realities. Steve was clear about how this perspective came from a postmodern, poststructural, and social-constructivist perspective. This emphasis on language and using language precisely is foundational to SFBT.

Using language that favors the presence of solutions rather than the absence of problems (MacDonald, 2011) is crucial with clients managing trauma as it focuses on what the client wants rather than trying to stop what happened or what is happening as a result of the traumatic experience. Wittgenstein proposed that language is the tool for thought, and thus the language we use in SFBT is the vehicle for helping the client change the way they think about the trauma and themselves. As language has the "ability to solidify certain views of reality" (O'Hanlon, 2003, p. 60), the language of the solution-focused therapeutic conversation is paramount to the outcome of therapy. SFBT thus reflects the social constructionist idea that the creative and descriptive nature of language constructs new versions of reality and thus ultimately creates change. Strategically and purposefully, the therapeutic conversation leads and guides the client to "clarifying how they would like their lives to be different, inviting new descriptions of what is possible in clients' lives, and by identifying resources that clients might use in changing their lives (Miller & McKergow, 2012). These strategic questions create new experiences, thoughts, and understandings because the "questions we ask shapes the answers our clients give us" (Dolan, 2007, p. 22). As the client answers the questions their attention shifts from a problem-saturated mindset into a new awareness of who they are, what strengths they have, what they want, and how they could get there. The premise that the language we use serves as an attention shifter is the foundational basis of SFBT. The solution-focused dialogue is "highly practical" (Korman & McKergow, 2009) and does not rely on technical language but rather emphasizes the client's words and hopes, which serves the approach well (MacDonald, 2011).

As clinicians and researchers have continued to evaluate what makes SFBT effective, which is especially important in an era where evidence-based practice (EBP) is stressed and often mandated, they have continually been led back to the importance of language. The Solution Focused Brief Therapy Association (SFBTA) has outlined that the therapeutic process of SFBT includes the following three components: (1) the belief that the mechanism of change does not take place *within* the client (either psychologically or biologically) but rather change occurs within the therapeutic dialogue between the client and the therapist; (2) effective therapeutic change should focus on *observable* communication (which means that change should be evaluated based on what is said and done in session, rather than on the intension of the clinician); and (3) the evidence base of SFBT is founded on a "solid experiment basis in psycholinguistic research" (p. 5). This is a fancy way of saying there is research to support the idea that focusing on language is valuable. Given the importance of language within a SFBT perspective, we want to mention some of the language components that might be useful for SFBT clinicians (for further details about these components, please see the Solution Focused Brief Therapy Association's treatment manual [www.sfbta.org]).

■ LANGUAGE COMPONENTS THAT CAN BE USED BY SFBT CLINICIANS

Lexical Choice

Because SFBT is so focused on language and the use of the client's specific language, SFBT clinicians need to be selective about which of the client's exact words and ideas they utilize. This careful selection of words, summaries, paraphrased statements, and questions is characterized as lexical choice. When working with clients managing trauma, SFBT clinicians specifically select and amplify the client's best hopes, personal strengths, factors of resilience, supportive friends and family members, and other details that help to develop a rich description of the client's preferred future. SFBT clinicians also work diligently to not choose to use or amplify words and ideas that are related to the traumatic experience or details of sorrow and pain. It is important to note that clients are free to talk about their trauma (and often come expecting to do so) and that SFBT clinicians do not ignore these details or encourage the client to stop talking about these experiences. Rather, by utilizing lexical choice well, SFBT clinicians simply select the words and language clients use that are in line with the preferred future clients would like to see despite their traumatic history.

Grounding

Grounding is a three-step, co-constructive process that takes place in any conversation that creates understanding between speaker and listener (Bavelas, De Jong, Korman, & Smock Jordan, 2012). This process follows the following steps: (1) the speaker presents new information, (2) the listener demonstrates that they heard and understood the speaker's message (this is often done by a slight head nod, audible noises such as *umm, hmm*, etc.), and (3) the speaker acknowledges the listener understood accurately and that the conversation can proceed. Although this sequence of communication interaction happens in every conversation, SFBT clinicians can use verbal and nonverbal language to ground (and therefore co-construct) conversations about desired outcomes and best hopes for trauma survivors. The following example will highlight the difference between a problem-focused interaction and a solution-building interaction.

Example 1: Grounding in a Problem-focused Way

CLIENT: Things have been very difficult since my recent sexual assault. I haven't been able to sleep well, I have horrible flashbacks, and I feel like I am constantly on guard waiting for something like that to happen again.

THERAPIST: Oh, wow! It sounds like these thing have really been troubling you. That must be very difficult.

CLIENT: It is difficult. In fact, it just seems to be getting worse and worse. I'm afraid I'm never going to get over this.

In this example the therapist highlights that they not only heard that the sexual assault had been difficult but added that "these things" (the results of the sexual assault) "must be difficult to manage. The client confirms that it has been difficult (thus completing the first grounding sequence), and adds that they are "afraid that I'm never going to get over this" (starting the second grounding sequence). One can notice that the impacts of the sexual assault in this situation are getting more pronounced through this conversation. Contrast this first example with a solution building grounding example below:

Example 2: Grounding in a Solution-building Way

CLIENT: Things have been very difficult since my recent sexual assault. I haven't been able to sleep well, I have horrible flashbacks, and I feel like I am constantly on guard waiting for something like that to happen again.

THERAPIST: Oh, wow! It sounds like this has experience has really affected you. I'm wondering how you have been able to cope despite having to manage all of this?

CLIENT: (Nodding) I guess I have just been trying to make it through one day at a time. Some days are better than others.

One can see the acknowledgment of the therapist is still there in the phrase "this experience has really affected you"; however, the therapist does not amplify the difficulty but rather begins a new grounding sequence by asking about the client's coping. The client completes the first grounding sequence by acknowledging that the therapist has understood and follows the therapist-initiated grounding sequence by mentioning that they are "trying to make it through one day at a time."

The outcomes of these two sequences are different; imagine the positive impact a full session of solution-building grounding sequences could have on the client and their increased capacity to manage their trauma. Imagine the details that could be elicited about the client's best hopes and their desired outcome.

Formulations

A formulation takes place when one of the participants in a conversation "describes, summarizes, explicates, or characterizes what another participant has said" (Garfinkel & Sacks, 1970, p. 350). Although formulations in therapy might be seen as just summarizing what the client has said, and therefore, are non-directive, an SFBT clinician understands that they can choose what to include in the summary they provide. The SFBT clinician makes a choice each time the client speaks about what their next utterance will be. If the clinician chooses to use a formulation, they can summarize everything the client mentioned in the previous speaking turn; however, they may choose to only include some of the client's message in their formulation, or they may choose to preserve what the client said with some additions or variations (the last choice is what therapists often call a "reframe"). Given the options available to clinicians we encourage SFBT clinicians to be purposeful in the choices they make and create formulations that are consistent with the theory of SFBT.

Example 1: Formulation That Incorporates Everything the Client Mentions

CLIENT: I have been really struggling with the flashbacks lately. They seem to be coming more and more. I'm not really sure what to do. It didn't use to be this bad.

THERAPIST: So, the flashbacks you have been experiencing are more frequent now and worse than they used to be; you also mentioned that you're feeling overwhelmed and you're struggling with what to do to proceed, did I get that right?

CLIENT: Yeah, you got it. I really need help … I really wish that these flashbacks would just go away.

You can see that the therapist mentioned each of the points from the client's first utterance (i.e., they are struggling with the flashbacks, that the flashbacks are coming more frequently [more and more] and that the flashbacks are worse than they used to be). You can see that the therapist also added an extra word that the client didn't mention (overwhelmed); this adds to the despair experienced by the client. The client then confirms that the therapist has provided an accurate summary of the statement.

Even though this therapist added very little, the client's language stays problem focused and seems to heighten a little (i.e., "I really need help"). It is clear that this therapist is impacting the direction of the client's language. Contrast this example with Example 2 provided below, where the therapist only formulates part of what the client mentions.

Example 2: A Formulation That Preserves Only Part of the Client's Language

CLIENT: I have been really struggling with the flashbacks lately. They seem to be coming more and more. I'm not really sure what to do. It didn't use to be this bad.

THERAPIST: So these flashbacks didn't use to be this bad. (Therapist pauses and the client nods.) Can you tell me what it is about you that helped you to cope with these flashbacks before, especially since there were fewer of them?

CLIENT: I'm not sure I did anything. I just think it didn't happen as much.

THERAPIST: What was different about you when these weren't happening as much?

In this example the therapist used a formulation during their first speaking turn to paraphrase that the flashbacks were happening less frequently. The therapist completely deleted the language associated with the idea that the client was struggling in their formulation. Instead the therapist used a question that incorporated the client's language to highlight that the client did manage the flashbacks when there were fewer of them. In this example the therapist was able to understand what the client stated without perpetuating the problem talk but rather moving toward the strengths of the client. The way clinicians (especially SFBT clinicians) use formulations will directly impact the outcome of therapy.

Not-Knowing Questions

A not-knowing question is just what it sounds like: it is a question that asks the client to provide the clinician with information that the clinician does not know yet. Not-knowing questions can be very simple (for example, "How old are you?"). Or not-knowing questions can be more complex: (e.g.,"What thoughts did you have while you were experiencing this trauma?"). Clinicians have significant power in the co-construction process because they ask most of the questions during a session. This question asking significantly determines what is and what is not discussed in a session. SFBT clinicians should be careful to ask not-knowing questions that lead clients to discuss their preferred future and best hopes.

Some examples of not-knowing questions that can be useful in a SFBT session are, "What are your best hopes?" "What is the very first sign you would notice that would let you know that this miracle had taken place?" "Who else would notice this about you?" and "What impact would this noticing have on you?" These not-knowing questions invite the client to provide information the therapist doesn't know, but in a solution-focused direction. SFBT clinicians should be diligent about asking solution-building, not-knowing questions.

Presuppositional Questions

A clinician does not know the answer to presuppositional questions in advance, but the way a presuppositional question is languaged implies something or makes an assumption about the way the client's answer should be framed. Questions (of any variety) influence the direction of the conversation by implying that a client should answer that specific question; questions that contain presuppositions influence the conversation in specific ways by narrowing the scope of possible answers. Clients are influenced to construct answers to presuppositional questions that fit the assumptions established in the question.

Example 1: Nonpresupposition Embedded Question

THERAPIST: Have you been coping with this traumatic experience?
CLIENT: I mean, I've been trying to.

In this example the answer to the therapist's question is wide open. The client can respond in any way, and the answer would make sense. Look at Example 2 below to see how a clinician can narrow the possible response somewhat by inserting a presupposition into the question.

Example 2: Small Presupposition.

THERAPIST: What have you been doing to cope with this traumatic experience?
CLIENT: I have been trying to get enough sleep and relax at times.

Notice that the assumption of "you have been doing something to cope" is included in the therapist's question because the language was changed to "what have you been doing?" The open-ended nature of this question is narrower and works to eliminate the option for the client to respond, "I haven't been coping." Although the client could have answered in this way, it is less likely because the therapist is explicitly asking what they *have* been doing to cope. Now, notice in Example 3 below how the therapist can introduce an even bigger presupposition into their question to further narrow the possible responses.

Example 3: Larger Presupposition

THERAPIST: What tells you that you have been coping in just the right way for you?

This question implies or assumes that the client has been coping, that the coping is positive, and that the client knows what is just right for them (thus making the client the agent of change). The specificity of this answer will be much greater than an answer to a less specific question with a smaller presupposition. A SFBT clinician can directly impact the co-construction of language by using presupposition well.

These components of language (lexical choice, grounding, formulations, not-knowing questions and questions with embedded presuppositions) should be used with deliberation and precision when conducting a SFBT session. By using these language tools the SFBT clinician will help co-construct a detailed description of the client at his or her very best. These language tools can be used differently at various stages of the SFBT session. Below a description will be provided of a typical SFBT session. These language tools can be used throughout the SFBT session.

■ THE SFBT ART GALLERY

As we look at buildings around us, we notice that some are new and some are old; some have been renovated, and others are still in their original state. Some are constructed in a modern style, while others are from architectural eras gone by. In order to understand the way a building looks and the function of the building, having background understanding about the structure of the building is helpful. When describing the components of a typical BRIEF session, Chris Iveson was the first to use the analogy of the SFBT art gallery. This analogy provides a common language that can be used to describe the process of how SFBT language is used in session.

Physical buildings often need to be repaired, updated, and modernized over time for various reasons. Parts of these buildings need to be modified for new purposes, parts may be torn down or eliminated, and yet other portions of buildings are rebuilt or added to. If we go back to a place from our youth that is familiar to us later in life, we are often surprised by the changes to the architecture and skyline. Things that once seemed familiar to us may be unrecognizable. This recently happened to me (Elliott Connie) when I went back to visit my hometown. As a boy, I spent many hours in the public library in my hometown of Franklin, Massachusetts. This was a place I would do my homework, hang out with friends, and avoid being at home. One of the rooms that fascinated me during these years was the microfiche room; this is a place where individuals could browse through large quantities of information long before the advent of the Internet. In the Franklin Library there was a large room dedicated to housing these oversized machines and the file drawers needed for storing this content. Recently I returned to Franklin as an adult to teach SFBT (one of my lifelong dreams). On this trip I returned to the public library for a trip down memory lane. I was surprised to see that the microfiche room had been completely remodeled and renovated. This space was now housing multiple computers,

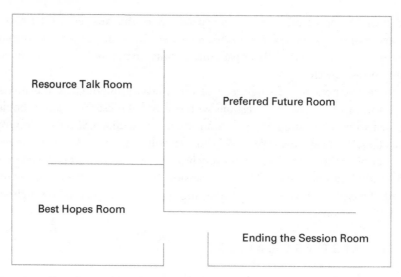

Figure 3.1 The solution-focused art gallery.

each with the capability of connecting to the Internet and accessing far more information than was previously available via microfiche. Although I am a nostalgic person and would prefer that many things stay the same, I understand that this renovation was necessary.

Similarly, the SFBT art gallery (structure of the session) has changed over time. This chapter will include a description of what the SFBT art gallery looks like now. It is important to note that understanding this session structure is important but that it is currently (and probably always will be) under construction. The current SFBT art gallery has four rooms that are visited during "the tour," or the SFBT session. The following rooms will be described in detail: (1) The Best Hopes Room, (2) the Resource Talk/Scene Setting Room, (3) the Preferred Future Room (the most important room), and (4) the Session Closing Room (See Figure 3.1).

■ THE BEST HOPES/DESIRED OUTCOME ROOM

The Best Hopes Room is the first room of the art gallery. This is the place where the clinician, in essence, gets "a ticket" to see the rest of the museum. In order to get a ticket (or permission to proceed to the rest of the museum) the clinician will ask what the client's desired outcome is. Without knowing what the client hopes the outcome of the session will be, an SFBT clinician has no idea what else should happen during the rest of the session. For example, this question might be something like, "What are your best hopes from our talking today?" or,

"What would you like to have happen as a result of this session?" The best-hopes question is intended to immediately get the session, and the client, focused on the desired outcome from therapy. The best-hopes question also serves as a contract between the client and the therapist about what the conversation for the rest of the session will focus on (Ratner, George & Iveson, 2012). This is important in sessions with individuals who are managing trauma, because this best hopes approach will tell you what he or she wants despite having experienced trauma. This question will help the client articulate what he or she would like to have happen when they know they are at their best despite having experienced something traumatic. It is important to note that this question is not aimed at ignoring the trauma or conveying that talking about the trauma is unacceptable, rather this question is aimed at understanding where the client would like to end up.

The desired outcomes portion of the session is the place where the SFBT clinician will most likely hear about the problem. Clients often come to therapy with the expectation that they will be asked to discuss their trauma and the surrounding events in great detail. Clients often believe that they are stuck because of their trauma and that in order to get unstuck they will need to talk in great detail about the traumatic event and the debilitating impact this trauma is having on their lives. Clients have often spent considerable time thinking about, reliving, and reexperiencing their previous traumas. They have developed a useful narrative or language around this experience and what meaning it has for them. For all of these reasons clients expect that they will use this trauma language during therapeutic encounters. The gallery-informed, language-focused SFBT clinician understands that this is acceptable. They do not try and stop the client from talking about their previous traumas or the resulting impact but rather listen with an attentive ear to the details that contribute to the client's desired outcome.

The very first question that should be asked in a SFBT session is some version of the best-hopes question. At the language level, this is important because it does not allow any room for problem talk to enter the session. The client and the clinician immediately begin thinking and (more importantly) talking about what will be helpful about this meeting. Clients might be caught off guard by this question and seem confused by it, or they might ignore the question altogether; after all, this is not what they were expecting to talk about during the session. The SFBT clinician remembers that the answer the client gives to this question (and every question) is exactly the right answer for them. This means that the SFBT clinician does not expect a certain answer, accepts the answer that is given, and uses the client's language to rephrase the best-hopes question in a way that might be more answerable for the client. Please note that we recommended rephrasing the best-hopes question. If the clinician does not understand the client's best hopes, or where the session is going, they cannot move on. We have to trust that our client can answer the best-hopes questions if we ask it in just the right way. We need to trust that they might need to tell us other things before they answer the question, but we also need to remember that it is our job to stay focused on the desired outcome. By incorporating the new language the client provided us from their initial response, we can ask the question again in a way that is better for each individual client. Through this process the client is teaching us how to be *their* therapist, rather than just *a* clinician. Learn from your client's response and use these responses to ask questions that will be helpful to your client in constructing a new reality.

The important part about the best-hopes room is to hold the presupposition that the client is amazing. The reason this is important, regardless of whether we are right or wrong, is that if we hold this view and perspective of our clients, we are much more likely to be curious about the client's amazing capabilities. If we lose this view of the client, we are no longer doing our job. It is vital that we hold this stance in order to ask them questions that elicit a description of their capabilities. Once we see them as amazing and are aware of their best hopes, we are able to move on to the rest of the SFBT session.

■ THE RESOURCE TALK ROOM (CLIENT LANGUAGE ROOM)

Although *the resource talk* room is one of the vital portions of a SFBT session, we were a little hesitant to include it here. Often the tasks associated with this room are misunderstood, and therefore clinicians consciously and unconsciously begin problem-solving or feel like they need to help the client to gain insight about the inner resources or strengths they possess; this is not the point of this part of the session. If this is not what this room is all about, then what's the point of talking about this at all? The point of this room in the art gallery is *language expansion*.

When clients come to therapy they only have language to describe their problems, traumas, and the things that are not going well (at least that's the language they expect to use in therapy). In the resource talk room we ask clients to step away from the problem for a moment and talk about other aspects of their lives. In this room we ask the clients about important places, people, and things in their lives. As the client talks about these important components, we are learning their language in the form of names of important people, qualities they value about themselves, places that they go when they are at their best, and things they value. It could be easy for an outsider watching this stage of the session to mistake what is happening for joining, developing a therapeutic relationship, or breaking down resistance; however, this is not the point of engaging in this kind of conversation within a SFBT session. Rather, the point here is to expand the vocabulary of the clinician to be able to co-construct a meaningful

conversation with *this* client. We are learning the unique language that is important to each client so that it can be used in later rooms of the SFBT art gallery. Just
like a traditional art gallery the rooms and wings tend to build on one another.
Some galleries are organized by eras or movements or geographical location of
the artist, while others may have an alternative organization. What an art con-
sumer learns in one room or wing of the museum will help them to make sense
of art they see later during the tour. This incremental building effect is similar
within the SFBT art gallery. The language the clinician learns during this portion
of the session will directly influence the questions they ask during later portions
of the session. The SFBT clinician is listening attentively for language that will
be helpful in developing a detailed description of the so-called preferred future,
which is the name of the next room in our gallery tour.

■ THE PREFERRED FUTURE ROOM

The preferred future room is the most important room of the gallery. In many
galleries the central attraction or the masterpieces are placed in positions of
great prominence; for example, the impressionist paintings in Art Institute of
Chicago are placed at the top of the grand staircase in the main hall of the gallery. Everyone knows that this room will be the highlight of the trip. Despite
this being the most important room, patrons are not usually directed to this ex-
ceptional room immediately as they walk in the door of the museum. Instead,
patrons are funneled slowly from room to room and wind their way through the
various rooms and exhibits throughout much of the rest of the museum before
reaching the apex of their museum experience. The patrons gain an appreciation
for what it took to create such a masterpiece before they have even seen it. Once
they get to the room in which the masterpiece is on display they will notice that
often this is the biggest room with the most expensive decorations. And it is
clearly the piece that is drawing visitors to the museum.

Just like this room in traditional galleries, the preferred future room is the
"main attraction" of the SFBT art gallery. This is the main reason the client
has come to therapy; this is the place where change happens, where details of
language are explored, and where the beauty of the session lies. *This is the masterpiece of the SFBT art gallery.* Just like other galleries, if an SFBT clinician went
directly to this room without visiting the preceding ones, they would miss important learning opportunities. The previous rooms give context for the answers
that are given here. There is no way to have an appropriate conversation that
needs to take place in the preferred future room unless one has visited the other
rooms first.

The clinician enters this room when he or she has a clear desired outcome
(best hopes) and the appropriate language gained in the resource talk room to be
able to ask *this* client a unique question. This is not an arbitrary preferred future

question; this is a customized preferred future question. Typically when a preferred future question has been discussed in other SFBT books there is a standardized miracle question outlined that could be used with any client. For example, "*Suppose that one night, while you were asleep, there was a miracle and this problem was solved. How would you know? What would be different?*" (de Shazer et al., 2007, p. 5). In the BRIEF art gallery this question is simply not adequate. By visiting the two previous rooms, the SFBT clinician is equipped to ask a personalized preferred future question to each client. Below is one example from Elliott Connie's session with a couple, Dave and Celeste.

> **Elliott:** I have an unusual question to ask the two of you. Suppose tonight as you are asleep a miracle happens that wiped away all of the problems that caused you to contact me. And instead of those problems, the high school feeling was brought back, where you felt like her protector and you felt safe, those high school kind of butterfly feelings were back and the high school, very fluttery feeling was back, just like that (snaps fingers). This miracle occurs overnight as you were asleep, but because you're asleep you can't know that it happened. You know, I mean, how could you, you were sleeping? When you woke up the next morning, what would be your very first clue that something was different, that this feeling was back?

There are two important distinctions about this second preferred future question that are important to point out. First, this version of the miracle question is specifically about the *presence* of the clients' best hopes rather than the absence of the problem that brought them here. This is important because by asking about the presence of the best hopes the client is free to talk about the differences they notice. If you simply ask about the absence of the problem, the client often gets stuck (after all, it is hard to describe something that *isn't* there!), or they revert back to using the language they are familiar with, the language of the problem. They say things like, "Well, I just wouldn't be feeling this way anymore." This does not tell us anything about how they *would* be feeling, it only tells us about how they *would not* be feeling. SFBT clinicians should frame their questions in a way that helps their clients talk about their best hopes and the signs they will notice when their best hopes are present. We should not be framing our questions in a way that leads clients merely to think about the problem being gone. For trauma clients their experiences can never be undone, but they describe futures where they are able to be their best selves despite the trauma history; we need to be asking about this *preferred future.*

The second important distinction about the second question above is that it includes the exact words that Dave and Celeste provided in the previous rooms of the art gallery. Elliott was careful to include phrases such as "the high school feeling," "you felt like her protector," "you felt safe," "those high school kind of butterfly feelings," and "very fluttery feeling" were all phrases that were introduced by Dave or Celeste previously. This preferred future question could not have been addressed to anyone else. No one else would have been able to understand this question because they had not co-constructed the language associated with this question. It is this level of specificity that we should be focusing when we ask clients these preferred future questions. The preferred future room, and asking the miracle question in this way, is one of the things that separates BRIEF from the rest of SFBT clinicians. Because we view this room as the most important and where change takes place, we believe that the time we spend in this room with our clients co-constructing a detailed description of their preferred future is *the* intervention. This part of the conversation will take the majority of the session (perhaps up to 40 minutes) and will be all the work that the client and clinician do together. The miracle question, or other versions of the preferred future question, are sometimes mistakenly confused with goal setting or finding out where the client would like to be. Please let us be clear: we do not view it this way. This is not goal setting! The time the client spends in this room with their clinician *is* the intervention; this is what helps them change and make changes in their lives.

This is the place where clients managing trauma get to begin describing how they would notice when their best hopes have taken place and what they will notice about themselves when they are again functioning at their best. By building their vocabulary related to their client's desired outcome, clinicians now have the ability to push their clients while also being safe. Because we are challenging them with their words, their language, and their worldview, this is experienced as a safe push rather than an unsafe one (which is often the outcome of pushing people to talk about the details of the trauma). Clients now feel empowered to talk about their best selves.

In the preferred future room clients are empowered as they are asked specific, detail-oriented questions about the presence of their best hopes. These detailed questions often walk the client step by step through their miracle day. Clients are asked questions like, "What time would it be when you wake up on this miracle day?" "Who would be the first person that would notice that you were different and that you were at your best?" "And if your happiness followed you to the dinner table, what would be different about the way you ate your dinner on this day?" These simple, straightforward questions help the client articulate minute details that would change on their miracle day. By thinking about and articulating these specific details, clients are literally creating a new reality through language. They are constructing a reality that is separate from the problem–dominated reality of trauma. During this conversation clients begin to imagine, perhaps for the first time, a reality that is not overshadowed by trauma or trauma symptoms. Mark McKergow refers to this process as "brain stretching." We are stretching client's thinking and experience in such a way that they are different people when they walk out of the session.

Once client and clinician have spent the bulk of the therapy session discussing the preferred future, the work for this session has been completed. It is now time to close the session in a way that accomplishes one goal: not ruining the work that has taken place in the preferred future room.

■ THE SESSION CLOSING ROOM

This may sound strange, but this room is only important because the session has to end at some point. Just like other galleries, once you have seen what you went to the museum to see, you are ready to leave the museum. Despite your being ready to leave, however, you cannot simply blink yourself out (although that would be nice, wouldn't it?). Given your lack of "blinking" ability, you must physically walk out. In exactly the same manner, you cannot simply blink to end the session and make the client disappear; therefore the final room in the gallery is only important because it *must* occur.

Gallery designers are smart people and know that people will want to remember the trip they made to the gallery. For this reason (and to make a little, or a lot, of revenue) most museums force their patrons to walk through the gift shop on their way to the museum exit. There is no way to get out of the museum without passing several monetary temptations that consist of cheap imitations of the real masterpieces housed in the museum. These imitations are nothing compared to the priceless memory that you can hold in your head. No one can change the lived experience you just had; this memory is something you create and carry with you.

In a similar way, we as SFBT clinicians need to resist the temptation to ask our clients to pick something up or take something with them, often in the form of psychoeducation, homework, or clinician-driven compliments. We are not salespersons trying to make a sale. Our job is to walk the clients through the gallery and help them identify what stands out to them. We need to trust that they have picked up and remembered what they needed to. If we are worried that perhaps they did not get what they needed, then it is helpful to remember that they would not have been able to answer the questions unless they had done exactly what they needed to do.

With clients managing trauma, it might be tempting to think that we need to provide them with psychoeducation about the things they might experience going forward, or give them homework assignments to help them "work through the trauma," or compliment them for coping so well and pushing through the difficulty and presenting for therapy. These clinician-driven approaches are simply cheap imitations of the co-constructed new reality the client is taking with them. It is vital to trust that this process works and challenge ourselves to stay out of the client's way. While we are resisting the urge not to do these things we should mention that the one thing that we commonly do to end a session is to ask the client to notice the details they mentioned in the preferred future room as they show up in their lives. The best way to avoid ruining the work that has been done is simply to ask them to identify the signs of the best-hopes/preferred outcome and the role he or she played in making these things happen. With this final question the SFBT session comes to a close. The session is now complete.

■ THE SCIENCE BEHIND SFBT

The potential benefits of a solution-focused approach extend beyond simply recognizing past successes and identifying pathways to preferred outcomes. The continuous strength-based language toward an ideal future is, in short, how change is prompted, but the mechanisms that explain why noticeable change happens are more detailed and extend further beneath the surface. There is a lack of empirical insight into the direct affective and neuropsychological results of the solution-focused approach, but the major components of the therapeutic model are consistent with well-researched studies in positive psychology on positive affect, which Miller (2011) defines as the degree a person experiences positive moods. Through connecting SFBT to essential components of positive psychology, it is easier to recognize the potential it has to offer, in terms of the benefits of both positive affect and changes in the brain. Effective in operationalizing components of SFBT, the depth of the field of positive psychology supports the utility of this approach in the face of circumstances of varying degrees of complexity or emotional intensity. Furthermore, because of numerous consistencies, the relevance of neuropsychological processes can cogently transmute to the comprehension of the efficacy of SFBT.

■ DEFINING HOPE IN SFBT AND POSITIVE AFFECT

Similar to the strengths perspective shift in social work in 1982 (Kim, 2008; Saleebey, 2006), psychology, in 1998, started to focus their attention to the positive resources that clients have rather than their pathological deficits (Seligman, 1999). Explicit commonalities between SFBT and positive psychology argue for the interchangeability of the mechanisms behind them. Crucial to both are hope and hopefulness. Equally worth noting, both also largely work with the same understanding of what the concept of hope is. Charles R. Snyder (1994) defined it as "the sum of the mental willpower and waypower that you have for your goals" (p. 5). Based on the study and implementation of SFBT and positive psychology, it appears as though both continue to draw on that definition. SFBT certainly incorporates the language of hope as integral to change. The approach necessitates frequent assessment of attainment certainty, often by use of scaling questions and constant navigation of solution pathways, all in order to try and reach a preferred future. The preferred future itself is fundamental in the construction and function of hope; this corresponds with positive psychology's understanding of goals as not only the natural means of thinking but as an essential component of hope (Cheavens, Feldman, Woodward, & Snyder, 2006). Hope theory asserts that sequences of human actions are guided by goals, and those with more hope have greater ease in connecting the present to the preferred future (Rand & Cheavens, 2009). Working under the assumptions of Snyder's definition and the large body of positive psychology that developed from it, using solution-building language in this approach is equivalent to building hope.

■ THE FUNCTION OF HOPE IN SFBT AND POSITIVE AFFECT

Beyond a similar understanding of hope, SFBT and positive psychology also share the development and utilization of it. The study of hope and hopefulness informs us that reducing hopelessness and building hope are not the same endeavors (Cheavens et al., 2006). This distinction mirrors SFBT's orientation toward the strengths that can help pave the way for the future rather than deficits that may have afflicted the past. The benefits described by hope theory would be less applicable to a therapeutic model that attempted otherwise. The reward of hope and positive affect are much more closely tied to progression toward goals rather than a fixation on reducing possible sources of dissatisfaction (Rand & Cheavens, 2009). A lack of emphasis on strength-based goal attainment could potentially invalidate the argument for interchangeability of components in trying to fit SFBT into the implications of positive psychology. Furthermore, there would be a gap in this asserted equalization because utilizing strengths and successes to achieve goals is a direct link to positive affect and its benefits (Cheavens, 2006). Hope precedes positive affect rather than existing as a product of it (Ciarrochi, Parker, Kashdan, Heaven, & Barkus, 2015). To reap its well-supported positive influences, it is far more effective to pursue hope as a target rather than as a by-product. Here lies another major alignment of SFBT with the concepts of hope theory and positive psychology. This approach's focus on using language that builds hope—the language of goal attainment that helps to synonymize understandings of SFBT and the implications of positive psychology—leads to the accessibility of hope theory, positive affect, and positive psychology in general to the interests of the effectiveness of the SFBT approach. This translation from psychological and neurological research to the therapeutic model allows for the discussion of the detailed benefits and positive changes presented in applying SFBT.

■ SFBT AND THE BROADEN-AND-BUILD THEORY OF POSITIVE EMOTIONS

Another similar concept in positive psychology is the difference between positive affectivity and positive emotions. Miller (2011) noted that positive affect refers to a person's mood, while positive emotions refers to the feelings a person experiences. Positive emotions theory also argues that positive emotions are not simply the absence of negative emotions (e.g., anger, sad, frustrated, hopelessness, etc.) or just a "good feeling" a client has but rather can serve as a therapeutic value in clinical practice (Fitzpatrick & Stalikas, 2008a). Most of the research and discussion in clinical practice viewed positive emotions as a desired outcome (i.e., I want to be happy again) and neglected the possibility of positive emotions serving as a vehicle for therapeutic change (Fitzpatrick & Stalikas, 2008b). In this sense, the concept of hope is often the positive emotion mentioned in solution-focused literature (Kim & Franklin, 2015). With the recent popularity of positive psychology and clinical studies on hope, there is an opportunity to reexamine how SFBT uses questions that elicit positive emotions in undoing the psychological dysfunctions of trauma especially and generating positive behavioral changes in clients.

Both Insoo Kim Berg and Steve de Shazer, two of the pioneers of SFBT, talked about the importance of increasing positive expectancy and fostering hope in clients when using the SFBT model (de Shazer, 1985; Berg & De Jong, 2008). Kim and Franklin (2015) discussed the positive emotional processes within SFBT and how the broaden-and-build theory of positive emotions (Fredrickson, 1998) may provide some of the most compelling evidence for explaining how SFBT works. This theory adds to our understanding of how SFBT creates better client–clinician relationships and engagement through the various techniques such as compliments, best hopes, miracle questions, and preferred future questions.

Broaden-and-Build Theory of Positive Emotions

Emerging out of the recognition that positive emotions were neglected in psychology research on emotions in theory building and hypothesis testing, Fredrickson (1998) sought to examine what role positive emotions play in individual's momentary thought–action repertoires and how this might guide specific interventions to improve psychological well-being. A client's thoughts and behavior can be influenced when they experience a particular emotion and over time leads to a set of behavioral responses to various situations. To help test the broaden-and-build theory, Fredrickson and colleagues conducted several laboratory studies that found support for the broadening of thought–action repertoires, undoing of lingering negative emotions, increasing resiliency, and improving psychological well-being.

Under the broaden-and-build theory (Fredrickson, 1998), positive emotions elicit thought–action repertoires that are broad, flexible, and receptive to new thoughts and actions while negative emotions elicit thought–action repertoires that are limited, rigid, and less receptive. The broadening aspect of this theory posits that after a person experiences a positive feeling, they are more open and more receptive to trying new things. Over time clients develop this broadened behavioral repertoire, which helps build their skills and resources rather than support their typical way of reacting. Positive emotions may be fleeting, but they have an accruing effect over time as clients continue to experience more and more positive emotions. Furthermore, positive emotions also have the ability to negate or undo negative emotions when a client experiences a greater number of positive emotions, which research suggests is a 3-to-1 ratio (Garland et al., 2010).

SFBT and Positive Emotions

While the broaden-and-build theory of positive emotions explains how positive emotions can influence a client's momentary thought–action repertoire, there is a lack of clarity on how clinicians can generate positive emotions when working with clients. Hence, SFBT is a prime therapy model to link this theory with clinical practice. SFBT is an example of a counseling approach that focuses on questions that help clients solve problems by building on their strengths. SFBT specifically focuses on language that increases positive emotion and is thus a potential method for facilitating effective change through language.

Orchestrating a positive, solution-focused conversation, sometimes referred to as "solution talk," is unique to SFBT and aims to create a context for change where hope, competence, and positive expectancies for change increase and a client can co-construct with the clinician workable solutions to their problems. Formulating answers to solution-focused questions requires clients to think about their relationships and talk about their experiences in different ways, turning their problem perceptions and negative emotions into positive formulations for change. SFBT clinicians listen carefully to each formulation made by clients during therapeutic conversations for specific words and openings in the conversations where the solution-focused clinician can punctuate client words and experiences and ask questions in unique ways that highlights strengths and solutions instead of problems.

SFBT techniques such as the *miracle question* are specific examples of clinical techniques that may be used to increase positive emotions by asking clients to shift thinking, feeling, and talking about their current situation. The miracle question helps clients visualize and describe a future where the problem no longer exists and also describe in vivid detail the areas of their lives when they are more competent, joyful, and hopeful. *Goaling language* is also believed to be important to the change process in SFBT and is co-created by the clinician and client; thus, it is something that is important to the client in achieving their preferred future. As the client finds small, incremental success in achieving their set goals, they become more hopeful, and this initial hope leads to bigger changes in their lives. The best-hopes question is another example of how SFBT creates positive emotions in their clients during sessions. By beginning the SFBT conversation with what the client views as their best hopes for our time together, clients are starting the counseling session thinking and reflecting on what positive outcome they hope for, how they've achieved it in the past, and what they need to do in the future to make that happen again. A review of therapeutic literature (Kim & Franklin, 2015) clearly supports the argument that the solicitation and reinforcement of positive emotions have been conceptualized by SFBT developers and clinicians as being important to the change processes within SFBT and that emotional processes should be viewed as resources that can help clients change. As positive emotions and thinking spiral clients to become more aware of their solutions and think creatively and generate new ways to problem solve.

■ THE NEUROPSYCHOLOGY BEHIND THE SFBT APPROACH

It is evident that positive affect is significant in personal growth, satisfaction, and accomplishment and involved in the client's progression through SFBT. Emotion, itself, whether positive or negative, is what establishes goals and orients behavior toward the achievement of goals (Davidson & Irwin, 1999). How emotional systems can guide goals and goal-oriented behavior proves germane to the discussion of the solution-focused approach's effectiveness and leads to a description of neuropsychological mechanisms responsible for the influences of positive affect and the utility of the components of SFBT.

■ THE ROLE OF REWARD IN POSITIVE AFFECT

The change the client experiences in SFBT can be partially explained by neuropsychological processes. While it is difficult to find empirical connections made specifically between neurology and major components of SFBT and positive psychology, there are several pockets of information with much depth on closely related subjects. The neurobiology of reward is one of the largest such bodies of research. Reward is a key antecedent of positive affect and could possibly explain several of the influential effects positive affect has on human cognition and behavior (Ashby & Isen, 1999). Neurobiological research synonymizes reward with the dopamine system rendering the neurotransmitter mostly responsible for the changes reward can yield, such as the improvement in creative problem solving that is associated with moderate amounts of positive affect (Estrada, Isen, & Young, 1994). The cognitive flexibility found in someone reaping the benefits of positive affect is the product of frontal cortical areas of the brain flooded with dopamine (Ashby & Isen, 1999). The connection between dopamine and human behavior as explained by positive psychology is so evident that research has found that those genetically predetermined to be more sensitive to dopamine are also more susceptible to positive affectivity and extroversion (Depue & Collins, 1999). Succinctly put, the benefits of SFBT, which have been described in terms of positive psychology, can possibly be explained in part by the dopamine system. The hope and strength-based goal attainment that induces positive affect is accompanied and supported by the good feelings and motivation of dopamine.

■ RESILIENCE IN THE PREFRONTAL CORTEX

Another neurological process related to the focal components of SFBT involves the system within the prefrontal cortex (PFC) that connects resilience to emotion. Affective resilience is associated with high amounts of activation in this area of the brain, and it is also relevant in the speed of recovery from negative stimuli (Davidson, 2004), which imparts its significance in the treatment of trauma. Resilience incorporates an individual's flexibility in adjusting to change, which might include unfortunate circumstances or constrained environments (Cohn, Fredrickson, Brown, Mikels, & Conway, 2009). The circuitry within the PFC is congruent with the influential role of emotion in building resilience, and both work well with the methods of change in SFBT. Just as research on the broaden-and-build theory suggests that happiness and life satisfaction are the products of circular aggregation between positive affect and broad-ranging resources (Garland et al., 2010), the wiring of the PFC, with regard to emotion and resilience, seems to demonstrate a similar circular building process. An abundance of positive emotion leads to greater resilience simultaneously while resilience helps to produce positive emotions (Cohn et al., 2009). This depicts a chain reaction beginning with the generation of positive affect, which directly induces both cognitive resources and resilience and consequently leads to more positive affect. SFBT's potential to generate positive affect allows the approach to be a gateway for clients into this upward spiral of well-being.

■ THE APPROACH AND WITHDRAWAL SYSTEMS

The relationship between emotion and goal-oriented behavior is clarified even further by the functions of the approach and withdrawal systems in the PFC. The former is described as being responsible for approaching behavior and for producing approach-related positive affect, "such as the emotion occurring as an organism moves closer to a desired goal" (Davidson, Jackson, & Kalin, 2000, p. 893). The withdrawal system is responsible for withdrawal behavior in the face of negative stimuli and the accompanying negative emotions (Davidson, Jackson, & Kalin, 2000). While both are systems within the PFC, there's evidence that supports that the approach system, along with its generation of positive emotions, is more associated with the left side; meanwhile, the withdrawal system is more associated with the right side (Davidson et al., 2000). That evidence helps to conclude that they could be separate systems within the complex network that guides emotion-related behavior and could be activated separately without consequence to the other. It would be ideal to induce positive affect for any of the many previously stated reasons. Therefore, treatment that revolves around goal-oriented approaching behavior, as SFBT does, should be well considered, especially in the cases of trauma in which there are potentially powerfully negative stimuli to which the client responds with avoidance. In cases like these, a clinician should be wary of provoking the withdrawal system of the PFC and be more interested in encouraging the positive emotions of the approach system.

■ PLASTICITY

Just as human behavior is, the human brain is malleable. In fact, susceptibility to a change in patterns is architecturally congruent between the two. The PFC has already been acknowledged as relevant to emotion-related behavior, but the amygdala is also implicated, especially in creating associations with stimuli (Davdison et al., 2000). Both neural regions can adjust and slowly reform over time (Davidson et al., 2000). This plasticity is a consequential part of the complexities of human adaptation. The potential for emotional systems to change and adapt can prove to be quite significant in cases of individuals attempting to intervene on their negative affective states and lack of life satisfaction: "It is likely that when trait-like regulatory strategies occur over a long duration of time, plastic changes in the central circuitry of emotion are produced" (Davidson et al., 2000). These regions of the brain can slowly accept new emotional patterns imposed on them as the norm. The pronounced plasticity of these areas of the brain sets up the potential for an echoing effect on the systems and behaviors they influence.

It is mostly undisputed that emotion can influence decision making. Consequently, one must acknowledge not only the power emotion has over behavior but how much emotion is embedded in the processes of building cognitive-behavioral patterns and learning responses to the environment. Plasticity in emotion and the neural circuitry behind emotion can translate into plasticity in behavior. The malleability of the emotion circuitry of the brain is in indirect contact with all the previously described systems, behaviors, and effects that emotion can influence. Therefore, a process such as that progressing through SFBT, one that might alter emotion and emotion-related behavior, has the potential to guide the direction of the consequences of emotion. As SFBT builds hope and imposes patterns of positive affect, the neural networks of the client are adapting to those changes, cementing his or her potential to attain the preferred future and satisfaction that he or she is pursuing.

■ REFERENCES

Ashby, F. G., & Isen, A. M. (1999). A neuropsychological theory of positive affect and its influence on cognition. *Psychological Review, 106*(3), 529.

Bavelas, J. B., De Jong, P., Korman, H., & Smock Jordan, S. (2012). *Beyond back-channels: A three-step model of grounding in face-to-face dialogue.* Retrieved from http://web.uvic.ca/psyc/bavelas/2012%20Grounding.pdf.

Berg, I. K., & DeJong, P. (2008). *Interviewing for solutions.* Pacific Grove, CA: Brooks Cole/Cengage Learning.

Cheavens, J. S., Feldman, D. B., Woodward, J. T., & Snyder, C. R. (2006). Hope in cognitive psychotherapies: On working with client strengths. *Journal of Cognitive Psychotherapy, 20*(2), 135–145.

Ciarrochi, J., Parker, P., Kashdan, T. B., Heaven, P. C., & Barkus, E. (2015). Hope and emotional well-being: A six-year study to distinguish antecedents, correlates, and consequences. *Journal of Positive Psychology, 10*(6), 520–532.

Cohn, M. A., Fredrickson, B. L., Brown, S. L., Mikels, J. A., & Conway, A. M. (2009). Happiness unpacked: positive emotions increase life satisfaction by building resilience. *Emotion, 9*(3), 361.

Davidson, R. J. (2004). Well-being and affective style: neural substrates and biobehavioural correlates. *Philosophical Transactions-Royal Society of London Series B Biological Sciences, 359*(1449), 1395–1411. doi:10.1098/rstb.2004.1510.

Davidson, R. J., & Irwin, W. (1999). The functional neuroanatomy of emotion and affective style. *Trends in Cognitive Sciences, 3*(1), 11–21.

Davidson, R. J., Jackson, D. C., & Kalin, N. H. (2000). Emotion, plasticity, context, and regulation: Perspectives from affective neuroscience. *Psychological Bulletin, 126*(6), 890.

Depue, R. A., & Collins, P. F. (1999). Neurobiology of the structure of personality: Dopamine, facilitation of incentive motivation, and extraversion. *Behavioral and Brain Sciences, 2*(3), 491–517.

de Shazer, S. (1985). *Keys to solution in brief therapy.* New York: W. W. Norton.

de Shazer, S., Dolan, Y., Korman, H., Trepper, T., McCollum, E., & Berg, I. (2007). *More than miracles: The state of the art of solution-focused brief therapy.* Binghamton, NY: Haworth.

Estrada, C. A., Isen, A. M., & Young, M. J. (1994). Positive affect improves creative problem solving and influences reported source of practice satisfaction in physicians. *Motivation and Emotion, 18*(4), 285–299.

Fitzpatrick, M. R., & Stalikas, A. (2008a). Integrating positive emotions into theory, research, and practice: A new challenge for psychotherapy. *Journal of Psychotherapy Integration, 18,* 248–258. doi: 10.1037/1053-0479.18.2.248

Fitzpatrick, M. R., & Stalikas, A. (2008b). Positive emotions as generators of therapeutic change. *Journal of Psychotherapy Integration, 18,* 137–154. doi: 10.1037/1053-0479.18.2.137

Fredrickson, B. L. (1998). What good are positive emotions? *Review of General Psychology, 2*(3), 300.

Garfinkel, H., & Sacks, H. (1970). On formal structure of practical actions. In J. C. McKinney & E. A. Tiryakian (Eds.), *Theoretical sociology: Perspectives and developments* (pp. 337–366). New York: Appleton-Century-Crofts.

Garland, E. L., Fredrickson, B., Kring, A. M., Johnson, D. P., Meyer, P. S., & Penn, D. L. (2010). Upward spirals of positive emotions counter downward spirals of negativity: Insights from the broaden-and-build theory and affective neuroscience on the treatment of emotion dysfunctions and deficits in psychopathology. *Clinical Psychology Review, 30*(7), 849–864.

Kim, J. S. (2008). Strengths perspective. In Terry Mizrahi and Larry E. Davis (Eds.), *Encyclopedia of social work* (20th ed.). Washington, DC: NASW, Oxford University Press.

Kim, J. S., & Franklin, C. (2015). The importance of positive emotions in solution-focused brief therapy. *Best Practices in Mental Health, 11,* 25–41.

Korman, H., & Mckergow, M. W. (2009). Inbetween—neither inside or outside. The radical simplicity of solution focused brief therapy. *Journal of Systemic Therapies, 28*(2), 34–49. New York: Guilford.

MacDonald, A. J. (2011). *Solution-focused therapy: Theory, research & practice* (2d ed.). Thousand Oaks, CA: SAGE.

Miller, D. N. (2011). Positive affect. In S. Goldstein, & J. A. Naglieri (Eds.), *Encyclopedia of child behavior and development.* New York: Springer.

Miller, G & McKergow M. (2012). *From Wittgenstein, complexity, and narrative emergence: Discourse and solution-focused brief therapy* (pp. 163–183). In A. Lock & T. Strong (Eds.), *Discursive perspectives in therapeutic practice. international perspectives in philosophy and psychiatry.* Oxford: Oxford University Press,

O'Hanlon, B. (2003). *A guide to inclusive therapy: 26 techniques for respectful, resistance dissolving therapy.* New York: W. W. Norton.

Rand, K. L., & Cheavens, J. S. (2009). Hope theory. In *Oxford handbook of positive psychology,* 323, 333.

Ratner, H., George, E., & Iveson, C. (2012). *Solution-focused brief therapy: 101 key points and techniques.* New York: Routledge.

Saleebey, D. (2006). *The strengths perspective in social work practice* (4th ed.). Boston: Allyn & Bacon.

Seligman, M. E. P. (1999). The president's address. *American Psychologist, 54,* 559–562.

Solution Focused Brief Therapy Association. (2013). *Solution focused therapy treatment manual for working with individuals* (2d ed.). Retrieved from www.sfbta.org

Snyder, C. R. (1994). *The psychology of hope: You can get there from here.* New York: Simon & Schuster.

4   SFBT and Violent Crime

■ JACQUI VON CZIFFRA-BERGS

■ INTRODUCTION

Violent crime is unfortunately part of our lives and affects everyone. No matter where you are in the world, there is a likelihood that one of your newspaper headlines includes a story about a violent crime (e.g., "Man brutally attacked," "Woman held at gunpoint by three men," "Children held hostage in armed robbery"). As clinicians we hear stories of violent crimes on a regular basis through various media outlets, and this is often part of our daily workload. I practice as a psychotherapist in Johannesburg, South Africa, and at least once a week my practice sees a client who has been a victim of a violent crime. According to Claymore (2016) South Africa is ranked the third most dangerous country in the world. As a clinician in private practice, I am continually confronted with trauma debriefing sessions with my clients. A violent crime can be defined as a crime in which an offender uses force or threatens a victim with violence, and in South Africa most cases of violent crime take place between people who know each other or live in the same communities (Institute for Security Studies, 2016). The high rate of muggings, home invasions, carjackings, rapes, assaults, and murders in South Africa is of grave concern. No matter how the violent crime is committed, the bottom line is that intentional harm was inflicted upon another person. This often leaves the victim of a violent crime with feelings of disillusionment, fear, and a loss of hope in life and in humanity in general.

However, depending on which part of the traumatic story you focus on, trauma can also highlight the human spirit's ability to survive and cope. How people survive and overcome a violent crime perpetrated against them is miraculous. People often find bravery and coping skills during a traumatic event they never knew they had and discover elements of themselves they never knew existed. Yes, a violent crime is devastating and terrible; however, it is not the whole story. A person's incredible ability to cope with the adversity of a violent crime and to survive the trauma completes the story. People "bounce back" (Bannink, 2014, p. 19), they are resilient, and they even grow in the wake of trauma. Emphasizing this aspect of the trauma story does not minimize the effects of trauma or negate the extreme pain people suffer, but it is important to stress the incredible effort people make in overcoming and coping with a violent crime.

This chapter focuses on how we can assist our clients to see their resilience, their survival mechanisms, and their ability to cope and even thrive after a violent crime. It looks at clients' managing trauma after a violent crime through a solution-focused lens and highlights the extraordinary ability of people to endure hardship, overcome fear, and live fulfilling lives.

■ IMPACT OF VIOLENT CRIME ON SOCIETY AND ON THERAPISTS

We all know that the trauma after a violent crime shatters a client's belief in safety, personal invulnerability, and trust in others. However, the results of several studies suggest that the trauma experienced after a violent crime need not be debilitating. When one highlights resources and resilience and focuses on hope and optimism, therapy shifts from post-traumatic stress to post-traumatic success (Bannink, 2014). In my past work, before solution-focused brief therapy, I would only focus on what happened, what went wrong, and how people felt after a violent crime had been committed against them. This left me drained and disillusioned with people, and I started dreading my work. I was trained in a classical medical model of trauma debriefing, and after hearing the same trauma story being retold for the second or third time, I could feel the secondary trauma infecting my soul, leaving me exhausted and scared to go outside. Previously, practicing from the belief that all people who experience a violent crime suffer from PTSD and that a form of abreactive therapy (healing by reliving an experience) is needed in order for my client to heal. This led to my becoming what Bannink (2014) calls a "victimologist" (p. 5). Without intending to do so, I was making my clients the victims of their own therapy, and I was becoming a witness or victim of their traumatic experience. Luckily, O'Hanlon (2011) dispels this myth and mentions that not all people who have experienced trauma suffer from PTSD. He challenges the concept that there are only negative effects after trauma, especially since a violent crime affects everyone differently. People respond differently in the wake of violence or when another person is intentionally trying to hurt them. Many different factors, such as the characteristics of the client, the type of violent crime, the meaning the client gives to the trauma, and sociocultural factors, influence how the client responds after the traumatic event.

Realizing that people are resilient and can experience growth after a trauma (Bannink, 2014) opened a whole new world for me. A new journey of *solution-focused strength rebriefing* started to take place, and I began to view the therapy process with a client who had experienced a violent crime as a *rebriefing of resilience* and a celebration of bravery rather than an interaction with terror by debriefing what went wrong. Looking through a strength-based resilience lens empowers my clients to get in touch with their inner resources and brings hope into the therapy room. Both client and clinician become co-therapists to hope and growth, and this leaves both parties feeling inspired, hopeful, and capable.

■ SFBT AS A GOOD FIT FOR CLIENTS WHO HAVE EXPERIENCED VIOLENT CRIME

Practicing and applying SFBT requires a specific way of looking at the world, at people, and at the change process. A solution-focused philosophy implies that you apply a strength-based orientation (Franklin, 2009) to the client who has experienced a traumatic situation. Seeing clients as resourceful and capable and not as victims of the trauma allows them the opportunity to take control, and practically and pragmatically create change. Solution-focused brief therapy is the study of "strength and virtue" and not of "disease, weakness and damage" (Bannink, 2014, p. 5), and differs from traditional trauma debriefing. Instead of focusing on the traumatic event, fixing the suffering and defusing the negative emotions, SFBT focuses on the client's "strengths and resilience," coping, and resourcefulness before, during, and after the violent crime and helps the client to cultivate a different way of looking at themselves and of approaching life (de Shazer, 2007, p. 14). Solution-focused brief therapy requires a mind shift from conventional trauma debriefing (Edwards, 2009) and defusing of emotions to a mindset of building and empowering a client to a healthier future. As Bannink states, "Treatment is not just fixing what is wrong; it is also building on what is right" (2014, p. 5). The true value of SFBT for clients who have experienced a violent crime is that the clinician is not trying to fix what went wrong and what others did but rather guiding our clients to remember and experience their resiliency. This approach allows the client to notice the best version of themselves and expand on the more minute aspects of control, bravery, and remarkable strength they exhibited.

Clients who have experienced violent crime do extraordinary things to get through the traumatic event. If we only focus on the traumatic event itself and how they felt while it was happening, we become "victimologists" (Bannink, 2014, p. 5), emphasizing the event and not the resilience of the person. I firmly believe that we need to become *resilientologists* instead and focus on the client's resourcefulness, coping, inner strength, and ability to bounce back. This does not mean that we sugarcoat the negative traumatic event but rather that we create new ways of looking at the client, the event, and their future.

■ TRAUMA CHANGES THE BRAIN

Once an act of violence has been committed, it leaves the client vulnerable and disillusioned. Take the case of a 25-year-old single mother named Jill, who has just arrived at her holiday cottage with her eight-month-old baby boy. She puts the baby to sleep and starts unpacking the groceries in the kitchen. A man walks in with a knife, takes her to the bedroom where her baby is sleeping, ties her up, and threatens to rape her. All she can think of is that she must get him out of the cottage and away from her child. Jill fabricates a story that she has hidden a lot of money on top of the kitchen cupboard and that she will show him where it is. As he unties her she breaks free and jumps through a glass sliding door, smashing the glass, and runs out into the street screaming for help. The man flees, leaving her and her baby alone. Two weeks later she enters therapy with a fear of being alone, fear of men, fear of being able to take care of her child, and a fear of the future. The traumatic experience has changed her brain and created a heightened sense of fear, interrupted her filtering system, and confused her sense of self (van der Kolk, 2014).

New research is showing that the brain changes in response to experiences "for better or for worse" (Bannink, 2014, p. 32). Clients who have experienced a violent crime tend to get stuck in a trauma pattern—they keep seeing the attacker's face, predicting a negative outcome, or reliving a traumatic scene. However, "Neuroscientists have discovered that the brain does not remain stable for the rest of its life but changes" (Bannink, 2014, p. 33); and thus, if trauma can change the brain then so, too, can therapy. New experiences create new neural pathways, and these new pathways become stronger the more they are used. For clinicians, this means we need to create a more resilient, strength-based experience of the trauma. If we keep focusing on the negative experiences of the trauma, these negative patterns or pathways established by the trauma will become stronger. Conversely, if we focus on the resilience during or after a trauma, these experiences will also get stronger and change the way the person perceives himself or herself and what happened, thus making it more likely that new positive long-term connections and memories will form.

By the time Jill arrives for therapy, her brain has established a clear neural pathway of fear and possibly depression—and an overwhelming sense of being an inadequate mother. Traditional trauma debriefing would encourage this young woman to retell what had happened, would focus on normalizing feelings, and would educate Jill in what she could still expect to happen to her after such a trauma. In solution-focused brief therapy, we strategically ask questions aimed at helping Jill's brain get out of the trauma rut by creating a new strength-based association of what she did to help herself. In doing so, we become "amygdala whispers" (Bannink, 2014, p. 7) to Jill's brain; rebriefing it on her strengths, her resilience, her coping, her abilities, and guiding her to a healthier future vision.

When we compare traditional trauma debriefing questions and reflections with solution-focused questions, one can clearly see what experience is amplified in therapy and therefore how the brain is encouraged to change.

Unintentionally, traditional trauma debriefing runs the risk of amplifying the negative experience (Table 4.1). By doing this it intensifies the negative neural pathway that was established by the traumatic event in the first place. Solution-focused questions and reflections, on the other hand, create strength-based and resource-filled experiences and establish a resilient neural pathway with a future focus.

TABLE 4.1. Traditional Trauma Debriefing

Questions and reflections	Client response	Amplified experience
Tell me what happened?	• He tied me up. • He nearly raped me. • He cut my face. • He threatened my baby.	• I got hurt. • I nearly died. • I had no control. • I was afraid.
Jill, what did you hear, see, smell, feel?	• I smelt alcohol on his breath. • I smelt old sweat. • It was so quiet around me. • My baby was sleeping.	• Highlights fear and being out of control. • Remembering what went wrong. • Encourages destructive recall.
So you felt scared and alone, Jill? Sounds as if you were very worried about your baby, Jill?	• Yes, I was very scared. • Yes, I got hurt. • Yes, I nearly died. • Yes, he could have hurt my baby.	• I was alone. • I have no control. • I was terrified. • I nearly died. • My baby nearly died.
Under these circumstances, Jill, it is natural to feel stressed and overwhelmed.	• I am allowed to feel this way. • I must feel scared. • I am allowed to feel like a bad mother.	• I am going to be scared forever. • I cannot look after my child. • I am not a good mother.
Jill you can expect negative symptoms after trauma, such as fear and anger.	• I will not sleep. • I will continue to feel scared. • I will not cope.	• I cannot do this. • I will always stay afraid. • My child will always be in danger.

TABLE 4.2. Solution-Focused Brief Therapy

Questions and reflections	Client response	Amplified experience
Jill, how did you get the idea to fabricate a lie and get him to the kitchen?	• I thought of my child's safety. • I needed to protect my son, get him away from my child. • I just did it, I did not think about myself, just about keeping my child safe.	• I think of my child first. • I am a good mommy who protects her child.
Jill, it sounds like you stayed in control. You kept thinking about your child and you made a plan.	• I had to get the guy away from him. • I had to do something. • I had to act.	• I take control. • I am a protective mother. • I make plans.
Jill, how did you manage to stay calm?	• I don't know, I just did it. • I kept saying to myself, "stay calm, stay calm."	• I trust my instincts. • I can calm myself down.
Jill, how did you find the courage to break through a glass door?	• I just did it. • I just ran.	• I am brave. • I am courageous.
Suppose your son were old enough to retell this story to his friends, what would he say he is proud of?	• That I am a brave, strong mommy. • That I'm not afraid. • That I will do anything to protect my child.	• I am a strong woman. • I am a plan maker. • I am a protective mother. • I am courageous. • I remember all the positive, brave and protective things I did to save my baby and myself.

Solution-focused questions elicit the client's inner resilience to cope with a trauma (Table 4.2). I believe that these questions are asked by a *resilientologist* and not a *victimologist* to encourage productive recall from the client. Steve de Shazer (2007) affirms that the questions we ask in therapy create a virtual reality for the client. The more we repeat and amplify the coping skills, abilities, and resourcefulness of the client, the more we create an experience of a resilient person. This changes the client's neural pathways and helps them get out of the trauma rut they are stuck in. For clients who have been victims of violent crime where someone did something harmful to them, solution-focused questions shift the attention from what someone did to them toward what they did to help themselves. This gives the client a sense of control and empowers the client to regain mastery of their lives.

■ PRACTICAL APPLICATION OF SFBT AFTER A VIOLENT CRIME

SFBT is aimed at strategically guiding clients to acknowledge their strengths and create a better, healthier future. After a violent crime, clients are often so stuck in the trauma rut of what happened that they cannot envision things being different. It is as though they are so disillusioned by the violent events that they have lost faith in their fellow humans and cannot picture a future with any hope. As solution-focused clinicians, we lead our clients from behind through a strategic journey of finding out what they want, empowering them to believe in themselves, creating a picture of new hope, and inviting them to change. The following discussion of the application of SFBT after an act of violent crime will include a detailed case study of a client who experienced a violent carjacking in front of his family. The process and application of SFBT starts with the client describing his best hopes and goals, rediscovering his strengths, envisioning a preferred future, and ending with an invitation to the possibility of change will be discussed in detail.

■ DESCRIPTIONS OF BEST HOPES

Solution-focused clinicians are first and foremost solution-builders and not problem-solvers. This means that the clinician is constantly collaborating with the client to lead from behind toward the client's goals and best hopes. The clinician's job is "to create a conversation and context where solutions can emerge" (Franklin, 2009, p. 138). The aim of the solution-focused therapeutic conversation is to discover what the client hopes to achieve from therapy. Typically the most common starting question is, "What are your best hopes from our work together?" This opening question sets the scene for what SFBT is all about and initiates the contracting process between the clinician and the client that the focus of the therapy is on the client's goals and needs and not on the traumatic event.

However, in my experience, clients who have experienced a violent crime do not initially answer the best-hopes question: they are stuck in the trauma rut to the extent that they do not seem to hear the question and just want to tell you what happened. If the client wants to tell the trauma story, then it is the clinician's job to acknowledge their need to talk but to also listen with a constructive SFBT ear and deliberately respond in a way that helps the client shift their focus to their resiliency and to rebriefing. What is crucial is that the clinician hears what happened but *only* validates and acknowledges the client's strengths and resources while reframing the trauma complaints into goals. Turning what the client no longer wants into what the client does want leads to understanding the client's best hopes or goals for the session. Thus, as the client is telling what happened, the clinician selectively reframes, reflects, and compliments only the resilience, coping, and values of the person while amplifying and reflecting only on what the client wants to replace the current trauma rut with.

■ BUILD A RELATIONSHIP WITH THE PERSON, NOT THE TRAUMA

Stories of violence and horror are full of drama and emotion, and the clinician can easily get hooked into the trauma story. So instead of treating trauma in SFBT, the shift is toward working with an individual client to build a relationship with the person and not the trauma. As Elliott Connie (2016) states, *trust over trauma*; you need to believe in the person and not in the event. It is vitally important to validate the person and not the traumatic experience.

Below is a session I did with a 40-year-old Zulu man named Desmond, who had been held up at gunpoint in front of his wife, mother, and child during a carjacking at his home. Desmond was left feeling disillusioned and disempowered, and as a Zulu man who is culturally responsible for the well-being of his family, he felt as though he had failed them. The following case illustrates the process of turning trauma complaints into goals and understanding his best hopes for the session:

> CLINICIAN: Desmond, how can I be helpful to you today? What are your best hopes for this session?
>
> DESMOND: On Friday after picking up my daughter from school, three guys with guns drove in behind me as I drove up my driveway. They forced us out of the car, I unclipped my daughter from her car seat and got out. They then forced us to lie down and stole our money, our jewellery and our car. My wife was in the house, thank goodness. She thinks I need to talk to someone. My wife says I need to debrief and tell the story but I am not sure. She wants me to feel like a man again.
>
> CLINICIAN: So your wife wants you to feel like a man again?
>
> DESMOND: Yes, I suppose I feel I did not protect my family enough or maybe I could have done more to protect them.
>
> CLINICIAN: Desmond, so you want to be able to feel like you protect your family?

DESMOND: Yes, it wasn't nice. I need this picture to go away that keeps popping in my head.

CLINICIAN: So you would like this picture to go away and you would like to find a new picture?

DESMOND: Yes, I do.

CLINICIAN: Desmond, I am a solution focused therapist and that means I look at things slightly differently, and I ask different kinds of questions.

DESMOND: (shakes head) Like how?

CLINICIAN: Well, I would like you to tell the story of what happened, but in a different way. I want us to look at it with a different lens and to retell and re-remember the story in a way you might not have thought or been aware of.

DESMOND: OK, I will try anything.

Even though Desmond did not answer the best-hopes question directly, he has clearly told me about three distinct goals for the session. I am now strategically aware that Desmond wants to:

- feel like a man again
- be able to know he can protect his family
- find a different picture in his head about what happened

In order for us to reach these goals it is essential that I help Desmond find his strengths again and empower him as a capable, resourceful man. Solution-focused brief therapy is not about problem solving but about helping the client discover the best version of himself. I call this *strength rebriefing* instead of trauma debriefing.

■ REBRIEF STRENGTHS

Yvonne Dolan (2012) states that in order for the person to recover from trauma, their perspective has to expand, and in order for their perspective on the experience to expand, they need to experience themselves as a strong and resilient person. Dolan emphasizes that clinicians can make the client the victim of treatment by over-emphasizing what went wrong and by building an alliance with the traumatic event. Solution-focused clinicians need to be mindful of whom we are building the relationship with and which part of the traumatic event gets amplified.

■ REBRIEFING STRENGTHS THROUGH SELECTIVE STRENGTH-ORIENTATED LISTENING AND REFLECTING

One of the most important aspects of SFBT and rebriefing strengths is to listen selectively to the trauma story for any signs of resilience and strengths in the client. Selectively only reflecting the strengths back is what Bill O'Hanlon (2011) calls "Rogers with a twist." We are still empathic and reflective but in a strength-based way. Only the coping, strengths, and positive handling of the trauma are reflected back to the client. In so doing the clinician is rebriefing the client on their strengths; helping the client remember elements of themselves that they might not have been aware of and thus amplifying the best version of the client. Selectively reflecting back strengths validates the person; it shows who they are and how they handle adversity. A solution-focused clinician listens past the trauma to the client's core values and how the client managed to survive. Selective listening is an attentive and mindful process that looks for the resourcefulness and resilience of a client and builds a relationship with the best version of the person and not with the trauma. This constant reflection of strengths becomes a positive reappraisal of the client's coping and ability to heal (Bannink, 2014) and empowers the client to act as a co-therapist in their own therapy. Debbie Hogan (2009, p. 181) says that instead of listening for "areas of pathology and dysfunction," the solution-focused clinician listens for areas of "competence and strengths."

> CLINICIAN: Desmond, I am curious, what did your wife do during this incident that you are proud of?
>
> DESMOND: She stayed inside the house and she didn't come out. Normally her instinct would be to come out fighting. But this time she stayed inside the house. She said when she saw me pulling our daughter behind me and talking to these guys calmly, she realised I had it under control and she could call for help. She called the security company.
>
> CLINICIAN: So she stayed in the house and called the security company?
>
> DESMOND: Yes, she did.
>
> CLINICIAN: Desmond, I am just curious; how come she stayed in the house and did not react like she instinctively would? What did she see happening that made her stay and not run outside?
>
> DESMOND: She told me that she saw me take my daughter and gently pull her behind me and she saw me talk to them. She said she knew I had this thing under control and she had to get help.
>
> CLINICIAN: So, Desmond, if your wife was here and I asked her what she saw you do that she is proud of, what would she say?
>
> DESMOND: She'd say me talking calmly and that I had it under control and that again she realised that I was protecting our daughter by pulling her behind me, there was no need for her to come running.
>
> CLINICIAN: Sounds like you had it covered?
>
> DESMOND: Yes.
>
> CLINICIAN: You had the whole situation under as much control as you could and you had your child protected?

DESMOND: Yes, I did.

CLINICIAN: That is great to know?

DESMOND: Yes, it is.

As the case example above shows, by selectively listening only to the above-mentioned strengths of Desmond, the clinician is choosing to preserve the details of resilience, omit the negative destructive effects, and contribute to a strength-based version of the client (Bavelas et al., 2013). Selectively reflecting resilience and coping builds or co-constructs a version of the client's life that is strong and capable. Solution-focused clinicians are thus building a relationship with the resilient client and not with the traumatic horror story. SFBT is a competency-based therapy that selectively reflects the strengths and amplifies the client's competency and puts these positive differences to work (Bannink, 2014).

■ INTRODUCING POSITIVE EMOTION AS PART OF STRENGTH REBRIEFING

A client who has experienced an act of violence is often saturated with negative emotions and negative associations. Adding positive emotions to a negative trauma story acts as an "antidote to the negative lingering emotions" (Bannink, 2014, p. 7). Including positive emotions into the therapy serves as a negative undoing effect, reintroduces and reminds the client of their strengths and becomes part of the process of rebriefing strengths. Ben Furman (2012) reiterates that bringing positive emotion into the trauma story creates a new experience and thus paints the story with a little color. By adding positive emotion and introducing the concept of pride rather than panic, new states of thoughts and behaviors are triggered, and the client's reality can completely change (Kim & Franklin, 2015). The trauma pattern is interrupted and the client "rewires his circuit board and thus breaks the negative patterns that have formed" (Kershaw & Wade, 2014, p. 8). SFBT helps introduce positive emotion after a traumatic event and thereby helps to broaden the individual's thought–action repertoire, thus helping the client to think and behave differently (Kim & Franklin, 2015). Introducing positive emotions such as pride changes how the client thinks about a traumatic situation. This ultimately changes the client's reality and creates a productive recall or a resilient memory (Short, 2014).

> **CLINICIAN:** Desmond, what did your mother do during this incident that you are proud of?
>
> **DESMOND:** She immediately took our dog that ran up to greet us by the collar. She held him tight.
>
> **CLINICIAN:** And you are proud of her for this?
>
> **DESMOND:** Yes, she knew that if the dog barked or went for them they would get panicky and do something stupid.

CLINICIAN: So you are proud of your mom for reading the situation well and keeping the dog calm?

DESMOND: Yes, she did, I didn't think about it, but yes, she did read it well. We all did.

CLINICIAN: So you are proud of all of you for reading the situation well, staying calm and doing what you needed to protect your child?

DESMOND: Yes, I am.

The broaden-and-build theory of positive emotions has developed strong empirical support for its claim that positive emotions can help generate change in clients (Fredrickson, 1998). Consistent with this hypothesis, SFBT incorporates specific techniques and questioning that can help create these positive emotions that will enhance clients' intellectual and social resources (Kim & Franklin, 2015). In the vignette above, the introduction of the positive emotion of pride counteracts the negative emotion and broadens the client's perspective of himself and his family. Research has shown that this undoing effect "promotes creativity and flexibility" and opens the client up to the possibility of a different future (Bannink, 2014, p. 9).

■ YES-SET TO STRENGTHS

Another way to amplify and rebrief strengths is to ask resilience-based questions where the obvious answer is yes. The yes-set is a term initially used by Milton Erickson in hypnosis (Short, 2014) and is extremely valuable in helping the client acknowledge their resourcefulness. In SFBT, clinicians apply the yes-set in order to guide the client to say yes to their strengths, resourcefulness, and resilience. The client is acknowledging and accepting their own abilities to cope in harsh circumstances. Constantly repeating strength-based questions, and letting the client amplify their own inner strength by saying yes to their strengths, repeatedly walks the neural pathway of resourcefulness and rebriefs the client as a strong, capable individual. I believe the yes-set colors the trauma experience with competencies. As MacDonald (2011, p. 11) rightfully states, "Language is a behaviour," thus by repeatedly hearing their strengths being acknowledged and affirming their own competency, the behavior description is more likely to become part of their belief system. Creating a yes-set can also be compared to Steve de Shazer's references to language matching, using the client's words but reframing them into a question where the obvious answer is yes. This keeps the clinician connected to the client's strengths and builds a resilient version of the client (de Shazer, 2007).

CLINICIAN: And I was just wondering about your daughter, Desmond, what did she do that you are proud of?

DESMOND: (gets emotional) When they forced us to lie down I pulled her away and lay on top of her and whispered in her ear to calm down.

Normally she is just a spontaneous kid, but this time she was calm and she listened to my voice. When I kissed her she stayed calm and listened to me because I covered her from this nonsense.

CLINICIAN: So during one of the most difficult events she listened to you?

DESMOND: Yes.

CLINICIAN: This spontaneous child calmed down and listened to her Dad?

DESMOND: Yes, she did.

CLINICIAN: And you lay on top of her to protect her?

DESMOND: Yes, I did.

CLINICIAN: You whispered in her ear and kissed her?

DESMOND: Yes, I did.

CLINICIAN: Under one of the scariest situations you showed your child love?

DESMOND: Yes, I did.

CLINICIAN: Does your wife know you did this?

DESMOND: Yes, my daughter told her.

CLINICIAN: So the one thing your daughter remembers is your love and your protection?

DESMOND: Yes, she does.

CLINICIAN: And the one thing your daughter wanted to share with her Mom is you kissing her?

DESMOND: Yes.

CLINICIAN: Desmond I am curious; what was your wife's reaction when your daughter told her about the kiss?

DESMOND: She said that's why she married me.

CLINICIAN: Yes, that is the reason she married you.

DESMOND: Yes.

CLINICIAN: This loving man who will protect his child no matter what?

DESMOND: Yes.

CLINICIAN: This loving man who whispers love calmly into his daughter's ear, who kisses his child while terrible things are happening. This is the reason she married you?

DESMOND: Yes.

By summarizing and paraphrasing only the resilient aspects of the story and repeating the strengths of the client back to them, the client always responds with a yes. This *echoing* of strengths and co-construction of a resilient conversation helps a new and "different version to emerge, a version that has the potential to open up new possibilities in the client's life" (Bavelas, 2013, p. 32) despite the trauma experience. As Bannink (2014, p. 36) states, "Repetition is the key in changing the brain," and by rebriefing the client's resilience, you re-program the fear perception, reset the filtering system, and empower the client with a sense of control (van der Kolk, 2014). The negative emotion and thinking has been de-patterned by the clinician's questions, and the client is now ready to look to the future. The clinician can therefore now ask leading questions about how the client wants things to be different and start unpacking a preferred future.

■ DESCRIPTIONS OF A PREFERRED FUTURE

Solution-focused questions change the trauma pattern by default and open up a range of new perceptions and realizations. Once the strengths have been rebriefed, solution-focused questions about the preferred future can be introduced. The client can now be invited to think differently and embrace their own inner strength and coping toward creating a healthier preferred future for themselves and their family. As soon as a strength-based version of the client is established, the client is ready for questions that pull them and their family into the future. By rebriefing the client on their strengths, the client is able to find stability and hope, which is another positive emotion (Kim & Franklin, 2015). By amplifying the client's resilience and integrating their strengths, the client is able to envision a different, more hopeful future for themselves and their family. Questions can now strategically be aimed at creating a future pull. Here is an example of the session with Desmond that illustrates his descriptions of a preferred future:

DESMOND: Doc, can I tell my family? They have been for debriefing at the trauma counselor, but can I tell them this?

CLINICIAN: OK, Desmond, let's suppose you went home tonight and you told your wife this version of the story, what would be different for her?

DESMOND: She would be so happy. She would hear me take back my power as a man, and she would know I am OK and that she is safe.

CLINICIAN: And suppose you went home tonight and you told your daughter this story, what would be different for her?

DESMOND: She would know we are a family of strong people who love each other and think quickly.

CLINICIAN: And Desmond, suppose you told your mother this story—what would be different for her?

DESMOND: She would feel relieved; she would dream about how strong we are and not just dream about how scared we were.

CLINICIAN: And Desmond, now that you have heard this version, what is different for you?

DESMOND: Looking at it from this angle I see we all did something we do not normally do. They can steal our money, our phones, our jewellery and our car; but they could not take my instinct, my inside. As a family we were united. We made decisions that actually helped us to be where we are today.

CLINICIAN: Yes, you all did what you would not normally do, yet what you did was the right thing to do?

DESMOND: Yes, it actually showed me my wife, my child, my own, and my mother's calm soul.

CLINICIAN: So it showed your calmness, your love, and your brave reactions to access a situation and take control.

DESMOND: Yes, and it brought us closer together and has made me realise things I did not notice before, like it showed me our insides—even in difficult situations we can still stay calm.

Asking a *suppose* question automatically implies that things will be different. Using the "presuppositional language" (Connie & Metcalf, 2009, p. 16) of *suppose* and *different* creates a vivid description of a different reality, a different perception, and a different picture of life after a violent crime. The miracle question is also a wonderful *suppose* question, and it can be utilized to create descriptions of a preferred future. I did not ask Desmond the miracle question, as in my experience working in a multicultural context, a miracle is not a concept readily accepted within certain African cultures. With Desmond I just used *suppose* and *different* to expand on how the future could change for him and his family.

▪ SUMMARY AND INVITATION TO CHANGE

Research shows that successful clinicians focus on their client's strengths from the beginning of the session to the end by referring back to the client's strengths and resilience (Bannink, 2014). Reminding clients of their resilience and coping increases the client's likelihood of continuing to use their strengths. Ending each session with compliments and a positive summary of all the resilient aspects of the person amplifies the resilient version of the client and emphasizes the positive abilities of the client. Inviting the client to go home and do something different reinforces the change that took place in the session.

CLINICIAN: So Desmond, here at the end of our session I just want to conclude with what really impresses me about what you have told me. Desmond, I am so impressed with how you all instinctively knew what to do to stay safe. I am so impressed by your wife's trust in your ability to look after her child, by your mother's calm reading of the situation and taking the dog under her control; but mostly Desmond, I am impressed by your ability to calmly and gently love and protect your child. Your ability to love while being threatened stands out for me. So Desmond, in this week to come I would like to invite you to go home and tell your family this version of what happened in your own gentle, loving, and protective way.

■ SUMMARY

People do not come to change their past. They come to change their future.
—Milton Erickson

SFBT is a hopeful and respectful way of helping clients manage the trauma of a violent crime by building a relationship with the client and not with the traumatic event. Solution-focused questions have a profound impact on clients who are managing trauma. The questions empower them to see themselves and their future differently and to change the neural pathways in the brain. By determining what the client wants from the therapy, or what the client's best hopes are for therapy, the clinician continues to serve the client's needs and does not impose preconceptions of what will be good for a client after a trauma. Rebriefing the client's strengths validates the client as a resilient person who has coped before and will continue to cope. I believe that working as a solution-focused *resilientologist* encourages strategic, brief, and effective therapy that creates a different version of the client after a violent act and restores hope. This process invites clients to dream again and take control of their lives. At the same time, doing therapy with a strength-based solution-focused lens also has a profound effect on the clinician. Being a part of a process where resilience and strengths are continuously mirrored is uplifting and impactful for both parties. One cannot help but admire one's clients and their abilities: it is a humbling, empowering, and ultimately hopeful experience.

■ REFERENCES

Bannink, F. (2014). *Post-traumatic success*. New York: W. W. Norton.

Bavelas, J., de Jong, P., & Korman, H. (2013). Microanalysis of formulations: In solution-focused brief therapy, Cognitive behavioural therapy, and motivational interviewing. *Journal of Systemic Therapies, 32*(3), 31–45.

Claymore, E (2016). South Africa ranked third most dangerous in the world. Retrieved TheSouthAfrican.com on the 11th of October 2017 from http://www.thesouthafrican.com/sa-ranked-the-third-most-dangerous-country-in-the-world/

Connie, E., & Metcalf, L. (Eds). (2009). *The art of solution focused therapy*. New York: Springer.

Connie, E. (2016). *Changing trauma flashbacks*. Paper presented at the Solution Focused Institute of South Africa, Johannesburg, 10 October 2016.

de Shazer, S. (2007). *More than miracles*. New York: Routledge.

Dolan, Y. (2012). Solution Focus for trauma: State of the art—brief solutions for trauma [Webinar]. Retrieved from http://psychotherapyconferences.com.

Edwards, D. (2009). Treating PTSD in South Africa. *Journal of Psychology in Africa, 19*(2), 189–198.

Franklin, C. (2009). Acceptance, transparency, research: Because others want to know. In E. Connie, & L. Metcalf (Eds.), *The art of solution focused therapy*. New York: Springer.

Fredrickson, B. L. (1998). What good are positive emotions? *Review of General Psychology, 2*, 300–319.

Furman, B. (2012). Enriching experience and putting trauma in its place. Brief solutions for trauma [Webinar]. Retrieved from http://psychotherapyconferences.com.

Hogan, D (2009). My encounter with the solution focused therapy model. In E. Connie, & L. Metcalf (Eds.), *The art of solution focused therapy*. New York: Springer

Institute for Security Studies. (2016). https://issafrica.org/crimehub/analysis/press-releases/sa-crime-stats-hope-amid-alarming-trends

Kershaw, C., & Wade, B. (2014). From Trauma to thriving: Neuroscience and hypnosis for successful living [Webinar]. Retrieved from http://psychotherapyconferences.com.

Kim, J. S., & Franklin, C. (2015). The importance of positive emotions in solution-focused brief therapy. *Best Practices in Mental Health, 11*(1), 25–41.

MacDonald, A. (2011). *Solution focused therapy*. London: SAGE.

O'Hanlon, B. (2011). Resolving trauma without drama. Brief solutions for trauma [Webinar]. Retrieved from http://psychotherapyconferences.com.

Short, D. (2014). Using Ericksonian hypnosis for trauma and memory reconsolidation [Webinar]. Retrieved from http://psychotherapyconferences.com.

Van der Kolk, B. (2014). How to help patient rewire a traumatised brain [Webinar]. Retrieved from www.nicabm.com.

5 Preventing Suicide in the Aftermath of Trauma

■ HEATHER FISKE

> Letting there be room for not knowing is the most important thing of all.
>
> —Pema Chödrön, "When Things Fall Apart"

■ TRAUMA AND SUICIDE

If only the magic wand in my office worked right, no one I know would ever have a flashback again. Flashbacks—a common response to traumatizing experience—are overwhelming and debilitating: "It's a full-on fight-or-flight feeling with no one to fight and nowhere to run" (Jessome, 2016, p. 9). The sense of helplessness that flashbacks engender, as well as the loss of physical, cognitive, and emotional control, can be pathways to hopelessness for those who suffer them. And of course, flashbacks (or "replays" as the client described in this article calls them) are just one of the possible negative outcomes of a traumatizing experience.

No wonder then, that the constellation of troubles and pains we call post-traumatic stress is strongly associated with suicidal ideation, behavior, and death, regardless of differences in age, background, or nature of the traumatic events (Gradus et al., 2010; Panagioti, Gooding, Dunn, & Tarier, 2011; Panagioti, Gooding, & Tarrier, 2009; Short & Nemeroff, 2014). This book is filled with useful practices for reducing the negative impact of posttraumatic sequelae and for identifying, facilitating, and enhancing the positive impact—that is, post-traumatic growth/thriving/resilience (Linley & Joseph, 2004; Nugent, 2014; Tedeschi & Calhoun, 2004). The finding that reducing post-traumatic symptoms leads to reductions in suicidal ideation (Cox et al., 2016) implies that all of these solution-focused practices may in fact be suicide prevention.

Suicide, which the World Health Organization (WHO, 2014) calls the "act of deliberately killing oneself" (p. 12), is the cause of 800,000 deaths worldwide each year. It is the second most common injury-related death and the second leading cause of death among those 15–29 years of age. It is estimated that there are at least 20 suicide attempts (i.e., a suicidal behavior that is nonfatal) for every death by suicide (WHO, 2014). These numbers exist in spite of the acknowledged reality that almost all suicide deaths are preventable. Suicide attempts and suicide deaths generate further trauma and elevated suicide risk for friends and family, first responders, and community members. The bottom line on the statistics of suicide and trauma is this: one preventable death is too many.

■ GETTING HERE: GOODNESS OF FIT

I began looking for more efficient ways of working with clients struggling with suicide during the 1980s, when I worked in a hospital with a small adolescent mental health team that was overwhelmed with referrals (four professionals; 60 to 90 referrals—most of them high risk—per month). Even young people who had already made suicide attempts were on waiting lists for months—an unacceptable situation. Solution-focused brief therapy (SFBT) was effective and much more efficient than the long-term treatments I had been using—and time matters with suicide risk. Also, I was increasingly impressed with the "fit" between SFBT and clinical work with people who were desperate enough to see suicide as a solution (Fiske, 2008). That fit arises from a number of factors.

1) SFBT is "hope-friendly" (Cooper, Darmody, & Dolan, 2003, p. 76). Uncovering histories of strengths, resources, successes, coping, and positive intentions builds hope that feeds positive therapeutic change (Kim & Franklin, 2015; Snyder, Michael, & Cheavens, 2000). A number of clinicians and researchers have focused on the "pragmatics of hope" in SFBT (Dolan, 2008), which focuses on how various aspects of solution-focused practice nurture and maintain clients' hope (Blundo, Bolton, & Hall, 2014; Dolan, 2008; Reiter, 2010; Taylor & Fiske, 2005; Wilson, 2015). Research findings have supported the hope-inducing properties of SFBT (McKeel, 2012), which were discussed in Chapter 3. And of course, clients are often demonstrating hope from the start just by being alive and in conversation with us. Cooper, Darmody, and Dolan (2003) noted this as well: "The act of asking for help is . . . 'hope-implicit' behavior" (p. 76). Solution-focused conversations also contribute to an "atmosphere of activated resources" that has been found to be a prerequisite for therapeutic change (Gassmann & Grawe, 2006). Attending to clients' strengths is also hope building for clinicians, and clinicians' hope is catching: clients who perceive their helpers as hopeful about them have better outcomes (Bachelor, 1991). The focus on client strengths and the resulting hopefulness supports vicarious resiliency in clinicians, a term and concept introduced by Hernandez, Engstrom, and Gensei (2010) to denote "the positive meaning-making, growth, and transformations in the therapist's experience resulting

from exposure to the client's resilience" (p. 72). Practicing SFBT thus contributes to the mental health and well-being of clinicians and may mean that they are more likely to remain patient and compassionate with frequent callers or repeat attempters.

2) Over time, solution-focused clinicians develop confidence in clients' strengths and capacities and an expectation that however dark the situation, there will be more to their conversations than explorations of pain and trouble. This confidence and positive expectation helps them to be comfortable confronting and acknowledging clients' pain and despair and discussing clients' thoughts and plans for suicide in a matter-of-fact way. That comfort is important in an area of practice where fear, avoidance, and denial often mean that people in suicidal crisis do not get the help they need. It is also important to note that in preventing suicide there are typically ethical and professional mandates as well as safety concerns that mean we need to have basic information about people's thoughts and plans for killing themselves.

3) Solution-focused approaches help clinicians to balance acknowledgement of the pain and trouble clients are experiencing and the possibility for change and healing (Butler & Powers, 1996). Consider for example the typical form of a solution-focused question about coping: "Given how difficult your situation has been for the last year, how you managed to come to this appointment/keep working/ stay alive/take care of your child?" The bleak worldview often associated with experience of trauma—especially long-term experience—makes acknowledgement critical if useful conversation is to occur.

4) Solution-focused language habits mean that clinicians will carefully unpack the life-affirming side of suicidal ambivalence, allowing discussions on the reasons and plans for living as well as reasons and plans for dying. When a person's worldview is dark and their focus has narrowed to the idea that suicide is the solution to their problems (SOS, "suicide the only solution"), this attention to the life-affirming side acts as a powerful "tap on the shoulder." That "tap" can ease cognitive constriction and encourage clients who may have been entirely focused on everything that is wrong to notice reasons for living and possibilities for change. Thus, SFBT rebalances the conversation, shifting away from a primary focus on reasons and plans for suicide that may, especially with repetition, be part of "rehearsing" and desensitizing suicidal action (according to Thomas Joiner's 2005 concept of the "acquired ability" to die by suicide). Furthermore, careful choice and construction of questions, compliments, and feedback to fit with the client's language (and therefore with the client's ideas and beliefs) is typical SFBT practice. This signals to the client that we are listening and not just

applying a formula or a one-size-fits-all approach. The use of the client's language greases the wheels of conversation and is especially helpful in a field where structured assessment and intervention formats can shut down the flow of conversation and impair relationship. For some clients who have had painful experiences and are seeing the world and themselves through a dark lens, adapting to their ways of speaking and thinking may mean modifying our language accordingly. This could mean, for example, asking reverse scaling questions from –10 to 1, or asking why things didn't get worse, or why the whole week wasn't as bad as the worst day.

5) Solution-focused use of the miracle question and other methods for helping clients to articulate details of their preferred futures is a unique contribution of SFBT practice. There are many good reasons for using these methods (de Shazer et al., 2007); when suicide is a possibility, some reasons are especially important. For example, both PTSD and suicidal behavior are associated with significant limitations in the capacity to think about a personal future (Brown et al., 2012; O'Connor, Smyth, & Williams, 2015) so having a structured way of developing and supporting such thinking is helpful. Contemplating a detailed "miracle picture" can be motivating and hope inducing, and the details of a "miracle" future often include things that people are already doing or at least beginning to do or thinking of doing. By identifying and noticing small steps that clients can see are both do-able and likely to make a difference. Small differences are often life saving in this work. Ed Shneidman (2005), the father of American suicidology, articulated that "there is a vital difference between 'intolerable' and 'just barely tolerable after all'" (p. 120). Preventing suicide is often a matter of discovering and reinforcing such differences, helping to make them "just noticeable" instead of invisible or overlooked.

6) Brigitte Lavoie (Fiske & Lavoie, 2016) suggests that SFBT may be a better fit for male clients than more traditional psychotherapies. Men are the highest risk group for suicide death, and most men are reluctant to seek help (WHO, 2014). Dulac (1999) has pointed out that traditional male values—staying in control, showing strength, maintaining a poker face, taking action, saving face, being successful, getting help only in crisis—are antithetical to the demands of traditional therapy. Those demands include: surrendering control, showing weakness, expressing emotions, talking, admitting flaws, accepting that one is not the expert, and committing to treatment. In SFBT, in contrast, the client decides the goal (thus staying in control), there is a focus on the client's strengths and successes, emotional expression is not required, clients identify action plans, the therapist assumes that the client is doing his

or her best and has good reasons for what he or she does, success comes easier when he or she is repeating something they already know how to do, and each session can be considered a single session.

7) SFBT modality utilizes strengths and abilities that are already present in clients, in their families and friends, in communities, and in helping systems. A suicidal crisis is not generally a good time to begin learning new coping techniques; and utilizing existing resources is more efficient, which is one of several reasons solution-focused therapy is "brief." And of course, recognizing that one has utilizable strengths that will help with one's problems is hope inducing for clients.

8) Lastly, because SFBT is not a problem-solving approach, it is useful with problems that cannot be solved. SFBT can help clients to focus on a future that is worth living despite loss, tragedy, or trauma.

■ APPLYING SFBT IN POST-TRAUMA SUICIDE PREVENTION

A lot of the key principles of a solution-focused stance are also useful when working with clients who are suicidal. These beliefs include such principles as:

- Change is always happening.
- The client is the expert in defining their problem and what they want.
- The client has the strengths and resources necessary for dealing with the problem(s) at hand.
- Small changes lead to larger changes.
- It doesn't matter where you start, so start with something that matters to the client.

A solution-focused stance also includes key practices, such as taking things slowly and staying mindful. The ability to remain slow and mindful even in crisis situations is fundamental to meaningful engagement with people in crisis. Staying mindful can be challenging in work with people who are suicidal, as it is all too easy for our minds to fill with risk-assessment protocols, diagnostic decision trees, and what I will record in the file or say to my supervisor. The solution-focused discipline of waiting quietly and expectantly to see what useful answers the client will come up with maintains conversational connection and creates room for a broad array of helpful possibilities.

The skill that underlies all other solution-focused practices is constructive listening and observation: watching and listening for the clients' strengths, capacities, good intentions, and improvements or successes. Among these "exceptions to the problem" are potential reasons for living. Scaling is one of the SFBT techniques that is most useful in "partializing" generalizing assumptions, breaking the overwhelming down into manageable bits, and making even small differences "just noticeable." In the present context, scaling is also especially helpful in providing a structured (i.e., safer) way to talk about emotional content that may be difficult for many clients to articulate. Concrete reminders to clients of hopeful signs, reasons for living, positive plans, and relationship supports are useful and necessary when clients are experiencing after-effects of trauma (which may include dissociation), or people who are in suicidal crisis (when logic is clouded, and it may be difficult to remember anything positive). Reminders may include notes or lists (e.g., of reasons for living), tattoos, or symbolic objects. "Rainy day letters" (Bannink, 2015; Dolan, 1991) are written when clients are feeling well and hopeful; include clients' own reflections on their strengths, accomplishments, reasons for living and future hopes and may provide much-needed reminders during more difficult times. A "medicine bundle" may serve a similar function (Dolan, 1991): based on American Indian practices, the bundle consists of a number of items that represent individual strengths, resources, positive emotions, and experiences. Similarly, David Jobes (2006) describes the development of a "hope kit," an idiosyncratic collection of "life-affirming items and meaningful mementoes that instill a sense of hope. Anything can be included that might remind the patient [sic] of why the struggle to live is worth fighting" (p. 83).

■ USEFUL QUESTIONS

All of the questions that I discuss here are second rate in a counseling session with suicidal clients. First-rate questions are those that are built on what the client says and on the direction and focus that are uniquely co-constructed in each session. But, of course, we have to start somewhere.

(1) *What are your best hopes for this conversation/consultation/group meeting?* This opening question, developed at Brief in London (Ratner, George, & Iveson, 2012), conveys helpful implicit assumptions (Bavelas, McGee, Phillips, & Routledge, 2000) that you have hopes or that you have more than one (or that you can select the best ones), that selecting best hopes is your responsibility, and that hopes are something we are interested in. The client can answer that there is no hope, although that answer is in fact rare, and clinicians need to know if that is true. Really the SFBT clinician is interested in knowing what the client wants. It's a challenging question, but if a solution-focused clinician has an opening agenda, it is to get an answer to this question and to do so *before* going on to develop a future picture or specific goals.

Elliott Connie (2013) describes this stage of SFBT as finding the direction or "destination" for collaborative work. We may not accept the first or second statement the client makes about what they want as the focus or destination of our work together, holding out for a more workable joint agenda. I tend to view suicide not as what clients want but as a means clients employ to achieve something they want, such as relief from pain, escape, rest, or safety. This makes asking a common solution-focused question such as "How will that be better for you?" reasonable even when the topic of conversation is the client's death. The answers inevitably relate to solutions for current life problems.

(2) *Suppose a miracle happened?* I find the traditional miracle question uniquely useful in this work, in part because there is often a correspondence between the question and the client's assumptions (i.e., that things are so bad that it would take a miracle to change them). Even without the power of the miracle question to ignite hope and to identify useful goals, the change that answering the question(s) typically produces in the client makes it a worthwhile intervention. As clients build their miracle pictures, there is often laughter, animation, evident relaxation of tension, eagerness to add details and tell stories, amazed delight at their own answers. At the *very least*, co-constructing a personal miracle picture gives clients a break and a different experience from the dark thoughts and feelings with which they have been preoccupied. Other future-oriented methods can also be helpful, such as a *letter from the future* (Bannink, 2015; Dolan, 1991; Henden, 2011), or *the older wiser you* question (Dolan, 1991), or the *suppose there might be some way forward* question (Bannink, 2015).

(3) *On a scale from 1 to 10 . . . If 10 stands for, the day after that miracle, and 1 stands for the worst day of your life, what is today? What is the range in the last month? Where do you need to be on the scale to be safe from killing yourself or to be safe from thoughts of killing yourself? What will be different when you are one step higher on the scale? What will be the first sign that you are moving in that direction?* In my opinion, the most fruitful use of scaling is not as a single question and answer, but as the scaffolding for a conversation about where the person is and their possibilities for change.

(4) *What would (someone important in your life) say?* Relationship questions are magic. A client may be totally unable to respond to a direct question but can answer in detail when asked what a good friend would say to the same question? Also, these conversations often offer useful information about relationship resources and reasons for living. I might ask questions like:

- *Who wants you to live?* (and who else, and who else . . .)
- *What would (that person) say that could be helpful to you?*
- *What would your best friend hope for you?*
- *What would your friend want you to remember?*
- *Where would your friend say you are on that 1 to 10 scale?*
- *How would your friend know that you are focusing more on life?*
- *What difference would that make for your friend?"*

(5) *What else?* Getting more examples and more details about exceptions, miracles, resources, and good reasons for trying once more is an effective tool for getting the good stuff into the room, making it real and live for the client. This question is another important counter to the cognitive constriction (or

TABLE 5.1.   What is Helpful in Solution-focused Conversations about Suicide?
Summary v. 3

- Be mindful.
- Go slow.
- Follow the client.
- Presuppose that the client has hope and reasons for living that you can help them *tap into*; after all, the client is still alive
- Listen with a constructive ear.
- Watch and listen for what is hopeful to the client & to the helper (about the client)
- Use the client's language.
- Don't have a conversation about suicide: have a conversation about
  - what the client (really) wants; the "destination"
  - resources/exceptions/coping (including reasons for living)
  - details of a preferred future/miracle picture
  - what the client is already doing that works, even a little bit
  - small possible steps
  - signs of change
- Use *partializing language*, including qualifiers and scaling
- Use scaling as a scaffold for a conversation about change
- Balance talk about risk and reasons for dying with talk about survival and reasons for living
- Use solution-focused questions as a tap on the shoulder
- Ask relationship questions; help the client utilize relationship resources
- Develop an idiosyncratic "safety plan" (i.e., a plan that gets the client's attention, makes sense to the client, and incorporates the client's resources and reasons for living)
- Highlight, reinforce, and celebrate positive change
- Work on maintaining positive changes
- Practices learned from the specific client

With thanks to Tom Strong (1997), who challenged us to get it down to one page.

"blinders" or "tunnel vision") common for clients in this situation and a useful way of highlighting and enhancing the client's reasons for living. Also, "Hope is contextual. It needs a place to roost" (Cooper, Darmody, & Dolan, 2003, p. 10). See Table 5.1 for other useful questions.

■ CASE EXAMPLE

The client in this case is a 38-year-old man named Rodney. He had emigrated from the Bahamas to Canada 15 years previously and was a social service worker in a homeless shelter. He was referred by his family doctor when he came to her office in distress, with high blood pressure, and told her about a trauma at work two months before involving his discovery of the blood-covered dead body of a client. For Rodney, the experience took him back to finding his father's body after his father died by suicide when Rodney was 12 years old. He told his doctor that he couldn't forget either death, couldn't sleep, and wanted to kill himself. I saw Rodney the same day.

Session 1

The transcript begins after a brief discussion about confidentiality and consent to treatment (a professional requirement for me) and the structure of the session, and is edited for length.

> CLINICIAN: So, what are your best hopes for this meeting?
>
> RODNEY: Hopes! Hopes. . . . (long pause, drums one foot on the floor, tears running down his face). I *hope* to overcome my fears. But I don't expect to.
>
> CLINICIAN: What will be different for you when you overcome your fears?
>
> RODNEY: I'm not sure how I would react if I was back in the same environment. Or in the same situation.
>
> CLINICIAN: And when you have overcome your fears?
>
> RODNEY: I think that after understanding it, maybe I could relate to it somehow. That's what my doctor said.
>
> CLINICIAN: Ah. And what will be different for you then?
>
> RODNEY: . . . If I could, could get over it faster, that's important. It just hits me and the whole thing comes back, it's a replay. And it goes on and on. It's depressing me. I'm on stress leave now, but I'll have to go back there. (cries, shakes his head) And I can't, I can't go back.
>
> CLINICIAN: This is so tough. So, whether you go back there or not—
> there are some things that you want to be different? One thing you said was, I think, getting over the replay faster.
>
> RODNEY: Yes. I feel so weak. I'm depressed. I don't want to get up. I don't want to talk about it. I just want to quit everything.
>
> CLINICIAN: That's how terrible this has been for you that right now you feel like you want to quit everything.

(Note: "right now you feel like you want to quit everything" is an example of a solution-focused *formulation* [Froerer & Jordan, 2013; Korman, Bavelas, & DeJong, 2013] that transforms the client's statement, "I just want to quit everything" by qualifying it in two ways: [1] wanting to quit is a "feeling" [and feelings can change] and [2] it is "right now" so it could be different at another time. If the client accepts the formulation, then the qualifications I presuppose in my reflection, with their inherent "partializing" possibilities, become common ground for us to work from [Healing & Bavelas, 2011].)

> RODNEY: Yes. I feel like that might be my destiny, be like my father.
>
> CLINICIAN: Like your father?
>
> RODNEY: He killed himself. I went in to wake him, just like the man at work (crying). And he was dead when I touched him. I can still feel him. I'm terrified someone else is going to die near me. My kids, I check on them over and over at night.

CLINICIAN: How terrible for you, to lose your father that way. And then this recent death at your workplace. Of course you are having trouble with this.

RODNEY: I don't think I can stand it. I go driving at night when I can't sleep and I keep thinking I could crash the car and end everything.

CLINICIAN: So you've thought about that, you've felt that bad.

RODNEY: Yes.

CLINICIAN: How have you decided to keep going in spite of how difficult it is?

RODNEY: Well, it's stupid, but we share the car, my wife and I. We're not together, but I live in the basement, and we try to help each other. She really needs the car to get to her work.

CLINICIAN: That's amazing to me, that when you are in so much pain you would still want to be fair in that way . . . to help her.

RODNEY: It's not really amazing. We're not friends. I thought we were but she's not there for me, it's just about what makes her life work better. She's like everybody else, thinking I should just bounce back and they should be able to depend on me.

CLINICIAN: People depend on you?

RODNEY: Huh, yes. I look big and strong and I went to school and I speak well, so anything tough they say, get Rodney to do it. Same as at work. Nobody cares.

CLINICIAN: Nobody?

RODNEY: OK my kids, they're little and loving. They just want me to be their dad and I don't know if I still can. They might be better off to just be with their mom.

CLINICIAN: They just want you to be their dad.

RODNEY: Yes.

CLINICIAN: Tell me about them. How many? Names? Ages?

RODNEY: My boy is Peter, he just turned 4. DeShawna, my girl, she'll be 2 soon.

CLINICIAN: What are they like? Good kids?

RODNEY: Well Peter, he's a rascal, nonstop action. But yes, a good kid. And DeShawna, she's a heartbreaker, smart as a whip and sweet as sugar.

CLINICIAN: What's Peter's favorite thing about you?

RODNEY: He loves to see me play soccer, or used to, he wants to be a soccer star like his old man. And we play together.

CLINICIAN: A soccer star dad! Wow!

RODNEY: Not lately, I can't get myself to go out. Coach is mad at me. And I'm way out of shape.

CLINICIAN: Until recently though?

RODNEY: Yes, I thought I could have a career when I was young. But then I had to grow up. Still always loved to play though.

CLINICIAN: Wow. And what about DeShawna, what's her favorite thing about you?

RODNEY: I would have to say tickling.

CLINICIAN: You tickle her, or she tickles you, or . . . ?

RODNEY: Both.

CLINICIAN: And lots of laughing I expect.

RODNEY: Oh yes (smiles). She has the best giggle, that girl.

CLINICIAN: How often do you see them?

RODNEY: Oh every day. And like I said, I check on them at night. Drives their mom crazy because I go up into her space.

CLINICIAN: You still manage to see them every day? In spite of feeling so bad, not even wanting to get up?

RODNEY: Well yes, they're my kids. It's not the same as before but when I'm with them I usually manage to be OK. Sometimes I even forget for a few minutes when I'm with them.

CLINICIAN: How do you do that? See them every day, and sometimes even be OK?

RODNEY: If you're going to be a dad, you have to be with your kids, be part of their life.

CLINICIAN: And that's important to you.

RODNEY: Yes.

CLINICIAN: Something you really want, to be their dad, be part of their life.

RODNEY: Yes. It's the most important thing there is.

CLINICIAN: Ah (writes). The most important thing. How do you think you manage to be ok with them, and sometimes even forget?

RODNEY: I'm just really focused on them, on their little world. And it would scare them to see me all upset. Sometimes though if they're playing and I'm there but not doing something with them, like if I'm doing the barbecue, I'll start crying. It just comes up.

CLINICIAN: Are there other times when you are less affected by what happened? Even a little bit?

RODNEY: The counselor I saw before—I just saw her twice, the insurance said she didn't have the right credentials and they wouldn't pay—

CLINICIAN: Oh, dear, that's a shame. How was it helpful to see her?

RODNEY: Well, she kept telling me to get out and get some exercise, play soccer again, or just go for a walk. And she showed me this breathing thing, in then hold then out, and count, and that one I did a few times.

CLINICIAN: And was it helpful?

RODNEY: I think so. It didn't stop the replay but it took the edge off some. Not as intense, maybe not as long.

CLINICIAN: Oh that's *very* helpful. And some really good evidence of how you will be able to deal with this well over time.

RODNEY: Maybe. I sort of forgot about it lately.

CLINICIAN: Ah, so good to remind yourself.

RODNEY: Maybe. I guess so.

CLINICIAN: Rodney, I have this strange question that I want to ask you. Would that be OK?

RODNEY: Yes.

CLINICIAN: Suppose that, after we finish this conversation we're having now, you carry on with the rest of your day, see the kids, barbeque, whatever you would normally do . . . and eventually tonight you go to sleep. And let's say that tonight you have a good sleep, OK?

RODNEY: OK.

CLINICIAN: And while you're sleeping, a miracle happens. And the miracle is, that these troubles that have brought you here today, they're gone, overcome. It's a miracle. *But,* because you're sleeping, you don't know that this miracle has happened. So tomorrow morning, when you wake up, what's the first thing you will notice that will tell you, something has changed for the better?

RODNEY: My kids are in the room.

CLINICIAN: Oh! Right there with you!

RODNEY: Yeah, they used to always stay with me when their mother went to her church group, two nights a week. Lately they don't because she knows I'm not doing so good.

CLINICIAN: So you'd wake up knowing they were right there.

RODNEY: Yes. I can always hear them.

CLINICIAN: . . . . hear them?

RODNEY: Yes, DeShawna she always makes these little noises just before she really wakes up (smiling). Like a bird. And Peter, he just thrashes around all the time, can't stay still even in his sleep.

CLINICIAN: So hearing them there, that would make a difference.

RODNEY: Yeahhhh . . . Yes, I guess it might.

CLINICIAN: How? How would that be better for you?

RODNEY: . . . It would mean I'm being their dad.

CLINICIAN: Ah, and I know how important that is for you. What about for them? How do you think it would be better for them?

RODNEY: I make them a cooked breakfast and walk them to day care. I work afternoon shift. Or I used to. So I have more time in the mornings than their mother does. They like that, or at least they like my breakfast.

CLINICIAN: What else will be different after this miracle?

RODNEY: I'll be stronger.

CLINICIAN: Stronger how?

RODNEY: Every way. Physically, to start. Maybe it's easier to feel strong that way first.

CLINICIAN: OK, so physically stronger first. Then what?

RODNEY: Then stronger in my feelings, emotionally. Less fear.

CLINICIAN: Ah, less fear. When you feel less fear, what will be there instead?

RODNEY: Peace.

CLINICIAN: *Peace.* Oh yes. What else will be different?

RODNEY: Maybe I'll be able to pray. I can't pray any more.

CLINICIAN: How will that make a difference, to be able to pray again?

RODNEY: I might not feel so alone. I always used to just talk to God, but I can't do it, and the pastor at our church just told me I was lucky and to trust in the Lord.

CLINICIAN: What else?

RODNEY: The replays, I'd like to say they'll just be gone.

CLINICIAN: Well it is a miracle . . .

RODNEY: Ok then they'll be gone. I'll be able to go to sleep easier, and I won't wake up in a panic, all confused about where I am and what's wrong. That's a big difference right there, not starting every day with my heart pounding and all sweaty.

CLINICIAN: A big difference all right. So how *will* you start the day?

RODNEY: Wake up natural, not sudden, just lie there with my eyes closed listening to DeShawna and Peter, think about making them pancakes.

CLINICIAN: And how will that kind of start make a difference as the day goes on?

RODNEY: Just be a better day. Relaxed. Feel like going for a walk, maybe even to soccer practice.

CLINICIAN: So with all these changes you just described after this miracle, who in your life will be the first to notice?

RODNEY: Well my wife will sure notice if I'm not coming upstairs all night to check on the kids.

CLINICIAN: Of course! And what else will she notice?

RODNEY: Maybe that I'm doing better, up and around and getting out and doing something. More active.

CLINICIAN: What difference will it make to her to see you up and around and more active?

RODNEY: She'll think that she can depend on me again, with the kids. So she can go out.

CLINICIAN: And the kids? What will they notice?

RODNEY: I'll be laughing, playing with them more.

CLINICIAN: What difference will that make for them?

RODNEY: Oh they love that.

CLINICIAN: How can you tell?

RODNEY: Not hard! They laugh and squeal and want more, more, more.

CLINICIAN: You've described a lot of things that will change for the better after that miracle: Peter and DeShawna in the room with you, hearing them, pancakes, playtime, laughing; being stronger, physically first and then other ways; sleeping better, waking up easier; being able to pray; having a sense of peace. When was the most recent time that you experienced even parts of that miracle picture?

RODNEY: Well it's been a while. Closest would be some of the time I spend with the kids.

CLINICIAN: OK, with the kids. So let's say on a scale from 1 to 10, if 10 stands for, I can be Peter and DeShawna's dad, and 1 stands for, I can't have anything to do with them at all, where are you now?

RODNEY: Oh, well I guess, I guess I must be about a three or four.

CLINICIAN: What makes you that high on the scale?

RODNEY: Not very high

CLINICIAN: Not a one or a two. Or a minus 50.

RODNEY: I guess not.

CLINICIAN: So what contributes to you being at three or four?

RODNEY: I do still see them every day, like you said. And I'm better with them than with other people. I get them fed, try to talk to them and play a little.

CLINICIAN: To me that seems like a lot, given how you've been struggling with this.

RODNEY: I guess.

CLINICIAN: So what would it take for you to go from three or four to a solid four? Just that much difference?

RODNEY: That's a hard question.

CLINICIAN: Yes it is.

RODNEY: . . . maybe if I can see some difference in the replays. They're the worst.

CLINICIAN: So at a four, how would they be different?

RODNEY: I don't know. That's not a big change, so it could just be they don't last as long, or not as strong, or maybe just the effects wear off quicker.

CLINICIAN: What's the longest time that the effects have lasted?

RODNEY: All day and the next morning.

CLINICIAN: . . . and the shortest so far?

RODNEY: Maybe an hour or two. But it's usually longer.

CLINICIAN: And what was different? Between the longest and the shortest?

RODNEY: Um. I think that the shortest was maybe when my kids were with me. So I had to be OK.

CLINICIAN: Good! What else?

RODNEY: It was light, not dark like the night it happened, so I could see where I was, I didn't stay confused as long about where I was. The worst is usually when I wake up. I keep a light on now.

CLINICIAN: And so that was helpful, to see right away and know where you were.

RODNEY: Yes for sure, and that it was here and now, not back then.

CLINICIAN: Good thinking. What else?

RODNEY: When I did the breathing thing, I think it was easier. Not as intense.

CLINICIAN: OK that's very helpful. What else?

RODNEY: That's all I can think of.

CLINICIAN: That's great, that's a lot of possibilities to start with. I have another kind of strange question for you.

RODNEY: OK.

CLINICIAN: I know that your kids are young, but it sounds like they have very distinct personalities, they make their feelings known.

RODNEY: You got that right.

CLINICIAN: OK, good. So, suppose that they could express their best hopes for you, that they had the words to do that. What would they say?

RODNEY: (crying) They, they just want me to be here, be with them, be their dad.

CLINICIAN: That's what they want, just for you to be here, be their dad. It's so clear.

RODNEY: Yes .

CLINICIAN: Both of them

RODNEY: Yes

CLINICIAN: OK. I think that I've run out of questions, is there anything else that we should talk about before I take that little break?

RODNEY: I can't think of anything.

CLINICIAN: Ok, so we'll take 10 minutes, and then I'll give you some feedback.
—10-minute break—

CLINICIAN: So, thanks for your patience while I was thinking about all this.

RODNEY: That's OK.

CLINICIAN: I'm amazed by some of the things that you have been doing.

RODNEY: Amazed?

CLINICIAN: Yes. This has been so very difficult for you, as it would be for anyone. A lot to deal with, and of course you are having reactions to it. What amazes me is what you have somehow been able to do in spite of all that. I have a whole list here (shows sheet). For example, coming in to see your doctor, and then to see me. You find it hard just to get up sometimes, much less push yourself to deal with this. And especially after having to stop working with the first counselor you saw; that can be so disheartening. You seem determined to find help. That determination is a real strength.

RODNEY: I guess.

CLINICIAN: And you were very clear and articulate about your hopes, about what you want to change.

RODNEY: I had a lot of time to think, maybe too much.

CLINICIAN: Well I think that some of your thinking has been productive. And although you're feeling lousy, you still made a lot of efforts to get some useful change going, like going to see your pastor and trying out that breathing exercise. Shows that determination again. Figuring out that there are some times that are a little better than others, and beginning to notice what makes a difference, like being with the kids, having a light on, knowing you're here and now, doing your breathing exercise.

RODNEY: Yes.

CLINICIAN: And this understanding you have that maybe to regain your strength you can start with physical strength first.

RODNEY: Seems that way.

CLINICIAN: And since you're an athlete, and have been all your life, I guess you have had injuries.

RODNEY: Oh yes. Some doozies, twice they told me I couldn't play anymore.

CLINICIAN: Wow! So obviously you know very well about making a comeback.

RODNEY: You could say that.

CLINICIAN: And of course you have very good reasons for being willing to do what you are doing to make this comeback.

RODNEY: You mean Peter and DeShawna.

CLINICIAN: Yes. I think you have some other reasons, too, but for sure they are the most important. So, I wouldn't presume to suggest how you begin to get physically strong again, because you know far more about that than I ever will. My only suggestion is to start slow, and then slow down even more, and give yourself credit even for thinking about it, that's part of starting.

RODNEY: OK.

CLINICIAN: And maybe later we can talk about how you do some of the things that have been a little helpful so far in a more deliberate way . . . get systematic about it.

RODNEY: OK.

CLINICIAN: But for now, whatever small beginnings you can make toward getting stronger again; and just notice when you have even the smallest, passing moment of peace.

RODNEY: (nods). Yes, OK. Thank you.

Session 2

CLINICIAN: So what's better?

RODNEY: OK, well, it's been up and down.

CLINICIAN: Of course, good.

RODNEY: But I figured something out.

CLINICIAN: Oh! Tell me.

RODNEY: For everything I need to do, if I'm ever going to get better, I need to be strong.

CLINICIAN: OK.

RODNEY: Just to get started, I need to be strong. To get myself out of bed, I need to be strong. To get strong, I need to already be strong.

CLINICIAN: That's a dilemma.

RODNEY: Yes, and I can't do that alone. And I haven't been able to pray. And my pastor here just made things worse. So I remembered that my mother's cousin's husband is a pastor in Hamilton, and I went to see him.

CLINICIAN: You went to see him! In Hamilton! How did you do that?

RODNEY: Used the car on Saturday when my wife wasn't working. I had to get there, I knew I'd be able to find him.

CLINICIAN: Find him?

RODNEY: I haven't seen him since I first came here, I didn't know their address or anything. I figured if I found a church and asked around, I'd find him.

CLINICIAN: Wow! That determination of yours . . . And what happened?

RODNEY: I found him, wasn't too hard. And he really helped me.

CLINICIAN: I'm so glad. How?

RODNEY: It was different than I expected. Not so much about God, more talking about me growing up, how he remembered me from family things at home. Just like Peter, always on the move, always happy as long as I had a ball. Not just soccer, any kind of ball game. They had a gym in his church and he took me in and we shot hoops.

CLINICIAN: You're kidding me.

RODNEY: For real.

CLINICIAN: And how did it all help?

RODNEY: I think I can pray now.

CLINICIAN: Oh, that's big.

RODNEY: Really big. It's what I needed more than anything else.

CLINICIAN: I am so amazed. I never could have thought of any of this . . . and that's the truth.

■ CONCLUSION

Writing about the work that we do, while a necessary effort to communicate and examine our practice, always leaves me uneasy, because generalizing is both unavoidable and dangerous. What is useful learning from reading, thinking, and talking about the work is still much less useful than learning from the work itself while doing it. One size fits one. The best we can do then, is to rewind and start fresh each time, letting past experience enhance our curiosity and flexibility and our confidence in client capacities. As Sir Laurens van der Post says, "May you go slowly, and all good things will come to you"—Sir Laurens van der Post (CBC I radio interview with Shelagh Rogers, May 12, 1996).

■ REFERENCES

Bachelor, A. (1991). Comparison and relationship to outcome of diverse dimensions of the helping alliance as seen by client and therapist. *Psychotherapy, 28*, 534–549.

Bannink, F. (2015). *101 solution-focused questions for help with trauma.* New York: W. W. Norton.

Bavelas, J. B., McGee, D., Phillips, B., & Routledge, R. (2000). Microanalysis of communication in psychotherapy. *Human Systems: The Journal of Systemic Consultation and Management, 11*(1), 47–66.

Blundo, R. G., Bolton, K. W., & Hall, J. C. (2014). Hope: Research and theory in relation to Solution-Focused practice and training. *International Journal of Solution-Focused Practices, 2*(2), 52–62.

Brown, A. D., Root, J. C., Romano, T. A., Chang, L. J., Bryant, R. A., & Hirst, W. (2012). Overgeneralized autobiographical memory and future thinking in combat veterans with posttraumatic stress disorder. *Journal of Behavior Therapy and Experimental Psychiatry, 30*, 1–12.

Butler, W. R., & Powers, K. V. (1996). Solution-focused grief therapy. In S. Miller, M. A. Hubble, & B. L. Duncan (Eds.), *Handbook of solution-focused brief therapy* (pp. 228–247). San Francisco: Jossey-Bass.

Connie, E. (2013). *Solution building in couples therapy.* New York: Springer.

Cooper, S., Darmody, M., & Dolan, Y. (2003). Impressions of hope and its influence: An international e-mail trialogue. *Journal of Systemic Therapies, 22*(3), 67–78.

Cox, K., Mouliso, E. R., Venners, M. R., Defever, M. E., Duvivier, L., Rauch, S., et al. (2016). Reducing suicidal ideation through evidence-based treatment for posttraumatic stress disorder. *Journal of Psychiatric Research, 80*, 59–63.

de Shazer, S., Dolan, Y., Korman, H., McCollum, E., Trepper, T., & Berg, I. K. (2007). *More than miracles: The state of the art of solution-focused brief therapy.* Binghamton, NY: Haworth.

Dolan, Y. M. (1991). *Resolving sexual abuse: Solution-focused therapy and Ericksonian hypnosis for adult survivors.* New York: W. W. Norton.

Dolan, Y. (2008). 'Pragmatics of hope.' Keynote presentation, Swiss Family Therapy Days, Fribourg, Switzerland.

Dulac, G. (1999). Intervenir auprès des clienteles masculines: Theories et pratiques québècoises. AIDRAH. Action Intersectorielle pour le Développement et la Recherche sur l'Aide aux Hommes. Centre d'études appliquées sur la famille École de service social. Motreal: Université McGill.

Fiske, H. (2008). *Hope in action: Solution-focused conversations about suicide.* New York: Routledge.

Fiske, H., & Lavoie, B. (2016). Fostering hope: Solution-focused stories about suicide prevention. Solution Focused Brief Therapy Association Annual Conference, Halifax, NS.

Froerer, A. S., & Jordan, S. S. (2013). Identifying solution-building formulations through microanalysis. *Journal of Systemic Therapies, 32*(3), 60–73.

Gassmann, D., & Grawe, K. (2006). General change mechanisms: The relation between problem activation and resource activation in successful and unsuccessful therapeutic interactions. *Clinical Psychology and Psychotherapy, 13*, 1–11.

Gradus, J. L., Qin, P., Lincoln, A. K., Miller, M., Lawler, E., Sørensen, H. T., et al. (2010). Posttraumatic stress disorder and completed suicide. *American Journal of Epidemiology, 171*(6), 721–727.

Healing, S., & Bavelas, J. B. (2011). Can questions lead to change? An analogue experiment. *Journal of Systemic Therapies, 30*(4), 30–47.

Henden, J. (2011). *Beating combat stress: 101 techniques for recovery.* Chichester, UK: Wiley.

Hernandez, P., Engstrom, D., & Gensei, D. (2010). Exploring the impact of trauma on therapists: Vicarious resilience and related concepts in training. *Journal of Systemic Therapies, 29*(1), 67–83.

Jobes, D. A. (2006). *Managing suicidal risk: A collaborative approach.* New York: Guilford.

Joiner, T. E. (2005). *Why people die by suicide.* Cambridge, MA: Harvard University Press.

Jessome, P. (2016). *Disposable souls.* Halifax, Nova Scotia: Vagrant.

Kim, J. S., & Franklin, C. (2015). The importance of positive emotions in solution focused brief therapy. *Best Practices in Mental Health, 11*(1), 25–41.

Korman, H., Bavelas, J. B., & De Jong, P. (2013). Microanalysis of formulations in solution-focused brief therapy, cognitive behavior therapy, and motivational interviewing. *Journal of Systemic Therapies, 32*(3), 31–45.

Linley, P. A., & Joseph, S. (2004). Positive change following trauma and adversity: A review. *Journal of Traumatic Stress, 17*, 11–21.

McKeel, J. (2012). What works in solution-focused brief therapy: A review of change process research. In C. Franklin, T. S. Trepper, W. J. Gingerich, & E. E. McCollum (Eds.), *Solution-focused brief therapy: A handbook of evidence-based practice.* New York: Oxford.

Nugent, N. (2014). Resilience after trauma: From surviving to thriving. *European Journal of Psychotraumatology, 5*, 1–5.

O'Connor, R. C., Smyth, R., & Williams, J. M. G. (2015). Intrapersonal positive future thinking predicts repeat suicide attempts in hospital-treated suicide attempters. *Journal of Consulting and Clinical Psychology, 83*, 169–176.

Panagioti, M., Gooding, P., & Tarrier, N. (2009). Post-traumatic stress disorder and suicidal behavior: A narrative review. *Clinical Psychology Review, 29*, 471–482.

Panagioti, M., Gooding, P., Dunn, G., & Tarrier, N. (2011). Pathways to suicidal behavior in posttraumatic stress disorder. *Journal of Traumatic Stress, 24*, 137–145.

Ratner, H., George, E., & Iveson, C. (2012). *Solution-focused brief therapy: 101 key points and techniques.* New York: Routledge.

Reiter, M. D. (2010). Hope and expectancy in solution-focused brief therapy. *Journal of Family Psychotherapy, 21*, 132–148.

Shneidman, E. S. (2005). How I read. *Suicide and life-threatening behavior, 35*(2), 117–120.

Short, A., & Nemeroff, C. B. (2014). Early life trauma and suicide. In K. E. Cannon & T. J. Hudzik (Eds.), *Suicide: Phenomenology and neurobiology.* Springer International Publishing: London.

Snyder, C. R., Michael, S. T., & Cheavens, J. S. (2000). Hope as a psychotherapeutic foundation of common factors, placebos, and expectancies. In M. A. Hubble, B. S. Duncan, & S. D. Miller (Eds.), *The heart and soul of change: What works in psychotherapy.* Washington, DC: American Psychological Association.

Strong, T. (1997). Can you get it down to one page? *Journal of Systemic Therapies, 16*, 69–71.

Taylor, L., & Fiske, H. (2005). Tapping into hope. In S. J. Cooper & J. Duvall (Eds.), *Catching the winds of change: Conference proceedings*. Toronto: Brief Therapy Training Centers International.

Tedeschi, R. G., & Calhoun, L. G. (2004). Posttraumatic growth: Conceptual foundations and empirical evidence. *Psychological Inquiry, 15*, 1–18.

Wilson, J. A. (2015). *Hope-focused solutions: A relational hope focus of the solution-building stages in Solution-Focused Brief Therapy*. Doctoral dissertation, Nova Southeastern University.

World Health Organization (WHO). (2014). *Preventing suicide: A global imperative*. Retrieved from http://www.who.int.

6 Interpersonal Violence

■ DAWN CROSSWHITE, JOHNNY S. KIM, AND STACEY ANNE WILLIAMS

Interpersonal violence is a societal issue that touches one out of three people as either an adult or a child. Its exact prevalence is unknown because interpersonal violence (also known as domestic violence) can present as abuse, violence, exploitation, or control by one person against another. This can present in any of the aforementioned ways against a spouse, intimate partner, former spouse or former intimate partner, children, the elderly, disabled persons, or pets. Interpersonal violence can also be referred to as domestic violence or intimate partner violence (IPV) and will be used interchangeably throughout this chapter. It essentially encompasses any act that is intended to intimidate, exploit, control, or take advantage of another person.

Reports of domestic violence are frequent, though exact estimates vary by country, by socioeconomic status, and by ethnicity (Alhabib, Nur, & Jones, 2009). Annually, this public health crisis affects millions of people worldwide (Stiles-Shields & Carroll, 2014). What is known about this public health epidemic has largely come to light since the movement to combat violence against women during the 1970s and 1980s: it was in these decades when violence against women began to be widely accepted as a major public health epidemic and a women's rights issue (Alabib et al., 2009; Stiles-Shields & Carroll, 2015). The history of the movement was traced further back by Fagan and Browne (1994) as it examined the modern women's movement, which began in the 1960s to study sexual violence against women perpetrated by their intimate partners and the shift toward victim-centered practices in the criminal justice system in the subsequent two decades. Until 21st century, research efforts have mainly collected data from female victims with male partners, which explains why the epidemic was originally called the "battered women's movement" (Stiles-Shields & Carroll, 2015, p. 637).

The reported lifetime prevalence rates of physical and/or sexual violence in studies of violence against women was studied by Alhabib and colleagues in a 2009 systematic review. This review identified 1,653 primary studies conducted worldwide that reported that anywhere from between 15% and 71% of women worldwide experience at least one episode of domestic violence in their lifetime. Most of the studies included in their meta-analysis were conducted in

North America, although Europe, Asia, Africa, and the Middle East were also included. A separate worldwide review (Garcia-Moreno, Jansen, Ellsberg, Heise, & Watts, 2006) of prevalence by the World Health Organization (WHO) reports that "A review of over 50 population-based studies in 35 countries before 1999 indicated that between 10% and 52% of women from around the world report that they had been physically abused by an intimate partner at some point in their lives, and between 10% and 30% that they had experienced sexual violence by an intimate partner" (p. 1260). Another review of 19 studies focused on the prevalence of physical violence within same-sex relationships and found that same-sex couples had higher rates than heterosexual couples; however, prevalence rates of same-sex domestic violence tend to demonstrate little congruency between studies. The review also found that lesbians, gay men, and heterosexual men are equally likely to abuse their intimate partners (Stiles-Shields & Carroll, 2015).

■ INTERPERSONAL VIOLENCE CHARACTERISTICS

Definitions of domestic violence and interpersonal violence vary based on agencies from which data is collected, the population being studied, and considerations of independent researchers. However, differing definitions tend to include some combination of physical violence, threats of physical violence or death, psychological abuse, emotional abuse, economic exploitation, surveillance, intimidation, and isolation. Acts or threats of violence against animals in the home and children may also be used to control family members and partners; for some people, violence against a third party can be a stronger motivator to adhere to the abuser's demands than violence directed at the victim (Morgan Steiner, 2012; Newberry, 2017).

Domestic violence is characterized by a cyclical pattern of abuse with several recognizable and predictable phases. First, there is the phase in which tension builds within the relationship. Smaller or less serious acts of abuse may occur, and the victim frequently uses appeasing behaviors and words in an attempt to mitigate the abusive behavior toward them or others in the home. If the victim does not have success in keeping the abuser's tensions down, the second phase begins. The abuse usually escalates into a larger or more serious event in order to exert power and control over the victim. In some cases, the second phase does not enter the third phase and instead will end in the death of the victim (Gonzalez & Corbin, 2011; Morgan Steiner, 2012). After this outburst of violence, the perpetrator may enter the third phase, which is characterized by a reduction in tension between the victim and the perpetrator. This may be a honeymoon phase, in a sense, as the perpetrator may ask for forgiveness, persuade the victim that they didn't mean the abuse, convince the victim that they will change their abusive ways, or that the abuse was the result of the victim's actions or thoughts and that it could have been prevented.

Victims may stay in such relationships out of necessity (such as economic dependency), codependency with the perpetrator, a belief that they are able to save or help the perpetrator, or for other reasons. Victims will most frequently feel an urgent need to leave after their lives or the lives of their children have been threatened, but they often do not realize that the violence or abuse will escalate when they are planning to leave, during their immediate exit, or shortly after their termination of the relationship. According to Gonzalez and Corbin (2011) 41% of victims reported that they were assaulted at least once by the perpetrator within two and a half years of exiting the abusive relationship; most of those were within the first six months after leaving. This dynamic may be complicated by the inability for same-sex couples to get safe emergency housing separately. Gender assignments in shelters are intended to keep heterosexual couples apart and thus may not guarantee that a female victim of IPV (with a female abuser) will be kept separated from each other if they seek shelter at a community agency. This is also true for men who find themselves in need of emergency shelter or temporary housing, although it is typically also more difficult to find shelters and emergency resources that include male victims of domestic violence (Stiles-Shields & Carroll, 2015).

■ RISK FACTORS

Interestingly enough, risk factors for perpetrating *and* for experiencing interpersonal violence have been found to be similar. Perpetrators of domestic violence whom identify as homosexual and those that identify as heterosexual have been found to have experienced similar events or mental health issues as well. Past exposure to violence (especially within one's family of origin), insecure attachment styles, substance abuse, alcohol abuse, depression, bullying, anxiety, engagement in risky sexual behaviors, post-traumatic stress syndrome, and complex trauma all contribute to being both a victim and a perpetrator of intimate partner violence (Stiles-Shields & Carroll, 2015). It has been noted that attitudes toward violence in victims of interpersonal violence tend to hold beliefs that justify abuse by men toward women in both the developed world and in developing countries (Fagan & Browne, 1994).

An important caveat to conducting such a review of rates of domestic violence is that under reporting of incidents of exposure is frequently a concern, and there is a higher number of people who experience abuse than there are people who are willing to *disclose* such abuse to a service provider (Alhabib et al., 2009; Stiles-Shields & Carroll, 2015). This could be a reflection of the victim's tendency to justify violence toward them and their perception that incidents shouldn't be reported because it was isolated or that it was justified. Bidirectionality is a history of being both a victim and a perpetrator of domestic violence and is more commonly found in same-sex domestic violence relationships than it is in heterosexual relationships (Stiles-Shields & Carroll, 2015). Particular challenges for same-sex domestic violence (SSDV) situations are that victims report being reluctant to report violence to police because they may expect oppression or discrimination from the legal system. They are also more likely to be mislabeled as "mutual batterers"—those who fight back with the intent of hurting their perpetrator—where their heterosexual domestic violence counterparts are given the label of self-defense when they fight back (Stiles-Shields & Carroll, 2015).

Women who live in small rural and isolated areas report the highest rates of prevalence of intimate partner violence as compared to those living in urban settings; they also have the least geographic access to domestic violence intervention service providers, counseling, emergency shelter, transitional housing, resource referrals, advocacy, and community-based health programs (Peek-Asa et al., 2011). Barriers such as geographic distance from resources and victims' isolation from communities must first be overcome in areas where public transit is not available or accessible, and if that is able to be overcome, rural victims are still twice as likely as their urban counterparts to be denied services due to a lack of staff, inadequate specialized services, and lack of funding (Peek-Asa et al., 2011).

■ CONSEQUENCES OF INTERPERSONAL VIOLENCE

Lasting consequences of experiencing domestic violence as a child and as an adult are varied and serious. Studies have found that there are increased rates of elective abortion among women who have experienced abuse and that women who have a history of abuse are more likely to terminate a pregnancy without including their partner in the decision or informing them of the pregnancy. Women who have experienced abuse are less likely to seek medical treatment and yet more likely to have serious injuries when they do seek treatment. They are also more likely to utilize emergency care services and attempt to commit suicide (Glander et al., 1998; Peek-Asa et al., 2011). Children exposed to interpersonal violence in the home are more likely to become perpetrators of IPV and victims of violence themselves. Children exposed to long-term domestic violence situations show altered brain development due to increased brain activity in the amygdala. The amygdala is the brain center that governs emotions, understandably resulting in alterations of personality, instances of acting out, trauma symptoms, and withdrawal. Girls are more likely to show signs of internalizing behaviors such as being withdrawn, depressed, and anxious. Boys are more likely to show signs of externalizing behaviors such as acting out and violence (Evans et al., 2008; Gonzalez & Corbin, 2011).

Many of those who have not experienced domestic or interpersonal violence personally find them asking the question, "why not just . . . leave?" This is a deeply personal question to survivors of domestic violence and one that needs to be considered when a safety plan is being developed. This plan frequently needs to involve removing children and pets from the home prior to the exit plan for the victim. Perpetrators of violence frequently know the important role that pets play for victims and that they can be used as a weapon to control the victim. Despite knowing this, many shelters and emergency services do not accept victims with their pets, forcing victims to choose between their own safety and that of a beloved animal. Many victims of IPV have an exceptionally strong bond with their animals; since isolation is used as a tool to keep victims away from other people and their communities, pets may be the victims' sole source of comfort or of a loving relationship. In this case, pets may be regarded as a member of the family, and they may provide an important role which the perpetrator does not fill for the victim or for children. A darker side to this reality, however, is that perpetrators may know that bonds with pets may be used specifically to control victims as a form of psychological abuse (Newberry, 2017; Morgan Steiner, 2012). Pet fostering may be an option for some victims to escape if friends or family cannot take the animal in themselves; shelters that can accommodate small animals, dogs, and even equines might be available to others, but victims of domestic violence may not know of that availability or these considerations may not be available in the victim's area or within easy enough accessibility to them in a moment of crisis (Newberry, 2017).

■ PRACTICAL APPLICATION OF SFBT

Intimate partner violence can involve both heterosexual couples as well as same-sex partners. Trauma in IPV is experienced by the victims but also can be experienced by the perpetrator and children who are exposed to it (Carlson, 2013). Given the wide variety of ways people may experience IPV in a relationship, we highlight some of the keys questions that may be more useful around this issue.

- Relationship questions allows the client to begin to see other people's points of view and experience more empathy toward others.
- Difference questions (asking what difference that would make) helps clients verbalize the impact of their actions beyond just themselves and often used after asking a relationship question.
- Socratic questioning allows the clinician to question the client's assumptions and beliefs. In turn, the client begins to see the possibilities of solutions and achieving their goals.
- Scaling questions allows for the client to break down their assumptions further. In a sense, grading the assumptions to better break them down into more manageable steps and help them move past their black-and-white thinking.

- Complimenting and focusing on client strengths is useful since so much of the messages clients hear from others are blaming, lack of control, self-doubt, and fear.

■ CASE EXAMPLE

Below is a counseling session involving a real case to illustrate ways to use the SFBT approach with a client who is the perpetrator of interpersonal violence. We intentionally chose an example where the client was the perpetrator rather than a victim; this was to demonstrate how this approach can be used with clients who are typically forced into more problem-focused or punitive approaches to behavioral change. This client has a long history of anger and violent behavior, with his first arrest occurring at the age of 12 for physical altercations.

The client in this case is a 34-year-old single father we'll call Michael. Michael entered in-home therapy, at the request of a child welfare caseworker, in order to gain full custody of his seven-year-old son, Joshua. Michael's first major criminal activity occurred at the age of 17 when he was sentenced to prison for seven years for attempted murder. Since his release, he has had several citations for various infractions ranging from alcohol use to harassment. It should be noted that Michael, the father, was not involved with the incident that had his son removed from Joshua's mother's care, and therefore Joshua has been placed with Michael. Michael has demonstrated that with support, he is able to take care of his son, but there are concerns among the child welfare case managers that Michael needs to address his anger. Professionals involved in this child welfare case are noticing that Michael's anger issues are beginning to affect his son's behavior and suspect that it will likely create more problems for Joshua in the future.

The session being used for this case illustration occurred approximately two months after the initial assessment. During the first eight sessions, there was a lot of work on getting the client to avoid problem talk and focus on the future, strengths, and solutions. Michael, as a result of the trauma he had experienced growing up, was very invested in problem talk because he believed it validated his experience. The clinician needed to take a few extra sessions to help reframe his beliefs so that he saw what the clinician saw, which was that he had many strengths. The clinician also worked on affirming the client's behaviors that would move him toward his ultimate goal of gaining full custody of Joshua. Through observations in previous sessions and staffing consults, it became apparent that Michael had a strong need to overpower the women in his life, including the female caseworker and female clinician. He was often flirtatious and had his shirt off during a couple of sessions as well, including this session. Below is a transcript from the ninth follow-up counseling session using SFBT, which was conducted at the client's home:

Counseling Session # 9

CLINICIAN: Hello, Michael, what is happening that is better today?

MICHAEL: Nothing! Everything sucks: my truck is broken; I haven't been able to work much, so I can't pay any of my bills (having an irritated tone while expressing animatedly with his arms).

CLINICIAN: It sounds like a lot is going on with you. With so much going on, I appreciate you being able to attend our session.

MICHAEL: Yeah, well, I wouldn't have if you didn't come to me.

(Joshua comes in.)

JOSHUA: Hi!

CLINICIAN: Hi, Joshua.

JOSHUA: Guess what? Guess what?

CLINICIAN: What's up?

JOSHUA: I got a star today because I didn't throw a fit or get in trouble.

CLINICIAN: Wow, that is so cool! Can I see it?

(Joshua runs off to get the star.)

CLINICIAN: Wow, Joshua, this is really cool. I'm so proud of you. I know you have been working really hard at being a good boy in school. What was different today that you didn't get in trouble or throw a fit?

JOSHUA: My teacher said I could get a star and I didn't want my daddy mad at me.

CLINICIAN: What a great day for Joshua, huh, Michael?

MICHAEL: Yeah, he is doing better in school but still getting in trouble. (To Joshua) OK, go outside and play so we can talk.

JOSHUA: OK, daddy, I will.

It has been discussed in previous sessions that Joshua does not like it when his daddy is mad because Michael yells, and it scares him. Rather than focus on anger of the father toward Joshua in the dialogue above, the clinician focuses the conversation on the fact Joshua didn't get in trouble and earned a star. The clinician pays Joshua a compliment and tried to get details about how Joshua made that happen. Joshua's response still focused on his dad not getting angry, but the clinician chooses to focus on the positive behavior instead and gets the father to acknowledge Joshua's good accomplishment so Joshua can hear it, too.

CLINICIAN: So, Michael, what are your best hopes for this session?

MICHAEL: I want my truck fixed and be able to pay my bills. (With a raised tone) Can you do that?

CLINICIAN: I cannot imagine how frustrating it is to be without your truck and dealing with the challenges of paying your bills. Since that is something I really cannot assist you with. How can I help you?

MICHAEL: You can't!

CLINICIAN: OK, how do you think talking about the problems with your truck and bills will help you reach your goals?

MICHAEL: It's not and I don't care! I'm fucking angry this is happening! You afraid of me? I like it when people are afraid of me, especially women!

At this time, Michael is talking with a raised voice more and with a more aggressive tone. He also starts to posture by sitting up taller, raising his arms and pushing out his chest. At this point, knowing he is trying to get a rise out of me, I remain seated with a relaxed position. I speak in a low, soft voice. I do this for a few reasons, the least of which my safety. I am in his home, taking away the security of an office setting and other people around to assist. To trigger Michael could put me at risk. Although, I have never felt threatened by Michael. More importantly, I wanted to role model for Michael how to respond verses react when someone is escalated. All he has know is aggressive and assaultive reactions when faced with anger. To put him into a solution frame of mind he needed to experience a different response to help slow his reaction down.

CLINICIAN: No, I am not afraid of you, Michael. Can I ask how does making women afraid of you help you reach your goal of getting full custody of Joshua?

MICHAEL: People should be afraid of me. You should be afraid of me because I'm a scary person. (With this, Michael flinches forward a bit.) I need to be scary so people don't take advantage of me or my family. I had a shitty life. My dad was a piece of shit and always beat us kids and my mom up. My mom did nothing to help us, especially me. It's my mom's fault that I first got in trouble with the law because she called the cops on me.

CLINICIAN: Tell me more about that time about how you protected yourself and your sister.

MICHAEL: My dad and I got into a fight. Instead of calling on him, which she should have because he was the adult, she called on me. She said she did it to help me because my anger was out of control and everyone was afraid of me. Well, my anger wouldn't of been out of control if that asshole didn't hit on us all the time. I was trying to protect me and my sisters. It's the same thing that happened when I went to prison. I am the protector! I have a right to protect my family and if you piss me off you will get hurt.

CLINICIAN: You have gone through a great deal in your life, and through it all you have survived by being a protector. That is amazing and an admirable quality to have.

(Michael interrupts)

MICHAEL: Yeah, it's like with Joshua's mom, she's scared of me. She knows not to mess with me or Joshua or I'll make sure she hurts.

CLINICIAN: Can you tell me more about what you mean when you say that?

MICHAEL: I don't like her. She's stupid and beneath me. I don't even know why I got with her. There was this one time when she got in my way and

I hit her. I told her to leave me alone. It had been a long day and I didn't need her naggin' in my ear. It was a long day with a lot going on.

CLINICIAN: How long ago did this happen?

MICHAEL: It was around 2011, a while ago. Why?

CLINICIAN: I was wondering because earlier in the session you stated everything sucked and telling me I should be scared of you, you didn't hit me. How do you manage to be resolute enough to change your behavior from hitting me to just raising your voice.

MICHAEL: I don't know, you didn't do anything to me and I'm changing my ways.

CLINICIAN: It shows tremendous growth that you are changing your ways and controlling your actions. Knowing that you have made these changes, I'd like to go back to our previous discussion around your need to be protective of your family and friends, which is an admirable quality to have. You also talk about liking to scare people and people being afraid of you. Despite liking to scare people, it is very clear that you care an awful lot about the people you love.

MICHAEL: Yes, I do.

CLINICIAN: That is wonderful and what your case worker and the Department of Human Services want to see from you so you to gain full custody of Joshua. I'm a little confused though because when people care about someone they usually don't want to scare them.

MICHAEL: I only scare the people that threaten my family and me.

CLINICIAN: I'm still confused then because Joshua has told us that when you yell he gets scared. How does the yelling protect him?

MICHAEL: Well, because then he knows who is in control and when I'm in control he is protected.

CLINICIAN: I see. I would like to try something, are you interested?

MICHAEL: Sure.

CLINICIAN: Great! OK, let us assume you are your seven-year-old self and, as you reported earlier in the session, your dad always yelled and hit you. How would you have liked your father to protect you?

(Michael seemed to struggle with letting go of his anger and irritation.)

MICHAEL: I wouldn't want him to be a weak dad, but I would have liked for him to talk to me.

CLINICIAN: Anything else?

MICHAEL: Do more things with me, like I do with Joshua.

CLINICIAN: So talk more with you when he got angry and do more with you. What do you think Joshua would say if I asked him the same question about you?

MICHAEL: He'd probably say the same thing I did. I know what you are doing.

CLINICIAN: What am I doing?

MICHAEL: You are trying to get me to see how the yelling feels for Joshua. Put me in his shoes.

CLINICIAN: You figured me out! So did it work?

MICHAEL: A little bit. I never really thought about Joshua feeling the same as I did when I was his age. It makes sense.

At this time, Michael begins to relax more as evidenced by his posture and tone. He still seems to be a bit agitated but more willing to look at the situation differently. As mentioned throughout the case illustration, Michael vacillated between a problem-focused stance and taking a solution-focused stance. However, once he was able to have more empathy for his son and see Joshua's point of view, he joined the clinician in seeing solutions and a way out of him anger.

CLINICIAN: Awesome! How can you motivate yourself to talking more to Joshua?

MICHAEL: I want to remember what is important to me, keeping my son. I love my son and want what is best for him.

CLINICIAN: Yeah, I know you love Joshua. He's a great kid. Michael, I know you want what is best for your son as well, you've said it time and time again. I'd like to go back to a question I asked earlier. How does making women afraid of you help you reach your goal of getting full custody of Joshua?

MICHAEL: (Michael sighs and thinks for a few minutes) I don't know. I haven't thought of it that way. I guess it wouldn't because there is nothing but women on my case (Michael laughs).

CLINICIAN: How do you think your beliefs about control and power influenced your beliefs about women?

MICHAEL: Hmmmm . . . good question. I'm smart and should have put the two together . . . (Michael goes off in thought. Michael stops talking and begins to process the question before answering. This is a new behavior for him, to stop and think before he responds to a question.)

CLINICIAN: What do you mean?

MICHAEL: Well, I hate my father because of how he treated me and my sisters. I have always had conflicting thoughts about my mom because she never stood up for us. I figured to protect I needed to scare everyone and didn't think about in terms of power and control, but I guess it could look that way. Huh!

CLINICIAN: On a scale of one to ten, 1 being no motivation and ten being completely motivated, how motivated are you to continue to look at the connection between your beliefs about power and control and the way you treat people, especially women?

MICHAEL: To be fair and honest I'll give it a five because I've believed this my whole life.

CLINICIAN: Fair enough. What would help you move to a six?

MICHAEL: (Takes a few minutes to think) Maybe talking to my mom to see what was really going on with her while we were growing up.

CLINICIAN: Alright. Since we are running out of time, what do you think about you having the conversation with your mom as your homework for the week?

MICHAEL: That's funny because I knew you were going to suggest that. Yeah, I'll do it.

CLINICIAN: Great, I look forward to hearing how the talk goes. I have to go. You did a really great job at allowing yourself to think at your beliefs differently today.

MICHAEL: Thanks. And thanks for not being judgmental, it makes it easier.

Client Update

The following session Michael talked about his conversation with his mom and her experience with his father. Michael reported that listening to her allowed him to understand himself more, especially when she gave further explanation about calling the police when he was younger. This session was the first time Michael allowed himself to contemplate his beliefs around power and control and the way he treats people. It took a couple more sessions for him to see that he could protect people, especially Joshua, without scaring them. It has been over a year and Michael did receive full custody of Joshua.

■ SUMMARY

The message the client received his whole life is that he is a "scary man," and the view he has of himself has been reinforced by others around this characteristic trait. The SFBT clinician intentionally emphasized that she did not think he was a "scary man" and rather treated him as a human being with worth and potential. The SFBT clinician didn't respond to his "scary stance" (aggressive posturing, threatening tone) by ending the session early due to his covert threats but instead focused on his positive traits and beliefs.

Often clients work with various systems (child welfare, corrections, legal, mental health) where the emphasis is on their behavioral and mental problems. The focus of system care often emphasizes his past behaviors and what he needs to become (in their expectations and view) in order to get full custody. In these situations, the power belongs to the various professionals in the child welfare, corrections/legal, and mental health system. Also, they have constructed a message that he is an aggressive and hostile person who poses a danger to others. The SFBT clinician switches that view to see how he is a protector and advocate of his son and family as well as himself. This case example changed the client's internal views of the situation by drawing out and highlighting his protective stance as understandable and a positive trait. Once the client realized that he is a protector, he was able to learn that he didn't need to be aggressive in order to be protective and found a better solution to being a protective man. Using Socratic questioning to allow the client to come to this realization himself helped move him beyond his defensive stance and allowed for change to occur.

■ REFERENCES

Alhabib, S., Nur, U., & Jones, R. (2009). Domestic violence against women: Systematic review of prevalence studies. *Journal of Family Violence, 25*(4), 369–382. doi:10.1007/s10896-009-9298-4.

Carlson, B. E. (2013). Intimate partner violence. In *Encyclopedia of social work online*. Retrieved from http://www.eswo.com. doi: 10.1093/acrefore/9780199975839.013.1151.

Evans, S. E., Davies, C., & Dilillo, D. (2008). Exposure to domestic violence: A meta-analysis of child and adolescent outcomes. *Aggression and Violent Behavior, 13*(2), 131–140. doi:10.1016/j.avb.2008.02.005.

Fagan, J., & Browne, A. (1994). Violence between spouses and intimates: Physical aggresion between men and women in intimate relationships. In A. Reiss & J. Roth (Eds.), *Understanding and preventing violence: Social influences,* Vol. 3 (pp. 115–292). Washington, DC: National Academy.

Garcia-Moreno, C., Jansen, H., Ellsberg, M., Heise, L., & Watts, C. H. (2006). Prevalence of intimate partner violence: Findings from the WHO multi-country study on women's health and domestic violence. *The Lancet, 368,* 1260–1269. doi:10.1097/01.aog.0000252267.04622.80.

Glander, S. S., Moore, M., Michielutte, R., & Parsons, L. H. (1998). The prevalence of domestic violence among women seeking abortion. *Obstetrics & Gynecology, 91*(6), 1002–1006. doi:10.1016/s0029-7844(98)00089-1.

Gonzalez, R., & Corbin, J. (2011). The cycle of violence: Domestic violence and its effects on children. *The Scholar: St. Mary's Law Review on Minority Issues, 13*(405), 406–432.

Morgan Steiner, L. (2012). Why domestic violence victims don't leave. Retrieved from https://www.ted.com/talks/leslie_morgan_steiner_why_domestic_violence_victims_don_t_leave/transcript?language=en.

Newberry, M. (2017). Pets in danger: Exploring the link between domestic violence and animal abuse. *Aggression and Violent Behavior, 34,* 273–281. doi:10.1016/j.avb.2016.11.007.

Peek-Asa, C., Wallis, A., Harland, K., Beyer, K., Dickey, P., & Saftlas, A. (2011). Rural disparity in domestic violence prevalence and access to resources. *Journal of Women's Health, 20*(11), 1743–1749. doi:10.1089/jwh.2011.2891.

Stiles-Shields, C., & Carroll, R. A. (2014). Same-sex domestic violence: Prevalence, unique aspects, and clinical implications. *Journal of Sex & Marital Therapy, 41*(6), 636–648. doi:10.1080/0092623x.2014.958792.

7 SFBT with Survivors of War and International Conflict

■ STEPHEN M. LANGER

■ INTRODUCTION

There has been a massive displacement of humanity through multiple regional conflicts and national civil wars contributing to perhaps the largest forced migration of humanity the world has witnessed since World War II. The United Nations High Commissioner for Refugees (2016) reports 65.3 million people around the world have been forced from their homes. These refugees are divided into two distinct groups: (1) internally displaced persons (IDPs), or individuals displaced within their own country; and (2) externally displaced refugees who cross country borders to flee war and persecution.

The Syrian refugee crisis has caught the world media's attention. However, there are many other current conflicts not covered in international news, including numerous areas in which war may be officially over, and yet refugee and war survivors problems continue unabated and under-reported. The most well-known refugee situation may be the ongoing problem of huge long-term refugee camps in the Middle East, including areas around the state of Israel, in Palestinian territory, and in the nations of Lebanon, Syria, and Jordan.

■ IMPACT ON SOCIETY

The refugee impact on society is significant. As an example, in 2006 after the Ugandan government declared the northwest part of the country a free-fire zone, almost 2 million people, half under the age of 15, were displaced from their homes and clustered around military encampments for protection (Oxfam Briefing Paper 106). These refugees were exposed to hunger, exploitation, disease, lack of sanitary facilities, and lack of medical care. During this time, I witnessed a woman in one of these refugee camps, suffering with broken legs, in shock, and dying due to a lack of medical treatment. Children's education was disrupted and violent deaths were three times higher than in Iraq after the U.S. invasion in 2003. The rebel group, called the Lord's Resistance Army (LRA), abducted more than 25,000 children during the war who were used as child soldiers, sex slaves, or porters (Oxfam Briefing Paper 2007). When some of these children were later freed by the LRA, often years after their abduction, their families were afraid to accept them back. The children, now in their mid-to-late teens, had experienced and carried out horrible orders, such as killing, torture, and/or rape. Their parents and other family members had good reason to be concerned about their own safety. The children desperately wanted to forget what they had done and what had happened to them and rejoin their families.

In the IDP camps, mortality rates are high, both from diseases and violence. With the scarcity of food and other resources, widows with their young children are a particularly vulnerable group. The families these widows married into no longer want them, nor can they provide for them. Culturally, the connection between the family and the widow is broken when the husband/son dies. In addition, the widow's family of origin does not want her back because they also cannot provide for her. Due to the extra layer of despair, they are preyed upon by members of the refugee community, as well as the young soldiers who are in the military camps near the refugee camps.

On a more global scale, regional wars like the current troubles in the Middle East have a vast impact beyond the area in which the conflict is taking place. There is a dramatic movement of people from Syria into neighboring countries and beyond into Europe. Turkey has taken in over 2 million refugees from Syria. Jordan and other neighboring countries have also taken on a flood of humans fleeing the conflict. Germany accepted more than 1 million refugees and other European countries have taken in smaller numbers. The European Union also accepted over 600,000 asylum applications in 2015, mostly from people in Iraq, Afghanistan, Syria, and Libya (Eurostat Statistics Explained, 2016). These asylum seekers come to their refuge countries struggling with having lost their possessions, not having jobs, and having to adjust to a foreign culture. Their war experiences and mistreatment as refugees have often left them traumatized. Some of them have been tortured by their own government or by forces fighting on the opposing side of conflicts. There are now large refugee camps that have essentially turned into established settlements in Palestinian areas and in neighboring countries.

■ HOW I REALIZED SFBT WORKED WITH SURVIVORS OF WAR AND INTERNATIONAL CONFLICT

I was invited to become a member of the clinical faculty of the International Trauma Treatment Program (2017) in 1998 by John Van Eenwyck, Ph.D. ITTP was founded to "provide in-depth training for professionals from countries experiencing war, organized violence, or other forms of political oppression" (Trauma Treatment Program, 2017). It was decided by ITTP that it would be useful to take practitioners from war-torn countries out of the conflict zones, bring them to the United States, and train them so they could take the skills back to their native countries, although there was still some ongoing in-country training.

Another reason I work with survivors of war and international conflict is because of my own family history. My family lived for centuries in Upper Silesia, which was part of Germany, until the end of World War II. At the end of the war both my father's and my mother's family fled their town just ahead of Soviet soldiers. According to eyewitnesses I spoke with, the Russians proceeded to ethnically cleanse the area by lining up all the males who were 14 and over and machine gunning them, as well as raping the women and then sending the women and children west, while replacing the population with Poles they had displaced from conquered areas further east. The stories of my family fleeing west—some of them dying in the process and creating new lives with just the clothes on their back—are part of my growing-up experience. I grew up with a palpable sense that war is an ugly affair and to be avoided at all costs. I also have a recognition of the suffering of people fleeing the depredations of war. I carry this understanding with me and have always wanted to use my skills as a psychologist to mitigate the effects of trauma and displacement on survivors of war and disaster.

I have traveled to Uganda, Serbia, Croatia, and Trinidad to train local practitioners in SFBT skills. My experience in Uganda was instructive. After training two members of a private indigenous Ugandan refugee agency in the United States in 2005, I was invited to Uganda to train their refugee camp workers. Uganda struggled with civil war for 20 years, starting in 1987, with a vicious conflict between the Lord's Resistance Army (LRA) and the national government. The LRA tactics had a number of consequences. The establishment of large refugee camps near Uganda People's Defence Force (UPDF) encampments became necessary, as 94% of north Uganda's population was displaced as the government created a "free fire zone" to fight the guerrillas. The government stated that anyone caught outside of safe areas would be considered enemy combatants. The phenomenon of "night commuting," involving children who were likely to be abducted, began as they traveled to towns to sleep in the streets and then return to their villages to work during the day. A rise in HIV infections in the camps developed from soldiers having sex or raping refugee females. The arming of the Karamajong nomadic tribe to resist the LRA, led to Karamajong raiding of other tribes for cattle, as well as raping and pillaging, making the area even more insecure. At one point in 2005, as the conflict intensified, over 1.2 million people became IDPs and were housed in huge refugee camps (Oxfam, 2017). Refugees had to deal with limited food supplies, dislocation, and the ever-present danger from guerrilla forces, who would attack under the cover of darkness. The women and older children would go out to their land during the day to work the fields and tend the crops, returning to the camp before nightfall to minimize the risk of being attacked by the guerillas.

I traveled to Uganda in 2006 and 2007 to teach refugee camp workers who were working with refugees and returning abducted children as the war was winding down in the north. Pilgrim (Pilgrimafrica.org., 2017), the organization that had invited me to go to Uganda, also had a secondary school for refugee and returning abducted children, where I also consulted. A critical element in training refugee camp workers is helping them understand how they can use the SFBT approach in a way that is consistent with their own beliefs about the people they work with. Most of the workshop participants had previously been trained in counseling by pastors or were Christian lay preachers themselves, so their approach was directive and prescriptive. They were skeptical of the cooperative and questioning SFBT approach, which assumes that clients already know what is good for them (de Shazer et al., 2007). To help workers make the transition to a more cooperative approach, I decided to illustrate how this non-directive approach actually worked with an interaction I had experienced earlier in my Ugandan stay. I told them about going to a market in Kampala where tourist items were sold. I had gone from booth to booth to find a place that had all the items I was interested in purchasing. I made a deal with the shopkeeper that I would buy all my various items from her if she gave me a good price and if I could take a picture of her with her favorite item from her small store. After our negotiations about the price of the items, she thought a while about what item she would pick as her favorite. She said she had never been asked this question before, and she had always thought of the items she sold as things tourists would like, rather than what she liked. She finally picked an item and posed with a colored sand and bead picture with a caption that read: "With God All Things Are Possible." As I showed the workers a slide of her holding her favorite picture, I pointed out that this demonstrated she believed in God without me having to preach to her about it. I suggested that they assume this with their clients as well and that they already knew what was right and good for them.

■ PRACTICAL APPLICATION OF SFBT WITH SURVIVORS OF WAR AND INTERNATIONAL CONFLICT

A SFBT approach is helpful in a number of ways, at both the individual and the group level. SFBT thinking and practice involves empowering clients to think and act for themselves and move toward their preferred futures. It is pragmatic and looks for the active ingredients in *what is working* and aims for *change in the real world*. The purpose of SFBT in consulting, teaching, and other applications is to make the active ingredients of change knowable and easily accessible while cooperating with the client (de Shazer, 1985). SFBT has a present and desired future orientation, as well as a strong emphasis on client strengths, resources, and abilities, while using the client's frame of reference. Because each individual and each group is unique an SFBT consultation always has to be tailored to that particular person or group—there are no "one size fits all" answers.

SFBT addresses fundamental human desires and works with the inherent capabilities individuals and groups bring to the table to help them move toward what they want for themselves and for each other. Since these two elements are universal to humans, the SFBT approach appeals to people across cultures, experiences, and values. As a result, SFBT is applicable in any situation where people are looking for something better for themselves or for others they care about. Refugees typically have many more challenges in their lives than most people and therefore tend to be much more open to ways of improving their lot. Each situation refugees face is ultimately unique, and helping them overcome or deal with challenges inherent in their circumstances deserves an approach that empowers them and is realistic in considering the particulars of the situation.

As a rule, I do my best to assist locally based workers to think and work in solution-focused ways. This way they can help the people they are in contact with on an ongoing basis and build local capacity for acting in solution-focused ways, rather than becoming dependent on an outside "expert." They can unleash their own creativity to move toward desired futures and solutions. The only time I work directly with refugees myself is when I am teaching, either by conducting a live interview during a workshop or by seeing a client with a refugee camp worker to train that worker, who will be able to follow up as needed after I have left.

Another issue when working as a SFBT trainer and consultant from a First World country, especially in Third World countries and war zones, is the expectation that you will bring bags of money to distribute, rather than providing training that will help increase local capacity to deal with the difficulties people are confronting. Typically, people I encountered in my work initially asked for money directly or indirectly as I consulted with them. I have found it most useful to address this straightforwardly, early in the interaction, by making it clear that the resources I have to offer are not monetary but a way of thinking about things that will help us move on to more helpful conversations.

Some Tools

There are a myriad of challenges facing refugees and others impacted by war. Most authors focus on overcoming responses to traumatic situations. This is certainly important, but others highlight different concepts such as "post-traumatic success" (Bannink, 2015), or "post-traumatic growth" (Calhoun & Tedeschi, 2013) after war experiences. Although I have seen my share of individuals who are eventually better people after a traumatic situation, I am concerned that by implying people need to emerge from trauma better off by calling it *growth* or *success*, the clinician is placing expectations on them that may be unrealistic. It can make them feel they have failed somehow if they are not in a better place after treatment; this is clearly not beneficial. Oftentimes just surviving a bad situation is good enough. And it is not my job to tell them what is best for them— they already know.

I have found it most helpful to first find out what a person wants from the interview and what their "best hopes" are (Ratner, George, & Iveson, 2012). If overcoming a traumatic event or events is a response to this question, I become curious about what happened and how they dealt with it, assessing their coping and adaptive responses to the event(s) with them. How they responded to the critical event is the focus of the questions. As they answer these questions, the emphasis will be on what they did to make the situation better—or perhaps what they did to keep it from getting worse. If their response is that they "just had to get through it," then that is discussed in terms of how they coped.

SFBT practitioners use a positive, collaborative, hopeful stance. They look for exceptions to the problems people bring to them, as well as previous solutions, strengths, resources and abilities their clients already have. Questions are used as a primary way of interacting with clients versus directives and interpretations. People are typically complimented for successes and what they are already doing that is helpful to achieving their preferred future, as well as encouraged to continue doing what is working (de Shazer et al., 2007).

Consulting with a Widow's Group

When I visited one of the refugee camps in northern Uganda, I was asked to consult with a widows' group. The husbands of the widows had died because of disease, warfare, or other causes. Most of these widows were taking care of young children and babies. These women and children were no longer accepted as part of their husband's families, and their family of origin did not want them back either. Food was scarce in the camp. They were on their own and had to find ways to feed themselves and their families. Just like other women in the camp, they would travel to their fields nearby to cultivate crops using hoes. Since they did not have the protection of a family or their men any longer, some men in the camp would take the women's hoes away, even though they depended on these tools for working the fields. This meant that the widows could not work, causing a life and death food crisis for them.

The widow's group gathered under a tree in the camp, and I was asked to join them. After I was introduced they asked if I could buy them hoes, since theirs had been stolen from them. I reminded them that if I provided them with the tools, it would not solve their problem, because the hoes I bought them would most likely just be taken from them again as soon as they left the relative safety of the camp. I suggested that we needed to find a better way. They agreed that just getting more hoes was not a good solution and that they needed to find a way to keep the hoes they had. Ultimately, the widows agreed that the camp authorities, who were elected by the members of the camp, had sufficient authority to prevent theft without serious consequences to the thieves. They decided to ask the leader of the camp to buy hoes and mark them clearly on the handle as owned by the camp administration. Each authorized group member would then check out a hoe from the administration on a daily basis, so that anyone who stole a hoe would be held responsible by the camp authorities. The widows were pleased to have come up with a solution to a serious problem and were hopeful they would be able to feed their families again at the end of the meeting by implementing their plan.

A Live Workshop Interview: Rose

During my second visit to Uganda, I agreed to a live session as part of one of the workshops. I was to meet with a 14-year-old girl named Rose, who had escaped from the LRA about two weeks before. This was a delicate situation, given that she had almost certainly had been sexually mistreated while with the LRA. What had happened to her while in captivity I regarded as private information, which is consistent with the tenets of SFBT. We do not have to talk about or even know about the problems of the past to have a useful therapeutic conversation (Berg & Miller, 1992). I began the session by asking Rose what she wanted out of our conversation. She wanted to talk about being "normal again," her goals for her life now that she was home, and what she could do to reconnect with her family. She was quite shy and a bit reticent at first, especially talking in front of all these adults who were intently listening to her every word; however, we were able to develop some ideas for achieving her goals.

In addition to reconnecting with her family, she wanted to go to school so she could attend a university and become a nurse. We discussed steps she had already taken in these areas and what the next small steps might be. At the end of the session, I complimented her on her fortitude, resourcefulness, and life goals. After we completed the interview many of the workshop participants wanted to know why she had been abducted and why the LRA had kept her—and how anyone could do something so cruel. I reminded them that SFBT only attends to the preferred future, not the problematic past. They realized that knowing these details would satisfy *their* needs, not hers. They agreed that working on what she wanted to talk about was best for *her*.

I later received an e-mail from someone from the workshop with the following message: "Just today one of your clients, a girl you counseled during that workshop when you were in Soroti met me and told me that she is now doing well and is in one of the technical institutes around even trying to help those other girls who have some problems like unwanted pregnancies at school and so forth." It was heartening to hear that she had not only continued to work toward the goals she had identified for herself but also decided to apply what she had learned in the workshop to help others in a similar situation. She was apparently doing well enough to help others.

Consulting with Gaza Parents:

Even though I trained several Palestinians from Gaza through ITTP, I was unable to visit the Gaza Strip myself; however, the trainees were able to tell me some of the ways they applied their knowledge of SFBT once they returned home. A group of Gaza parents were troubled by how their anger, anxiety, and fear affected their children, especially when there was shelling and the threat of Israeli soldiers or factional fighters breaking down doors and entering family homes with guns drawn. The miracle question was asked: "If anger, fear, anxiety were gone during an attack—what would be different, how would you behave and act?"

Instead of continuing to talk about how bad the situation was and how powerless they were to change their circumstances, the parents began talking about how they wanted to react to the attacks and how to model that for their children. They became aware of social resources within the family, such as a grandmother who would gather the children and hold them when an adult was being questioned by armed men, how other families were coping with the situation, and how their religious faith kept them going, even in the worst of circumstances. When the people shifted from problem-talk to what they could do about the problem, even in a limited sense, it created hope. One group spent two hours working out 10 steps parents could take to handle children's reactions to shelling and invasion. They created a guide for other parents and distributed it throughout the neighborhood.

Preventing Suicide Bombing

Refugee camp workers were concerned about several adolescents in one of the camps who wanted to become suicide bombers. The SFBT-trained worker decided to visit the families of these kids to see how he might be able to help prevent them following through with their intentions. He started by asking the family members (with their teens present) their best hopes for their teenagers as they aged to adulthood. They were able to describe a preferred future for their child in a detailed way that was better than dying in the Israeli conflict. Given that the parents were highly motivated to ensure their child would not die, they also were willing to organize around making the preferred future happen for the teens. The parents and other family members would describe small steps each of them could take to help the teens achieve their better future, along with what the teens could personally do to make a good future for themselves. They answered the scaling question about how far toward this preferred future they had gotten already and what the next steps might be. They agreed to check in with each other on a regular basis to see how far they had gotten and if any modification of the plan was in order. All these boys are still alive a few years later.

Syrian Torture Survivor Intervention in Croatia, Germany, and Austria

Recently I helped the Rehabilitation Centre for Stress and Trauma in Zagreb along with their partner organizations in Germany and Austria develop an initial four-session group intervention based on SFBT principles. This was part of a larger effort to reintegrate about 220 torture survivors among refugees from Syria. This subgroup of Syrians is considered one of the most vulnerable groups among the refugees and has a high priority for services by the European Commission.

In the first session, group activities start with introductions and then having group members pair up and describe recent successes to each other. Then, the partner gets to introduce the other member of the pair to the whole group. Best hopes are described to the group and recorded. Answers to "What do you want to deal with first in order to feel better around the past experiences that brought you to this group?" and "What is each one of you already doing that helps you feel better, even a little bit?" are recorded to identify common elements and what might be useful from the contributions of the other group members. Scaling questions are used to assess how well participants see themselves as handling their difficulties, and they are asked what they know about themselves so that the number is not lower and what would be different if the number was one number higher. Feedback about how helpful the session was is requested, and a task of noticing what participants want to continue to have happen around the issues being worked on is given for the next session.

In the second session, participants are asked what is better in their everyday life; or if nothing is better, they are asked how they managed to not feel worse. The trauma response and what they feel they can and cannot change about their experience is discussed. They are also asked which elements of the trauma response they have already taken care of and how this came about. They are asked to imagine having a reunion two years in the future, having somehow overcome the difficult thoughts and feelings they have been experiencing and that the traumatic experiences they had are now a part of an older and wiser side of themselves. What would they and others notice that was different and an indication that they had succeeded? The participants are asked to scale where they are already with regard to their future selves. What would be the first signs that they are higher on the scale? What can each of them do to be a bit higher on the scale? Feedback is given by the participants about what impressed them about what others in the group have said. This feedback is written down for each group member and signed by the member to acknowledge it.

The third session starts with a question about what strengths the person has that might move them up the scale of improvements and what strengths their families or friends might say they can use to move up the scale. They are asked about secret strengths that nobody else knows about and how they learned these things about themselves. They are asked what strengths they want to develop or improve on to achieve their goals. They also discuss what tells them that making these improvements is possible and who might help them achieve these improvements. They put together a chart of who helps them or could possibly help them, including family, friends, other people, and organizations. They are asked who has helped them so far in overcoming their difficulties as refugees and trauma survivors and how they can widen their support system. They also talk about what they might recommend to others in their situation. Individual plans of action are developed. They are asked to state how confident they are that they will move up on the scale when they apply their strengths fully over time. They are asked to write what they value most about each other and each participant picks out their favorite statement and reads it to the group.

The fourth session's focus is on the plan of action each participant has developed. They are asked which items on the plan they have already started and what support they might still need to fulfill their plan. They are asked to scale their confidence about being able to achieve their desired outcome and what might increase their confidence level. The participants are asked to develop a list of tips to other persons in similar situations that will be included in a published booklet for other torture survivors. They are asked to scale their mastery over the problems that brought them to the group so far and asked how they might be able to continue making improvements. Finally, each participant puts an anonymous note in an envelope of each of the other participants about what they were impressed with about that person that the individual can read and return to when they face obstacles and setbacks.

As of early 2017, in Croatia, 29 refugees (14 males and 15 females) had taken part in the pilot phase of the group intervention. The majority of participants were living in reception centers, waiting for their asylum application to be processed. Apart from consequences of traumatic experience many struggled with anxiety and uncertainty whether asylum would be granted, as well frustration about living in poor conditions in crowded reception centers. It appeared that the SFBT intervention in the group setting, even though it was envisaged to address consequences of severe traumatic experiences, is potent in overcoming other difficulties these refugees faced in this context.

The first question asked in session one, about recent successes, set the tone for the intervention, focusing the clients on their strengths and resourcefulness.

The first reaction of some participants (both male and female) was to burst into tears. They recalled all the hardships they had survived to get to where they found refuge and all that they had left behind. This was then used in the SFBT conversation to focus on their strengths, abilities, and resourcefulness, which almost immediately changed the tone of the group interaction. In the final evaluation after four sessions, participants were asked what was most helpful during the last four weeks. A number of them instantly responded that this way of talking and thinking was helpful to them and that the initial conversation in the first session made a strong impression on them.

Discussing trauma symptoms in the second session by focusing on what has already been taken care of also contributed to hopefulness and resilience and to the confidence in their sense of agency. It appears that the group setting itself contributed to the effectiveness of the intervention, as well when the participants motivated each other to recall even the smallest steps toward recovery and which strategies they used successfully.

The future-oriented questions produced interesting responses. For many participants integration in the new society was strongly connected with overcoming trauma-related symptoms. Being able to competently communicate in the local language, having a good job, and starting a family were identified as evidence of recovery connected to the preferred future. This is also in line with the SFBT idea that solutions are not necessarily directly related to the identified problem.

Third and fourth sessions had an energizing effect on participants and contributed to their connecting with each other and increasing mutual support (Knezić, personal communication, 2017). This intervention is part of a larger program of rehabilitation, empowerment, and integration of asylum-seeking torture survivors and will be implemented in 2017 and 2018. These refugee centers have taken a step toward helping people in a SFBT way manage being mistreated. The implementations of this project will be assessed as the project moves forward.

■ MOST IMPORTANT SF QUESTIONS YOU ASK IN SESSION?

The most important SF questions I ask are ones that make the survivors aware of the resources they bring to their situations. In most instances refugees and displaced people are hyperaware of their surroundings, as well as of the new circumstances they find themselves in; they are also aware of all the new things they are required to do to cope with the challenges they face. While trying to adapt, they are also cognizant that so much around them is out of their control. As a result, they tend not to be as aware of what they themselves bring to the situation or what they are doing to succeed in their new surroundings.

Questions about their contribution to making things work for them are key to helping them gain a greater sense of agency. *What do you know about yourself that gives you hope that you will get asylum? What do you know about yourself that makes people want to help you?* Scaling questions about how the person is doing is helpful to elicit the information needed to base the questions about the person's contribution to their own status. It is important to keep in mind that these are unusual questions for most people, even in more ordinary contexts, and may therefore be difficult to answer. Clinicians may have to wait for the person to think before responding or redirect the person to the question after receiving an initial response. Don't be surprised if the first answer is: *I don't know.* As Steve de Shazer said, *I don't know* means *Shut up, I'm thinking* (de Shazer, 1996, personal communication).

Many cultures in the world are more collectivist-oriented than individualistic (Kim, Hong, & Sangalang, 2014), so when working with refugees from these countries it is also important to elicit the person's contributions to the betterment of their community or their family. Relationship questions (Berg & Kelly, 2000) that consider the client's perception of what others think of them and how they impact others is a good way to get at not only what strengths the person is bringing to the situation but also how those strengths interact with the people they relate to.

Finally, asking questions about what the person's hopes are, both for the session and for themselves, is a useful way to create a constructive framework for the work at the beginning of a session. It can become a touchstone throughout the interaction for everything else that occurs in the exchange.

■ CASE STUDY

Masud is a Palestinian from Gaza who was applying for asylum in the United States.[1] He was a journalist and a critic of the Hamas government when it came to power. He was detained and tortured by people associated with the government and risked death if he returned to his home. To obtain his college education, he went to Iraq, as there are no universities in Gaza. While he was studying to become an Arabic–English translator at a university in Iraq, the United States invaded the country, and he had to endure many hardships to survive in a war zone while finishing his degree. Since he came to the United States he has given many talks about the current situation in Gaza. He earned a master's degree in international relations and conflict resolution a few months before the interview. His family, including his wife and two young children, still lived in Gaza at the time he was interviewed.

1. Many thanks to Janet F. Sorensen for transcribing Masud's interview.

CLINICIAN: Hi, Masud. I'm curious about what your best hopes are in talking with me today about the issues you are confronted with about being a refugee here and how you are dealing with it?

MASUD: I think my best hope is just to have peace in my life and to have a betterment for my own children, and to raise awareness about the suffering and agony of my oppressed people. This is my best hope of being a refugee in another country. I think being a refugee is not a choice. It is really a struggle, hard work, working day and night, suffering from unrelenting anxiety and fear every day because we don't know where you are heading to.

CLINICIAN: I understand that you have recently done a number of things to try to establish your status here in this country. How is that going for you?

MASUD: It was really hard, being from another country, being from Palestine. I can imagine if I am from Syria, being Arab or darker skin, being labeled as a Muslim, being without legal status, without a green card or U.S. citizenship, it was really hard. Social Security, it was really hard for medical insurance. If I can do anything, I have to do it double and triple just to make it happen. It is hard in everything that you can imagine. It is hard to make a living. Most of the jobs, you should be a U.S. citizen. Because I finished my masters in international relations, I can work with a U.S. State Department and International Organization based in Washington, DC. One of their requirements is that you have to be a U.S. citizen. It is really hard, agonizing, unrelenting anxiety and fear. But, you know we have hope that things will go right.

CLINICIAN: What gives you that hope for yourself... that things will go right?

MASUD: Because I believe there are good people everywhere that are vouching for you, that are supporting you, and they know where you are coming from. What gives me hope, that I am surrounded by human beings and not surrounded by people who are bad. So this is what gives me hope.

CLINICIAN: Given that you've seen there are good people around, how does that help you then in doing what you need to do?

MASUD: It helps me a lot. It helps me a lot in understanding some cultural roles that I was unfamiliar with. It helps me to establish my roles in a place that I have community with so I can have like, some social connections and have people I can ask for their help in terms of getting aware of too many issues. That's why I'd rather live in a place where I can be surrounded by love and compassion and by understanding, so I can move on and carry on in my own path to peace and to establishing myself.

CLINICIAN: So on a scale of zero to 10 where zero is you haven't established that path at all and 10 is you are solidly on that path and things can go as smoothly as possible for you from here on out, what number would you give yourself so far?

MASUD: Six

CLINICIAN: Six. OK, wow! So what tells you that it's already at a six. What do you know about your situation and yourself that you can say it is a six?

MASUD: Because I have been here for three years, and I have achieved my master's degree . . . and this was the plan, my own plan. I have achieved my master's degree. I got some legal documents that I can work. I have got my social security number. I have too many legal documents that can give me relief or can help me out, that I am OK. I am six out of the scale of ten. If I get this I will be number eight and if I get this I will be number 10. So for me what I mean like, if I get my asylum interview I get number seven. If I get my unlimited social security number, my travel document, I will be a number eight. If I get my green card after one year it will be a number nine. If I get my U.S. citizenship after five years I will be a number 10. So, as you know between, actually, there are too many challenging situations I can imagine, but these are like the numbers. So every number will carry one year or two years with it.

CLINICIAN: So you are at a six now, what else makes it already a six, because it seems to me that's an impressively high number?

MASUD: I think because within my stay I establish good connections. I am a public speaker for refugee cases for human rights; I call it the social stamina or the social connection. I can pass through a lot of difficult situations because I am a public speaker. The audience feels like they should do something because they are imaging themselves as if they are in my own country. So I think having social stamina, social connections helps. You know, I lived here for three years, so I have been in 75 churches speaking about Palestine, about trauma healing, about social justice issues, and was speaking in some colleges and universities and that gave me some credibility and authenticity to talk about things that matter to people who are for peace and for trauma healing and for justice.

CLINICIAN: You've mentioned a number of things. One of them is social stamina, and I'd like to go through each of them one at a time. Is this a social stamina that you had before already or did you discover this during your time being a refugee and dealing with these issues?

MASUD: I think it is a survival skill that you will develop when you are in survival mode. Where I lived I used to be introvert. I liked to read a lot. I liked to be with myself. When I traveled I found for myself I cannot be introvert anymore. I have to have connections. I have to build connections. I have to work hard to build these connections, networking, networking, and networking, because I believe for a long time that networking is the best way that I can advance a lot of things. English is not my first language. I can have friends who can edit my work. USA is not my first country so I have people who can teach me about social norms, culture norms, religious understanding that I may be unfamiliar with.

CLINICIAN: So did you discover the social stamina after you left Gaza or did you already know that you had it when you were in Gaza?

MASUD: I think I had it, but I have to use it when I need to use it. I had one experience when I was in Iraq, as a student. I used to be a very concerned student, just sitting in the house reading. I want to show to my family that here is the best son for you, and I don't want to fail. When the U.S. war erupted there, everyone left, and I stayed in Iraq because my family was really poor, and they cannot afford for me to go to university. So I get a scholarship in Iraq . . . I have to do it, even in the war. That's what gave me some hope, and I was proud that I finished my bachelor's degree in Iraq in 2005 in a time when there was no one international student in Iraq. Because I want to have a good life. I want to be educated. I believe in education, and that's why I came to U.S. I came as a student. But I live in a country that I have a status under until now, which is not a very easy status. It is inhumane. It is like you are not a human being. You hear every day those Palestinians are subhumans or they are. . . no one can criticize them. It is very hard for me that I would be labeled as not a human being in the 21st century. So, it gives me, every day, dehumanization, and demonization. I can feel it. I can feel it when I am in the airport. I can feel it in the Egyptian airport where they treated us as we are cows or dogs, where sometimes we are dogs. They put us in a very small area where you can't go to the bathroom. You don't have towels and you don't have water. It is very dehumanizing. That is why when we leave we are looking for a better future and we are not taking anyone's jobs. We are creating our own work.

CLINICIAN: It sounds like you've really been in a lot of really difficult situations. It's really impressive how you've used your social stamina to get through that. Another thing that you mentioned that I'm kind of curious about is this: you said that you found people who care about you and that you discovered that there were people who cared about you here in the U.S. I'm curious, what is your sense of what it is about you that people would care about you rather than not care about you? What do you know about yourself?

MASUD: I really have no answer to this question but I can give you a general answer.

CLINICIAN: Well, I'm asking you what it might be about you in particular that people care about you?

MASUD: Maybe because they think sometimes that I am smart. I can contribute to where they are. Maybe they think that I am outspoken and in the same time I am very honest and I am very humane but I have to share things that should be shared. This is out of my love for humanity, out of my past experience that people are ignorant sometimes about something. That is fine, but when they are woefully ignorant about something, that is not fine. I am helping people as much as I can who want to be different, who want to be taught.

CLINICIAN: What other qualities do you have that helps people to care about you do you think?

MASUD: I just assume actually, because I don't know.

CLINICIAN: Of course.

MASUD: I think maybe it's their compassion. I think maybe sometimes some communities it is guilt and some communities it is understanding, deep understanding.

CLINICIAN: Ok, and what do they see in you, do you suppose, that makes them care about you rather than not care?

MASUD: (Pause) I have to dig deeper in myself to understand. I understood your question, but I can't give you a clear answer on the spot, why they care about me that give them the time or the space to look for me and to think about me, care about me, I think they can see my eyes, they can see myself.

CLINICIAN: And what do they see in your eyes?

MASUD: They can see that I am very passionate, I am very compassionate, and I am looking to do something that is so beautiful. We are human beings and we are hardwired to be social. I think when they look at you, when they hear your voice, as much honest as you are, they will like you and they will try to do the best they can to help you in passing situations, difficult situations. It is like about maybe your official appearances maybe, and maybe about your psychological disturbing feelings. What I mean by psychological disturbing feelings, that you are longing for your country, longing for peace everywhere, that you are longing for seeing your kids as happy as they can be, longing for your country to be free and to be in peace. Because I was thinking of my life, how can I do something for my own country, for my own children that they won't go through what I have gone through? I want them to feel peace and to experience, because they never knew what does it mean, peace? They are normalized about a situation that should be abnormal and should be opposed anyway. So I can answer your question about why they are caring about me.

CLINICIAN: What is it about you that they care about? What do they see in you? That is true about you?

MASUD: As I mentioned, maybe I am passionate and compassionate, or they think I am passionate or compassionate, I cannot think about themselves. Or maybe they think I offer something to them or they are understanding their own works, where I came from, and sometimes it rings true to them in some ways.

CLINICIAN: OK. Tell me more about that. What about you helps your story to ring true? Because they read about this in the newspaper all the time or see it on TV, and yet what is it about you that they end up caring about you when you talk about this?

MASUD: Because being in the United States and United States has gone through the civil war for four years a long time ago and they got the civil rights movement in the Sixties in the United States and people are connecting to the Jim Crow era or George Wallace in 1968, or when you are talking about racism against African Americans.

CLINICIAN: Right, so what about you, though? That brings that out in them?

MASUD: Because I am connecting to them. This is my job. I am connecting things together. I am helping people to see the difference. This is good when you are a voracious reader and you are reading about other cultures, when you are reading about other histories, that you are not the only one, or you are not the only oppressed one. So you can make connections. You can make some kind of connecting tools.

CLINICIAN: So you said you wanted to have peace in your life, you wanted a life for your children, so let's talk a little bit about that. You have two kids at home, right? So what are your best hopes for what you can do for them?

MASUD: Do the best I can, and I am doing the best I can. I am sparing no effort. I am using, investing in every microsecond to establish a better future for them, and I have suffered a lot seeing them grow up without me, seeing them in a very war-ridden and war-torn place, which is Gaza, and I am away. They experience three wars in seven years. They have experienced a lot and I was away, and I have some guilt about this. So that's why I'm doing the best I can in a place that I can be, in a way that I can feel OK, just to see them again, and I suffer. It is not a good journey. To be honest, United States is very tough when it comes to understanding. For instance, I can give you instances about the Syrian refugees. The refugees are dying out of dictatorship, out of global powers, Russia and United States, and they are going everywhere. The only two countries that are not accepting refugees are the United States and Russia. The United Stated accepted 10,000, which is nothing, while Jordan accepts 2 million, Turkey one million and a-half. I understand these are adjacent countries. I understand the U.S. can accept Mexican people like at the border, they are coming legally or illegally, but I am telling about only these. In Europe, in Germany, thousands and thousands were accepted and they were opening their borders to welcome them because they knew they can bring value, economic value. Yes, there are some bad people. Of course! You will have 1% as in your country you have a lot of bad people as they have a lot of bad people. They are humans. That's why we have police, that's why we have social system, that's why those are coming as transient immigrants. So they will live a life as you live and they create a lot of opportunities. Survivors can create opportunities.

CLINICIAN: So what's your sense of how your children think of what you're doing to be their dad?

MASUD: I think they love me, they say and I can feel when I call them, "we love you Dad" "We love you so much." And, I think they love me so much not because I am away. They have the sense that our dad is doing the best he can and something will culminate very good. We will have a better future. We will have a better life. Really they don't understand that it is not as they imagine. They cannot understand about this better life. They don't know that U.S. is going into upheaval in terms of social and political awareness. So for me, I think they like their dad, they love their dad, their dad is everything they have and they can feel this from words, from their hearts, virtual hugs, and virtual kisses. I can see that.

CLINICIAN: I understand you have Facetime with them or time with them on Skype?

MASUD: But what aches my heart, that I live in a country that you have just four hours of electricity every day. So when they call me even when I am in a meeting or at dinner with my friends, I have to leave my friends and excuse myself because I have time limits for calling. We are in the 21st century and people are having just four hours of electricity and within the four hours of electricity the electricity will run out and they cannot wash their clothes, they cannot go to take showers, and it is very horrible situation, but they have meaning in life. This is the good thing.

CLINICIAN: Do you help them to have meaning in life?

MASUD: Yes, I help them to see me as their role model. I am telling them very honestly what I am going through. "I am doing this, Papa, that, I am doing this, and I am doing this" and they are really, like, my daughter, today, she took the highest mark in the school.

CLINICIAN: Congratulations!

MASUD: Thank you. She took the highest mark in the school and she said, "I am so happy, Papa. I want to be a surgeon. I want to be a doctor." Because she works so hard while she is a kid, because she knew that her dad will be angry if she takes lesser marks because I survived a lot for them. I did everything for them. That doesn't mean that I have to punish them if they have lesser marks but they knew that their dad would be happy because he is struggling. He is away. They knew that.

CLINICIAN: Do you think in a sense she had those high marks for you, too, not just for herself?

MASUD: I think it is for me in a sense, that she can share her love because she asked that I want my Dad to see them. When I talk with her every day she is talking actually about herself, like, grades, about her school, that I am the first one and I will be the most qualified student in the class and she is really smart. I mean, it's not because she's my kid, but she's really smart.

CLINCIAN: And she's your kid! (laughing)

MASUD: Yes, to be honest about that, yes.

CLINICIAN: Then you also were talking a bit about raising awareness as far as your best hopes, and it sounds like you are doing a lot of that already. How do you fit your own life into this raising awareness and taking care of yourself, because you have so many things that you have to do just being a refugee and going through all the processes to deal with and surviving as well as getting your status and all that here in the U.S.?

MASUD: I think it is about compassion. It is also about when I travel or when I walk in the streets and I have coffee with someone and he asks me some question, "Where are you from?" I answer I am from Palestine. "Oh, it is part of Israel?" So that is my interest. Even I have to organize my day by hour. I have back-to-back plans every day and I would love to speak for people for free sometimes. Because, for instance, if you live in Olympia all of your life and someone says, "Oh, there is no Olympia, Washington," which is the capital of Washington State, what do you think? And you know it is a very historical place, for instance. Someone else says, "Oh, you are from Palestine? Oh, is it part of Israel or is it part of Egypt?" And you are talking about a country that was established since the dawn of civilizations. It was before religion came and before cultures.

CLINCIAN: So how do you take care of yourself then given that you have this mission to raise awareness among people, and there are so many opportunities to raise awareness and yet you also have to do things for yourself. How do you do that?

MASUD: Plan.

CLINICIAN: The example you mentioned just a minute ago was that somebody in the street says, "Well, isn't that part of Israel or Egypt?" and then you start educating them. Those are not planned things so I could see it disrupting your ability to take care of yourself because you could end up doing that instead of doing what you need to do for yourself.

MASUD: I think being activist or being for social rights either here in the United States or everywhere is not something that is a choice. It is moral and ethical principles that you have to abide by. Activism is in your blood, where you go, and that's what is a good thing about refugees. They can bring their talents and skills with them, which may be different than what's in the place they are coming in, in a different way, a different move, different emotions. I have answer for your question I think, that I plan it. I plan my day and then I make sure that I do the most urgent, the most important tasks for my day and also do the voluntary work every day, either in social media, in academic settings, or in social settings. This is what I believe. Sometimes it is frustrating that you spend your days, your time, to share and to raise awareness about things and you see there is no change. But I believe there will be a change. I believe. I can see it. Very small but it will go bigger and bigger. But just keep going and don't be disappointed. This is how it goes. Change take years. I am happy to be part of that movement and that's why I am well recognized by social activists and peace activist persons in the United States. They email me every day. I have no time to reply. Also in your question, sometimes I have to check what's the most important thing where I can fit in. That's why I fit in the trauma healing and social justice. I fit in international connections and understanding and problems. I cannot fit in everything. That is why now I filter and choose what I have to do. This is what I can do.

CLINICIAN: How do you make those choices?

MASUD: By knowing myself. By knowing my limitations. By knowing my own academic background. By knowing where I can contribute, where I cannot contribute. By being honest about my own future desires, what I want to be and about what mission that I hold dear, what mission that I love. I am a person who believes in all religions and at the same times disbelief in all religions when it comes to heresy, discrimination, bigotry, homophobia, Islamophobia, Christian phobia, Jewish phobia, Gentile phobia, everything phobia. I am a human being who believes in this and this is who I am, and I want to change because I use very all-inclusive principles in my life. So how you can make it, why do you have to talk about this? Because this is who you are. Some people, they have different sexual orientations. It is who they are. I am who I am. So you have to accept me, and you have to recognize me and my contribution to myself and to the world and to the people who are around me.

CLINICIAN: Is there anything else that you wanted to say before we finish up?

MASUD: I want to say something about refugees. Back in the day there was boats laden with hungry Jews who came from Poland and the United States refused to allow them in the country. It was the same history that is going on all over the world. Those people are smart. They are survivors. They don't choose who they are. They don't choose to be political. They want to survive. They have kids. It is a human condition to take care of your kids. It is a human condition to go into the boat and drown yourself for your kids. It is a human condition. It is not because they are Huns or they are coming to take your own country or they are coming to take your own resources. Because if you want to talk about resources, those people are the scapegoats of international powers and they are paying the price every day. 50,000 child-workers in the world. 50,000, can you imagine, in the world! If there are five kids working in the United States how much media attention would they get? 50,000! In Palestine you have 93% of traumatized kids who are involuntarily urinating every day, who are having so much social anxiety and psychological trauma. What I mean, those refugees can bring change in the world and they have done that in Saudi Arabia. Saudi Arabia was nothing when the Palestine refugees came and changed Saudi Arabia. People from gulf countries they are couch potatoes. The Palestinians came and reinvented these countries by their hard work, by their labor, and by their survival needs. Survival can bring change. So this is what I say. I say refugees are a good and powerful intervention in any country they will come in. Dearborn, Michigan is a good example. You can look at the economic living three years ago and can look how much money was brought to this area. The refugees can do a lot of work and they can bring their talents, their skills, their social understanding, and their own trauma also, and they can use it for a good reason.

CLINICIAN: So I am assuming that you intend to do the same, not just them, but you also.

MASUD: Everyone has his own path. I have more academic background and not hands-on experience so everyone has his own skills and that is what gives variety. And that doesn't mean they have nothing here but they can bring their own cuisine. They can bring their own sense of humor. They can bring their own sense of dancing; variety. What makes America great as I believe, is that it is diverse and it is powerful and everyone is joining to protect it. It's not like just one social grouping or one social sect or cult. That's why it is very powerful in that sense, as I believe in that actually.

CLINCIAN: Well, thank you. I appreciate your taking the time to do this.

MASUD: Of course. Thanks for having me.

■ SUMMARY

The world is facing an unprecedented crisis responding to a vast number survivors of war who become refugees or are internally displaced. SFBT has a potentially large role to play in helping these people deal with and overcome the significant effects of displacement and trauma. Rather than focusing on the problems they have faced that cannot be changed, within SFBT sessions clients are invited to explore what they can do themselves and how they can assist relief workers in supporting them to move forward in a hopeful and empowered way. The SFBT approach provides a number of tools to help people affected by war get on with their lives with all the inherent challenges that entails, while fully respecting the sometimes unimaginable difficulties they have survived.

■ REFERENCES

Bannink, F. (2015). *101 solution-focused questions for help with trauma*. New York: W. W. Norton.

Berg, I. K., & Kelly, S. (2000). *Building solutions in child protective services*. New York: W. W. Norton.

Berg, I. K., & Miller, S. D. (1992). *Working with the problem drinker: A solution-focused approach.* New York: W. W. Norton.

Calhoun, L., & Tedeschi, R. G. (2013). *Post-traumatic growth in clinical practice.* New York: Brunner Routledge

de Shazer, S. (1985) *Keys to solution in brief therapy.* New York: W. W. Norton.

de Shazer, S. (1996) Personal communication, September 15.

de Shazer, S., Dolan, Y., Korman, H., McCollum, E., Trepper, T., & Berg, I. K. (2007). *More than miracles: The state of the art of solution-focused brief therapy.* Binghamton, NY: Haworth.

Eurostat Statistics Explained: Asylum Statistics (2016). Retrieved from http://ec.europa.eu/eurostat/statistics-explained/index.php/Asylum_statistics, March 15, 2017

International Trauma Treatment Program. History of ITTP. Retrieved from http://www.ittp.org/about/history.html, August 2017.

Kim, J., Hong, J. S., & Sangalang, C. (2014). Solution-focused approach with Asian American clients. In J. Kim (Ed.), *Solution-focused brief therapy: A multicultural approach* (pp. 55–71). Los Angeles: Sage Publications.

Knezić, D. (2017) Personal communication, January 15, 2017.

Oxfam Briefing Paper 106, *The Building Blocks of sustainable peace: The views of internally displaced people in Northern Uganda.* Retrieved from www.oxfam.org.uk/bp106-building-blocks-peace-uganda-110907-en.pdf, August 2017.

Oxfam America Research Report (2007). *Between hope and fear in northern Uganda: Challenges on the ground and an urgent need for peace.* Retrieved from oxfamamerica.org/research&publications/html

Pilgrimafrica.org. Retrieved from https://www.pilgrimafrica.org, August 2017.

Ratner, H., George, E., & Iveson. C. (2012) *Solution focused brief therapy: 100 key points and techniques.* London: Routledge.

United Nations High Commissioner for Refugees. Statistics, figures at a glance. Retrieved from http://www.unhcr.org/en-us/figures-at-a-glance/html 12-31-2016.

8 Substance Abuse and Recovery Through SFBT

■ SWATHI M. REDDY, KRISTIN BOLTON,
CYNTHIA FRANKLIN, AND
KARLA GONZALEZ SUITT

■ INTRODUCTION TO SUBSTANCE USE DISORDERS, TRAUMA, AND SFBT

The 2014 National Survey on Drug Use found that approximately 21.5 million people suffered from substance use disorders (SUDs) in the United States. A total of 17 million people reported an alcohol use disorder, 7.1 million people reported an illicit drug use disorder, and 2.6 million people reported both an alcohol and illicit drug use disorder (Substance Abuse and Mental Health Services Administration [SAMHSA], 2015a). Studies have found that anywhere from 30% to 60% of those seeking treatment for SUDs have experienced trauma (Back et al., 2000; Brady, Back, & Coffey, 2004; Dansky, Brady, & Roberts, 1994; Jacobsen, Southwick, & Kosten, 2001; Stewart, Conrod, Samoluk, Pihl, & Dongier, 2000; Triffleman, Marmar, Delucchi, & Ronfeldt, 1995). According to the *DSM-5*, a diagnosis of substance use disorder is based on evidence of impaired control, social impairment, risky use, and pharmacological criteria. Substance use is also highly comorbid with other mental disorders including trauma (SAMHSA, 2015b).

Solution-focused brief therapy (SFBT) has been used in clinical settings for clients who abuse substances (de Shazer & Isebaert, 2003; Hendrick, Isebaert, & Dolan, 2012; Juhnke & Coker, 1997) and research has started to emerge that shows that SFBT may also be a good intervention for clients who experience comorbid mental health and substance use conditions including trauma (Kim, Brook, & Akin, 2016; Mason, Chandler, & Grasso, 1995; McCollum, Trepper, & Smock, 2004; Pichot & Smock, 2009; Spilsbury, 2012). SFBT may be a practical intervention for clinicians working with clients who abuse substances because research indicates this population has a tendency to drop out of treatment after the first few sessions. Thus, the brief model of SFBT is well suited to accommodate clients because initial sessions rely heavily on determining a client's needs to find benefit in therapy rather than conducting lengthy evaluations of the client as typically performed with the traditional medical model of treatment (Berg & Dolan, 2001).

This chapter will describe how SFBT has been used in the treatment of substance use relying on the clinical literature to illustrate interventions. Specific ways to engage clients with substance use will be covered including the questions to ask to promote change. In addition, this chapter will describe a case where SFBT has been used with a client with alcohol use disorder and explain how SFBT may be used in groups to treat substance use. Finally, this chapter will discuss the emerging outcome literature on SFBT with clients who have substance use including studies that assess substance use and trauma.

■ SOLUTION-FOCUSED BRIEF THERAPY AS A METHOD OF TREATMENT FOR SUBSTANCE USE DISORDERS

SFBT has been applied in substance use treatment since the early 1990s, and there was increased output in the literature in the mid-1990s. Three books have been devoted to the application of SFBT with substance use treatment, while a number of books contain at least one chapter on applying SFBT with clients managing substance use (Berg & Miller, 1992; Miller & Berg, 1995; Pichot & Smock, 2009). SFBT has also been implemented in treatment centers around the world, including the United States, Belgium, Poland, and Iran (de Shazer & Isebaert, 2003; Nameni, Shafi, Delavar, & Ahmadi, 2014; Smock et al., 2008; Szczegielniak et al., 2013). The primary goal of substance use treatment is to decrease or eliminate substance use in clients entering these settings (de Shazer & Isebaert, 2003; Pichot & Smock, 2009). SFBT differs from traditional substance use treatments because it provides clients with an opportunity to set their own self-determined goals, which will oftentimes have little or nothing to do with substance use (de Shazer & Isebaert, 2003; McCollum, Trepper, & Smock, 2004). Examples of self-determined goals may include saving a marriage, keeping a job, or getting back a driver's license. The role of the clinician is to orient clients toward achieving their set goal and assisting clients in building their own solutions to promote change. In the process of setting and achieving their own goals, clients often come to their own recognition of how substance use may be inhibiting their lives. The clinician also asks questions that help clients identify how their life would be lived without the interference of problematic situations such as DUIs, court dates, and family problems. To develop solutions around the substance use, it is also important to work with the client and explore past experiences of what has worked to cut down or discontinue substance use. The clinician uses a non-directive and collaborative process to help clients recognize that their solution and substance use are connected but also that their problems extend beyond reduction or ceasing of substance use to additional aspects of their lives that also need change (Hendrick et al., 2012).

■ MOTIVATION TO CHANGE

Clients with SUDs present to therapy with varying degrees of desire to change behaviors. Crucial to the success of clients presenting with SUDs, solution-focused practitioners start where their client is or adapt to their clients in order to improve engagement and rapport. Some SFBT clinicians follow the stages of change process (Hendrick et al., 2012). The six stages in the process of change include: pre-contemplation, contemplation, determination, action, maintenance, and sometimes relapse (Prochaska, DiClemente, & Norcross, 1992), and these change processes are widely used in substance use treatment. It is important to recognize these stages as part of a cycle, and clients may move from one stage to the next at any time.

The role of the solution-focused practitioner is to help the client regain control of their lives in the safest way possible regardless of what stage of change they may be in when they see a clinician. Solution-focused practitioners follow the client's lead and refrain from directing the client in how to address substance use. Rather, the practitioner's role is to place more focus on emotional attunement of the client's experiences as they engage the client toward a shift in meaning through the process of co-construction. The co-construction process means that words and meanings are grounded and negotiated between client and clinician and that new meanings about the clients' experiences are shifted in the course of a solution-focused conversation. The co-construction of meaning is key to the change process implemented by the SFBT clinician (Franklin, Zhang, Froerer, & Johnson, 2016). During the SFBT conversation, for example, a client may shift the meanings concerning their substance use to understand that the substance use is related to the stresses in their marriage and the emotional pain they experience from the multiple abuse situations they have faced. Drinking is a way of coping that does not work so well, mainly because it only keeps the client trapped in an unsatisfactory and unacceptable life situation. The client likes to drink and uses it to cope; however, this also means they have resigned themselves to the unbearable situation. Confronted with this new meaning, the client may choose instead to focus on a solution to improve their life situation.

■ SOLUTION-BUILDING CONVERSATIONS

The clinician facilitates a conversation during the first session that allows the client to identify what they want out of the conversation and also to discuss their own feelings about the substance use (Gordon, 2007). What do they want out of this discussion? What do they like about the substance use? How did they get referred? And how do others view their usage (Dolan, 1991)? Deciding which behaviors to address first will ultimately depend on the client presenting for treatment (Brown & Wolfe, 1994). Some clients may say they want to change, and others may say they do not want to change and why they have to show up for treatment, for example. To accommodate different types of clients, the clinician may ask a client to describe instances where they do not drink or the smallest signs of progress if the person expresses a desire to cut down their usage. Regardless of the client's readiness to directly address their substance use, a slow progression of focusing on small changes is preferred in order to build competencies or control over undesirable behaviors without producing resistance or fear. Creating a context of competency and hope is implicitly achieved through use of solution-focused questions, as clients are encouraged to be in charge of their therapy by participating and developing their own treatment plan. This client-centered approach to therapy is especially useful for clients in recovery because they learn to view their personal actions to be associated with desired changes. The clinician proceeds with the client by asking questions to build rapport and to begin a process of goal setting and change.

Questions and Reflections That Build Cooperative Relationships for Solution Building. Solution-focused techniques are especially beneficial in establishing rapport and building therapeutic alliance with the client (de Shazer & Isebaert, 2003). Especially significant for clients in recovery, capturing opportunities to highlight their strengths fosters an encouraging relationship (Lutz, 2014) because clients may be more accustomed to a more confrontational and critical approach coming from family members and treatment providers. Engaging with your client through complimenting strengths not only allows for discovery of positive differences between the person and their substance use but also contributes to building self-efficacy, which is beneficial for recovery. Pointing out the client's well-developed skills, for example, even if these are related to obtaining drugs, should be framed as strengths as the client was most likely incorporating strong networking and entrepreneurial skills to sustain their drug habit. Clinicians should also pay attention to the positive differences, which may include remaining abstinent for a period of time, managing difficult feelings without relapsing, or attending a 12-step meeting. Identifying strengths with clients exposes tremendous resiliency and abilities that may not have otherwise been pinpointed. Examples of questions to discover strengths include:

- What has been going well in your life?
- What are some things that you enjoy or are good at?
- What else do you like to do?
- How did you become interested in this?
- Where did you learn the skills to do this?
- It seems like you've learned a great deal about . . .

- How did you figure out how to cope with your feelings like that?
- What I see about you is that you are good at . . .

Amplifying Ambivalence. In order to begin goal negotiation with clients who express ambivalence about discontinuing drug use, asking clients about their "good reasons" for using drugs respectfully explores how the client has benefited from the drug (Lutz, 2014). Rather than confront your client's denial, this method is preferred because after a thorough exploration on how drugs have been useful, the client eventually comes to recognize the various ways in which drugs have become unhelpful. If clients are unable to acknowledge this, asking clients if they are currently accomplishing their plans may assist in stimulating how their choices are affecting what they want or don't want in life. Examples of amplifying ambivalence questions include:

- You must have a good reason to use drugs?
- How helpful are drugs for you?
- How else are they useful for you?
- How helpful would your family say drugs are for you?
- How much do you want to stay sober?
- Was it in your plans to be in rehab/fail school/be on probation?
- What would you need to begin doing differently?

Exception Questions. Exception questions explore times in a client's life where an identified problem, such as having a drink, could have occurred, but did not (de Shazer & Isebaert, 2008). These exceptions are explored with the client in detail, determining who was involved, what was the situation, when did this happen, and where, to further the client's progress. Examples include:

- Tell me about a time when you could have used substances, but did not?
- What was different then? What's been better?
- Was there a time this week that you were tempted to drink, but you resisted? How were you able to do that?
- What has been your best day?
- What happens as the problem ends or slowly begins to fade?
- Why do you believe the problem is not worse?
- How have you managed to not relapse?

Relationship Questions. Identifying the important people in your client's life will be an advantage when exploring the impacts of substance use (Gordon, 2007). As a consequence of addiction, many clients have lost the trust of their loved ones, and relationships have been damaged. Exploring the most appreciated characteristics of the client's important persons will continue to aid in discovering additional relational supports and those that need to be mended. Repairing relationships become paramount for client's recovery and through relationship questions, clients are provided the opportunity to think about their choices that have affected loved ones and what these losses mean to them. Examples of relationship questions include:

- What will your children notice when you remain alcohol free for an entire week?
- Who in the family notices the good decisions you are making?
- Who in the family will trust you first?
- How did making better choices help you in school/work?
- How did making a safe decision improve your relationship with your parents/ significant others?

Miracle Question. The miracle question is used as a method of goal setting and to explore next steps. Clients are asked how they see their life differently when the problem disappears (de Shazer & Isebaert, 2008). There are many adaptations of the miracle question; however, the version that follows was how the question was initially asked by de Shazer (1988):

> Now, I want to ask you a strange question. Suppose that while you are sleeping tonight and the entire house is quiet, a miracle happens. The miracle is that the problem which brought you here is solved. However, because you are sleeping, you don't know that the miracle has happened. So, when you wake up tomorrow morning, what will be different that will tell you that a miracle has happened and the problem which brought you here is solved? (DeJong & Berg, 2008, p. 84)

The client's answers to the miracle question are co-constructed with the practitioner. Clients are able to use these details of what changes occur after the "miracle" has happened to begin building enhanced meanings about their exceptions, recognize past solution behaviors, and begin setting the tone for defining goals.

Goal Setting. Determining the focus of therapy may come from the client's response to the "miracle question," or by other means of setting a client goal. With this information, the practitioner and client then discuss what else is needed to make the solution happen not just momentarily, but long enough to sustain the client's vision of his or her future. The clinician assists the client to visualize what they want their life to look like when the problem is solved and to identify times when solutions have already happened (de Shazer, 1994; Hendrick et al., 2012). Throughout the SFBT process, clients consistently collaborate with the practitioner to revisit goals (de Shazer & Isebaert, 2003; Hendrick et al., 2012). Using the client's detailed descriptions of what thoughts, emotions, and relationships will be present after their problem has ceased, enables clear and specific steps, which are typically practical to implement in the person's daily life. These steps, however, may not be easy to carry out but rather will take hard work. For this reason, the clinician also continuously assesses the client's commitment and asks the client whether they can carry out identified steps to accomplish their goal. Questions to use for goal setting include:

- How do you want your life to be different?
- What are some "pieces of the miracle" that may already be present?
- What changes are needed in your everyday life?
- What has to happen for it to be worth your time to come here today?
- Suppose after we talk today your life would be different—what would have to happen for this? What do you want to happen instead?

Scaling Questions. Solution-focused clinicians can use "scaling" questions throughout treatment in order help clients assess their progress, confidence, and commitment in therapy (McCollum, Stith, & Thomsen, 2012). Scaling is especially helpful for clients working to minimize substance use as they create measureable goals to achieve their ideal life when their problems have miraculously disappeared. Examples of scaling questions include (Lutz, 2014):

- How helpful are drugs for you on a scale of 1–10, where 10 is most helpful and 1 is the opposite?
- How helpful or unhelpful would those closest to you say drugs are for you from 1–10?
- How much do you need to stay sober from 1–10? What makes the number not lower? What else makes it not lower?
- How much would those closest to you say you need to stay sober from 1–10?
- How confident are you that you can remain sober from 1–10? What would it take to raise it by one point?
- How confident are those closest to you that you can remain sober from 1–10? What makes it not lower? What else makes it not lower?

Compliments. Use of compliments throughout sessions serves as positive client feedback from the counselor. As previously mentioned, compliments offered to the client promote development of client competencies, which is conducive to achieving the goals. Complimenting clients regularly involves highlighting their character, determination, skills, coping abilities, and other attributes that will help them achieve their goals.

Breaks for planning feedback. Practitioners are encouraged to take breaks near the end of the session to collect their thoughts. By taking a moment to plan feedback, practitioners are able to develop additional compliments and begin thinking of the next steps to propose to the client. Steps proposed are based on what the client wants to happen and can do well, and on what has been co-constructed as a solution during the session.

Homework. The use of homework promotes self-responsibility, which is seen as the key to change (McCollum et al., 2012). Rather than focusing on the client's lack of responsibility, solution-focused clinicians approach responsibility in a positive and affirmative manner. By building upon previously identified areas of responsibility, practitioners are able to hold clients accountable for the change they desire.

When clients receive treatment for substance use, the main focus of SFBT is to identify exceptions (de Shazer & Isebaert, 2003). For example, exploring with the client how they overcame the urge to drink if he or she states they had an urge to drink but refrained. Using a daily log with clients may be beneficial in identifying further exceptions and may also be used to help clients track their change. Inpatient clients are encouraged to keep a daily log about their urges to use and how they handled these cravings (see Figure 8.1) while outpatient clients are asked to complete a daily log if they acted upon their urges to specify how they were able to discontinue use at the point at which they stopped (see Figure 8.2). Outpatient clients are also asked to complete questions found on the inpatient log after substance use has occurred or if the client experiences cravings but does not act upon these urges. Encouraging clients to complete these log forms enables a client to focus on their objectives and work toward the specific steps needed to achieve their goals.

Name: _____ Date: _____

1. On a scale of 1 to 10, how strong was the urge to drink alcohol or use drugs?

2. Where were you when noticed this urge occur?

3. Who were you with when you experienced the urge?

4. What were you doing when you experienced the urge?

5. How did you stop this urge?

6. On a scale of 1 to 10, how difficult was it to stop this urge?

Figure 8.1 Inpatient treatment daily log to be completed by client when cravings to use substances emerge. *Source*: de Shazer and Isebaert (2003)

Name: _____ Date: _____

1. What day and hour did you drink alcohol or use a substance?

2. What kind of alcohol/substance did you use?

3. How much did you use?

4. Who were you with?

5. What were you doing when you decided to drink/use?

6. Where were you?

7. How were you able to stop at the point at which you stopped?

8. On a scale of 1 to 10, how difficult was it to stop drinking at that point?

Figure 8.2 Outpatient treatment daily log to be completed by client after substance use has occurred. *Source:* de Shazer and Isebaert (2003)

Unique to SFBT's approach, therapy ends when a client has determined they have made enough progress and no longer need to continue treatment (de Shazer & Isebaert, 2003). This means therapy may end before a client reaches their stated goals. However, it is important to keep in mind the client is the expert in their life and may decide to terminate if they feel their life has sufficiently improved since the onset of therapy. Clients are encouraged to return to therapy for any reason in the future if they so choose.

■ CASE STUDY

Julia, a 50-year-old Hispanic woman, has been a victim of domestic violence and lives in poverty. Her ex-husband abused her and had several affairs while they were married. Julia experiences depression and has a history of suicide attempts. Her youngest son has been diagnosed with schizophrenia and is currently in treatment for substance use. The following case example presents a segment from the first session with Julia. The clinician utilizes a number of solution-focused techniques including scaling questions, goal setting, complimenting, strengths identification, breaking for planning feedback, and assigning home-work. The conversation below begins with a scaling question regarding Julia's preferred future. The clinician builds on Julia's intrinsic motivations and her desire to change for her family, highlighting the importance of relationships within her family including siblings and grandchildren and also on her past successes in controlling her drinking. This case demonstrates SFBT's adaptability to Spanish speaking clients and has been translated into English.

Case Example

CLINICIAN: And at what number would you like to be at?

JULIA: Ay! At 10.

CLINICIAN: At a 10! And what does a 10 look like for you?

JULIA: A 10 would be that they give me a cup of wine or a cool beer and that I don't feel anything to drink it and that I am able to ask for a mineral water or a glass of water. To know how to control that situation, that is what I can't do right now. Umm . . . what else? To manage my life well and to dress up a lot as I did it before because I am just abandoning myself to . . . I just don't mind how to dress, I have never been so dirty and ridiculous. I do not smell well . . . I want to be clean . . .

CLINICIAN: Ridiculous?

JULIA: Ridiculous! Because I do it!

CLINICIAN: I got it perfectly! You want to stop doing it.

JULIA: And that's it . . . to love myself more, to learn how to love myself more. And with so much love, go forward and love my grandchildren, my seven grandchildren, my sisters, I saw my sister so bad when she was connected to the breathing apparatus and I cried and I remember that I saw her and my brother and I were . . . we are the best drinkers, but none of us drank a cup because of her. Because of our love for her, and we were one week without drinking anything. We did a barbecue and we drink tea, and I said I have to love too much my sister to have done this sacrifice of not drinking anything.

CLINICIAN: That's what caught my attention, Julia! You can go without drinking! It is not easy but you can do it.

JULIA: Yes! I did it.

CLINICIAN: You are able to do it for your family and you want to stop drinking. What number of the scale would you like to be at next week, being very realistic because the 10, that is very high.

JULIA: A six or seven

CLINICIAN: Like a six?

JULIA: Yes.

CLINICIAN: And what would you have to do to get to a six?

JULIA: Not drink. Not to drink anything and not to have that need.

CLINICIAN: Huh? You said not drinking at all would be a 10? What would it take to get up to six?

JULIA: I do not want to drink. So, passing one day without drinking anything.

CLINICIAN: Okay passing one day without drinking anything would be a six.

JULIA: If I pass a day, God helps me and I can pass day by day, that He helps me and I will do my best and tomorrow another day without drinking. If it was possible just arrive to next week and to be in six I would go from one day to the next.

CLINICIAN: Okay, perfect. One day then another day. So, as you may notice, these sessions are a little different from others and I want to get out a little bit early to take a break and while we take the break I want to ask you to respond to this evaluation of today's session, can you?

JULIA: Yes.

CLINICIAN: Thank you.

Break for planning feedback and return to session

CLINICIAN: So, after all that we have talked about today, I feel that you have many resources. Despite your desperation at the beginning, I believe that you are a super hard-working woman and that you have a high capacity of reflection regarding what is happening to you. And you are able to say I need to go only one day without drinking to get to another day. That is what it takes to go forward, and that ability is not in everyone.

JULIA: No, not in everyone.

CLINICIAN: And that is a tremendous. . . it's a huge resource that you have. An ability that you can take advantage of. And moreover, you have the capacity to realize, to know what's useful for you to go forward and what you need to do. Despite that you say that you feel alone and that you don't see people helping you, you mentioned that you feel proud of your children, that even if you don't speak all what you would like, you guys have a relationship and communicate with each other. Your sisters also are there. You said you love each other.

JULIA: Yes.

CLINICIAN: And maybe you don't help each other a lot but you know you count on them

JULIA: With them, yes. With all of them.

CLINICIAN: You are a tremendously hard-working woman, and I believe that that . . . you are intelligent and have known how to move forward besides all things you have been through in your life.

JULIA: All the difficulties. I have moved forward.

CLINICIAN: Besides all things, you have been able to stop drinking in the past.

JULIA: I have been more than eight months without drinking.

CLINICIAN: You have done that! Wow! And you have done it alone! And that is so valuable. So, from now to tomorrow what could you do to go a little bit toward that six?

JULIA: Living the day by day . . . I will be the happiest woman if I achieve today not to drink anything. I can do it then tomorrow.

CLINICIAN: OK.

JULIA: That's why I will fight today, to try to do a lot of things at home to keep myself occupied . . . despite I left the food ready yesterday, but it doesn't matter I will be with my son, to watch at last a good movie . . . and that's it.

CLINICIAN: And that's super important. You have a lot of things to do, and through this conversation I have seen that even when in a moment you saw everything black, at the end you have a lot of positive things in your life.

JULIA: At the beginning I did not want to say anything . . . but, I myself opened . . . I go home more peaceful, a little bit. . . that's true . . . I did not want to come, it is raining, the day is very ugly to stay home quiet and cozy, and I said—this will be expensive . . . and then one cannot go back in time and if I do not do anything right now . . . God knows what stupid stuff I will do. And I did well, it's good to come here.

CLINICIAN: What I am going to ask you is that when you achieve this [goal]. . . of not drinking for one day, you pay attention to how you are, how you feel, and also pay attention to how you are in relation with the other people who are with you.

JULIA: OK.

The case presented is an example of a solution-focused session with an individual with a SUD. The practitioner used solution-focused questions to assist the client in changing the undesired behavior (in this case consuming alcohol). In addition, the practitioner encouraged the client to be in charge of her own goal of not drinking by participating and developing her own treatment plan. The practitioner built on exceptions with the client and helped her to acknowledge her own strengths to overcome the trauma and adversities in her life. The practitioner built on the client's own competencies and followed the client's solution of one day at a time without drinking, but also helped her to modify her unrealistic expectations and way of thinking by defining the meaning of one day without drinking as helping her get to the next day. She helped the client to identify her own resources to get through the one day without drinking by discussing how she could manage the rest of that day. The clinician also continuously complimented and built on the client's strengths including her decision to come to the session and organize her life in a way that would help her not to drink.

■ SOLUTION-FOCUSED GROUP THERAPY

SFBT has frequently been applied within a group modality. The application of SFBT to groups for substance use has several benefits and allows practitioners to serve multiple individuals more efficiently (Smock et al.,

---

BOX 8.1 ■ Solution-Focused Group Therapy Session Format for Substance Abusing Individuals

Solution-Focused Group Therapy Session Format

- Ask group introduction question. Invite group members to identify themselves when they answer the question.
- Group leaders silently identify common themes from group answers and find a broader theme that includes all the common themes. This is done by having the group leaders write down a common theme.
- Group leaders reflect out loud the theme of the group.
- Group leaders ask the group's permission for the group to address the theme identified unless another issue (emergency) needs to be addressed.
- Ask a future-oriented question based on the theme.
- Get as many details as possible about the future-oriented question asked.
- Listen for any exceptions mentioned by the clients, and follow up any exceptions by getting as many details as possible.
- Ask scaling questions to determine client's current level of progress toward his or her goal.
- Find out what the client has done to have reached and maintained his or her current level of progress.
- Find out where the client thinks other people in his or her life would rate him or her and what the client is doing that would cause them to rate him or her there.
- Ask group members what role the theme plays in working toward their miracles.

Source: Smock et al. (2008)

2008). Conducting SFBT in a group format is advantageous because of its ability to reduce substance use through a synergistic environment that promotes solution building and increased self-reflection. Additionally, group settings can be supportive while encouraging responsibility because participants have more opportunities to see the effects of success between group members and are held increasingly more accountable. Box 8.1, taken from Smock et al., 2008, outlines the group session format that was used in a substance use group treatment program. The group sessions last between 1.5 and two hours, for an average of six sessions.

■ OUTCOME STUDIES ON SFBT WITH SUBSTANCE USE DISORDERS

Literature has shown the effectiveness of SFBT when treating individuals with substance use; however, more efficacy studies are needed to determine with what conditions and which clients SFBT may work well on. In 2000 Gingerich and Eisengart conducted a review of SFBT outcome studies. Of the 15 studies they identified, two of these studies evaluated SFBT with substance users. The first study found 36% of the group that received SFBT met the study's standard of recovery after the first two sessions, whereas the comparison group only had 2% of their participants reach recovery after two sessions (Lambert et al., 1998). The second study used a single-subject design and found SFBT was effective in reducing the client's alcohol use; however, the results did not conclude that the client's behavior change was a direct result of SFBT due to many threats of internal validity (Polk, 1996).

Smock et al. (2008) conducted a randomized controlled trial among level 1 substance abusers. The authors evaluated the effects of solution-focused group therapy (SFGT) and found when compared to problem-focused psychoeducation, SFGT was the only group that showed significant improvement from pre- to post-treatment.

Kim et al. (2016) conducted the first randomized controlled trial design evaluating SFBT effectiveness on parents presenting with substance use and trauma-related problems in the child welfare setting. This study is particularly important given the prevalence of comorbidity between post-traumatic stress disorder (PTSD) and SUDs. The study found that the application of SFBT with dually diagnosed individuals could be just as effective as evidence-based interventions such as Cognitive-Behavioral Therapy and Motivational Interviewing in reducing substance use and trauma-related symptomatology. However, more studies are needed to explore the treatment effects of SFBT with SUDs and with clients who have also experienced comorbid trauma related disorders.

■ SUMMARY

SFBT is a non-confrontational, strengths-based approach that may be used to help clients decrease or abstain from substances while improving their relationships and life circumstances and developing healthier coping skills to manage painful feelings. The application of solution-focused techniques is instrumental in creating shifts in meaning and perspectives where clients learn to regain control of their lives and find success in a life of recovery. This chapter described how SFBT has been used in the treatment of substance use relying on the clinical literature to illustrate interventions. Specific ways to engage clients with substance use was covered including the questions to ask to promote change. This chapter further described a case with a Hispanic woman with an alcohol use disorder who had experienced many adverse life events and illustrated how SFBT interventions are used. In addition, SFBT has frequently been applied in a group treatment modality and this chapter introduced a group protocol that has been used with success in a substance abuse treatment program. Finally, this chapter summarized the emerging outcome literature on SFBT with substance use disorders including one study that specifically addressed substance use and trauma.

■ REFERENCES

Back, S. E., Dansky, B. S., Coffey, S. F., Saladin, M. E., Sonne, S. C., & Brady, K. T. (2000). Cocaine dependence with and without posttraumatic stress disorder: A comparison of substance use, trauma history, and psychiatric comorbidity. *American Journal on Addictions, 9*(1), 51–62.

Berg, I. K., & Dolan, Y. (2001). *Tales of solution: A collection of hope-inspiring stories.* New York: W. W. Norton.

Berg, I. K., & Miller, S. D. (1992). *Working with the problem drinker: A solution-focused approach.* New York: W. W. Norton.

Brady, K. T., Back, S. E., & Coffey, S. F. (2004). Substance abuse and posttraumatic stress disorder. *Current Directions in Psychological Science, 13*(5), 206–209.

Brown, P. J., & Wolfe, J. (1994). Substance abuse and post-traumatic stress disorder comorbidity. *Drug and Alcohol Dependence, 35*, 51–59.

Dansky, B. S., Brady, K. T., & Roberts, J. T. (1994). Post-traumatic stress disorder and substance abuse: Empirical findings and clinical issues. *Substance Abuse, 15*(4), 247–257.

De Jong, P., & Berg, I. K. (2008). *Interviewing for solutions.* Belmont, CA: Thomsen Brooks/Cole.

de Shazer, S., & Isebaert, L. (2008). It's a matter of choice. In P. de Jong, & I. K. Berg (Eds.), *Interviewing for Solutions* (pp. 309–312). Belmont, CA: Thomsen Brooks/Cole.

de Shazer, S., & Isebaert, L. (2003). The Bruges model: A solution-focused approach to problem drinking. *Journal of Family Psychotherapy, 14*(4), 43–52.

de Shazer, S. (1994). *Words were originally magic.* New York: W. W. Norton.

de Shazer, S. (1998). *Clues: Investigating solutions in brief therapy.* New York: W. W. Norton

Dolan, Y. (1991). *Resolving sexual abuse: Solution-focused therapy and Ericksonian hypnosis for adult survivors.* New York: W. W. Norton.

Franklin, C., Zhang, A., Froerer, A., & Johnson, S. (2017). Solution focused brief therapy: A systematic review and meta-summary of process research. *Journal of Marital and Family Therapy, 43*(1), 16–30.

Gingerich, W. J., & Eisengart, S. (2000). Solution-focused brief therapy: A review of the outcome research. *Family Process, 39*(4), 477–498.

Gordon, A. B. (2007). *Solution-focused approach with clients facing diverse challenges.* Retrieved from https://www.fadaa.org/webinar_files/SFBT%20Webinar%20Diversity%20Handout.pdf

Hendrick, S., Isebaert, L., & Dolan, Y. (2012). Solution-focused brief therapy in alcohol treatment. In C. Franklin, T. S. Trepper, W. J. Gingerich, & E. E. McCollum (Eds.), *Solution-focused brief therapy: A handbook of evidence-based practice* (pp. 264–278). New York: Oxford University Press.

Juhnke, G. A., & Coker, J. K. (1997). A solution-focused intervention with recovering, alcohol-dependent, single parent mothers and their children. *Journal of Addictions & Offender Counseling, 17*, 77–88.

Jacobsen, L. K., Southwick, S. M., & Kosten, T. R. (2001). Substance use disorders in patients with posttraumatic stress disorder: A review of the literature. *American Journal of Psychiatry, 158,* 1184–1190.

Kim, J. S., Brook, J., & Akin, B. A. (2016). Solution-focused brief therapy with substance-using individuals: A randomized controlled trial study. *Research on Social Work Practice.* doi: 10.1177/1049731516650517

Lambert, M. J., Burlingame, G. M., Umphress, V., Hansen, N. B., Vermeersch, D. A., Clouse, G. C., et al. (1998). The reliability and validity of the Outcome Questionnaire. *Clinical Psychology and Psychotherapy, 3,* 249–258.

Lutz, A. B. (2014). *Learning solution-focused therapy: An illustrated guide.* Washington, DC: American Psychological Association.

Mason, W. H., Chandler, M. C., & Grasso, B. C. (1995). Solution-based techniques applied to addictions: A clinic's experience in shifting paradigms. *Alcoholism Treatment Quarterly, 13,* 39–49.

McCollum, E. E., Stith, S. M., & Thomsen, C. J. (2012). Solution-focused brief therapy in the conjoint couples treatment of intimate partner violence. In C. Franklin, T. S. Trepper, W. J. Gingerich, & E. E. McCollum (Eds.), *Solution-focused brief therapy: A handbook of evidence-based practice* (pp. 183–195). New York: Oxford University Press.

McCollum, E. E., Trepper, T. S., & Smock, S. (2004). Solution-focused brief group therapy for drug abuse: Rationale, content, and approaches. *Journal of Family Psychotherapy, 14,* 27–42.

Miller, S. D., & Berg, I. K. (1995). *The miracle method: A radically new approach to problem drinking.* New York: W. W. Norton.

Nameni, E., Shafi, A. A., Delavar, A., & Ahmadi, K. (2014). The effectiveness of combination of structural and solution-focused family therapy in treatment of the substance abuse and the family function improvement. *Journal of Sabzevar University of Medical Sciences, 21*(1), 155–163.

Pichot, T., & Smock, S. (2009). *Solution-focused substance abuse treatment.* New York: Routledge. Taylor & Francis.

Polk, G. W. (1996). Treatment of problem drinking behavior using solution-focused therapy: A single subject design. *Crisis Intervention 3:* 13–24.

Prochaska, J. O., DiClemente, C. C., & Norcross, J. C. (1992). In search of how people change: Applications to addictive behaviors. *American Psychologist, 47*(9), 1102–1114.

Smock, S. A., Trepper, T. S., Wetchler, J. L., McCollum, E. E., Ray, R., & Pierce, K. (2008). Solution-focused group therapy for level 1 substance abusers. *Journal of Marital and Family Therapy, 34*(1), 107–120.

Spilsbury, G. (2012). Solution-focused brief therapy for depression and alcohol dependence: A case study. *Clinical Case Studies, 11*(4), 263–275.

Stewart, S. H., Conrod, P. J., Samoluk, S. B., Pihl, R. O., & Dongier, M. (2000). Posttraumatic stress disorder symptoms and situation-specific drinking in women substance abusers. *Alcoholism Treatment Quarterly, 18*(3), 31–47.

Substance Abuse and Mental Health Services Administration. (2015a). Behavioral health trends in the United States: Results from the 2014 National Survey on Drug Use and Health (HHS Publication No. SMA 15-4927, NSDUHSeries H-50). Retrieved from http://www.samhsa.gov/data/

Substance Abuse and Mental Health Services Administration. (2015b). *Mental and Substance Use Disorders*. Retrieved from https://www.samhsa.gov/disorders

Szczegielniak, A., Bracik, J., Mróz, S., Urbański, M., Cichoblaziński, L., Krzysztof, K., et al. (2013). General level of knowledge about brief solution focused therapy (BFST) in Polish addiction treatment centers. *Psychiatria Danubina 25*(2), 236–240.

Triffleman, E. G., Marmar, C. R., Delucchi, K. L., & Ronfeldt, H. (1995). Childhood trauma and posttraumatic stress disorder in substance abuse patients. *Journal of Nervous and Mental Disease, 183*(3), 172–176.

9 Infidelity in Marriage and Relationships

■ ELLIOTT E. CONNIE

When I was 12 years of age I was playing Little League baseball with my neighbor Kyle from across the street; he was also my best friend. From the time we met earlier that year, we spent just about every day together. We were typical best friends growing up outside Boston in the early 1990s. We snuck out to chase girls, played video games, and walked around talking just like the youth did in the movie *Stand By Me*. Most of all, though, we played sports. Nearly every day after school we dropped off our school things and ran out to play whatever sport was in season. It didn't seem to matter to us what sport it was—baseball, basketball, football—whatever it was, we were always together playing something. Our friendship grew, and we got so close that we did everything else together as well.

Because of our close friendship, it was not surprising that when our Little League asked the players to stand around town with donation cups to raise funds (that's what we did before the Internet and crowd funding) Kyle and I decided to team up. We decided to stand outside a local supermarket and asked the families to donate their change. This was an annual routine for the league we played in, and this was a pretty typical day for us. It was a typical day until something amazing happened that I will never forget; this amazing thing completely changed both of our lives forever.

A cute girl about our age came walking toward us, along with her family. She seemed a bit flirtatuos with Kyle. As you might assume, most 12-year-olds would respond with a combination of glee and awkwardness. We learned that this girl's name was Jennifer because she introduced herself to us and slipped her phone number to Kyle. He spent the rest of that day floating on an adolescent cloud nine. He could only have gotten to this "cloud" by a cute girl expressing even the slightest interest in him. However, after a few weeks of phone calls Kyle and Jennifer drifted apart.

Now fast forward to our senior year in high school, when all of a sudden Jennifer reappeared in our lives; however, this time she was dating another friend of ours. By this time Kyle had grown from a slightly shy adolescent to a very shy late teen. We would be at parties where Jennifer was present, and Kyle would always whisper in my ear that he had a crush on her, not realizing it was the same young girl from years ago; in fact, none of us realized it. He made me promise not to tell her of his feelings, which was typical of his shyness. Over the next few weeks it was not a hard secret for me to keep—after all, he was my best friend. However, the secret soon got much tougher to keep when Jennifer revealed to me that she had similar feelings for Kyle. Interestingly, she didn't remember that Kyle was the same boy she had met all those years ago outside that grocery store either.

I was able to keep this secret for about year. Now in my first year of college, I was visiting a friend who had attended school with Jennifer. During my visit I ran into Jennifer and expressed that Kyle still had a crush on her. Shortly after our encounter she reached out to Kyle, and their remarkable relationship had officially begun. In time, Jennifer realized that Kyle was the boy from the grocery store because she found a pamphlet he had given her. She had written his name on the pamphlet so she would never forget him and eventually packed it away, only to have it resurface years later to confirm that her current boyfriend was the boy she had met (and had a crush on) all those years earlier.

It didn't take long for them—and all of us who were lucky enough to be around them—to be aware of how special this relationship was. I had known Kyle since middle school; now that we were in college, I had never seen him so happy. In fact, I was jealous, not because he had found love but more because Jennifer had taken my best friend away from me. The time we used to spend playing video games and hanging out was now being filled by her. Over time, I learned to view it more as gaining Jennifer, as opposed to losing Kyle. Eventually this couple got married and went on to build an amazing life together. Kyle completely dedicated his life to Jennifer and to their growing family that eventually included three children. Even now, when I am around Kyle and Jennifer it is clear how dedicated they are to one another and to their family.

This is a true story: Kyle is really my best friend, and this is exactly how he met his wife. I have always been amazed by their story, and I was there from the very beginning. However, love stories like this are not unique. In my time as a therapist working with couples I have come to think of this position as the best job in the world. I think this because I have had the privilege of listening to countless love stories where the origins of the couple's love was just as unlikely, or even more so, than the story of Kyle and Jennifer.

So when couples such as this experience a ripple in their relationship it should come as no surprise that they often experience this as a traumatic experience. Just as I wrote in the first chapter, the trauma in relationships is not as important as the hope in relationships. In fact, assessing for the trauma violates the solution-focused approach itself.

In thinking about writing this chapter I was not sure how to express my thoughts. As is with many things related to SFBT, it is hard to express how problems are resolved. This is because the problem is not the direct focus of the professional, which means that the conversation becomes about something else entirely. That something is based on the client's desired outcome from the therapy, even if there is a trauma present. This means that a professional using this approach must resist the urge to explore the trauma—or its impact on the relationship and on each partner—and go about the business of accomplishing a detailed description of the couple's preferred future.

Getting this detailed account of the preferred future can be a significant challenge for many professionals. This is because our training teaches us that understanding the problem is vital. This need for understanding usually correlates with the severity of the problem presented in therapy. Effective use of the SFBT approach requires the professional to resist this urge and continue focusing on developing a preferred future description with the couple, remembering that this is more powerful than assessing the trauma. By taking this step, the clinician ensures that the client is able to resolve the problem in whatever way they need to. This is done with the guidance of the clinician through the process of questioning, as opposed to the clinician attempting to solve the problem for the couple.

To demonstrate this, I'd like to use a transcript of a session I conducted with a couple. I know that in many texts such as this, the author would write about the assortment of problems that could occur in couples therapy or the many ways that the partners could experience trauma symptoms. However, since the SFBT approach is based in language and depends on the professional's ability to develop questions that elicit a detailed description of the couple's preferred future, I thought it best to use a transcription.

As with most sessions, at the time of the appointment I didn't have any information as to the problem that brought the couple into therapy. Here is how the session progressed.

■ DAVE AND CELESTE

> E1: Elliott (E): Ah, OK. Hi, guys. How are you?
> D1: Dave (D): Good.
> E2: My name's Elliott, and you are?
> D2: Dave.
> E3: Dave, nice to meet you. And?
> C1: Celeste (C): Celeste.
> E4: Nice to meet you Celeste. Um, my name's Elliott Connie. Please call me Elliott. And do I have your permission to call you Dave? (D: Um hmm.) And I can call you Celeste? (Celeste nods). So what are your best hopes from meeting with me?

D3: Umm, not getting divorced and her putting her wedding ring back on.

E5: Okay, so umm, how would you know that we were having a conversation that was leading to you guys not getting divorced? Like, what would you notice differently happening?

D4: To, to, to tell me that we weren't going to get divorced?

E6: Um hmm. What would be happening instead?

D5: Being happy.

E7: OK. When you're happy what do you do?

D6: Umm . . . I'm not pissed.

E8: What do you . . . instead of pissed you would call that?

D7: Angry.

E9: And instead of angry, what would you rather have?

D8: Um, I'd rather just, I'd like to look forward to coming home. You know. (E: OK). I would like to look forward to . . . to being around her more.

E10: And if we had a conversation that led to you feeling like you were looking forward to coming home, as opposed to headed toward divorce, you'd be pleased?

D9: Yes.

E11: That would be a good thing. And, Celeste, what about you? What are your best hopes from this meeting?

C2: I'm not feeling very hopeful, honestly.

E12: OK.

C3: Um, but I guess, best hopes (E: Yeah), waving a magic wand. We would be friends again.

E13: Hmm. And if we had a conversation that led to you guys being friends again, you would be pleased?

C4: Yeah.

Notice how in the first part of the session I am working to establish a desired outcome from the therapy and not to uncover the root of the problem, or even what brought them to therapy. I do this by asking each partner what their "best hopes" are from the work that is about to ensue.

E14: Awesome! OK, well before we chat about that, it's kind of helpful for me if I can get to know you guys a bit and give you a chance to know me. Is that OK?

C5: Sure.

E15: So, where are the two of you from?

D10: Uh, we both grew up here in Dallas.

E16: Local, local guys.

D11: Yeah.

E17: How long have you been together?

D12: Uh, 10 years (looking sideways to confirm with Celeste).

C6: Yeah.

D13: I don't like . . . I hate the way I looked at her like, "five, ten years, right?"

E18: Yeah, well I probably would have . . . I have my wedding date engraved (D: Oh) on my ring so I would never forget, so that's not unusual.

D14: Well, good thing hers isn't engraved on her wedding ring. She couldn't look at it.

E19: She couldn't look at it right now?

D15: No.

E20: Hmm. Um, what do you guys do for fun?

D16: Um, well, I'm a standup comic, so that is . . . that is my fun.

E21: By profession?

D17: Yeah. Yeah, it's . . . it's gettin' there.

E22: Excellent, excellent. And, ma'am, what do you do for fun?

C7: I paint.

E23: What do you paint?

C8: Um, landscapes, acrylic on canvas or acrylic on board.

E24: Hmm, and do you do that by career?

C9: No.

E25: So what do you do for a career?

C10: Um, I take care of our daughter. I'm an at-home mom.

E26: And your daughter's name is?

C11: Zoe.

E27: And, how old is Zoe?

C12: Five.

E28: She's five years old. Wonderful. Um, what is your favorite quality about Celeste? What do you like most about her? I assume that since you're here, there are things you would like to see change, but tell me something about Celeste that . . .

D18: Uh, she's very kind. She's very . . . she's very . . . she's very kind.

E29: How does she demonstrate her kindness?

D19: Um, I mean if you, if . . . it's kind of annoying in a way, but uh, strangers. I mean, there was this, a bad storm once and she literally sent out a blast e-mail to all my comic friends and was like, "Hey, if you guys need a place to stay, you can come over." Didn't ask me, you know (E: Right), we've got like a two-bedroom apartment. But um, I mean I understand, it was, it was just very . . . stuff like that you know. Homeless people, there have been several dogs and cats in the house that weren't ours that we semi-adopted. So, there's . . . I mean, I know it's a good quality, but at the same time it's, I'd appreciate a heads up.

E30: Right, but it is a good quality?

D20: It is a good quality, yes. Very kind soul.

E31: And what is Dave's best quality?

Long pause while Celeste thinks.

D21: Wow.

C13: His optimism or enthusiasm.

E32: How does he demonstrate his optimism and enthusiasm?

C14: On stage honestly. I get to see that on stage. Maybe not so much at home.

E33: Right, but on stage you enjoy to see it?

C15: I used to, yeah.

E34: But you enjoy it's in there?

C16: Yeah.

E35: Very good. OK. Um, do you have any questions for me? Is there anything you'd like to know about me?

D22: Um, what do you . . .what is your therapy that you teach?

E36: Um, the type of therapy that I teach and practice (D: Yes) is solution-focused. Any questions about how that works?

D23: Have you used it on yourself?

E37: Have I used it on myself (Dave nods)? Wow, that's a great question. No one has ever asked me that before. Um, I guess I'd probably have to say yes. (D: OK) I'd have to say (D: OK) I've practiced it . . .

D24: Did it work?

E38: I hope so.

C17: Is it like uh, new paradigm that you have to . . . you know, solution therapy, do you apply that to just relationships or do you apply that to other aspects of your life?

E39: No, I mean, I apply it to other aspects of my life. It's, it's a way of working with people that kind of gets you focused on what you'd like, as opposed to what you wouldn't like. You know most, most therapies and other aspects of our lives are focused on figuring out when something's wrong and removing it. This is about identifying what we would like to be right and creating it. It's kind of different.

C18: It is.

E40: You guys OK to go through it?

D25: Yeah.

C19: Yeah, I'll try anything right now.

At this point in the session I am spending time learning details of the couple's lives, so the questions asked throughout the session can be personalized. For example, I now know the couple has a daughter named Zoe. This will allow for questions such as "What would Zoe notice?" and so on. By using Zoe's name specifically, and other exact details, the conversation belongs to this couple. The questions are more tailored to them, and therefore they feel less "technical"; this is a true hallmark for using this approach effectively.

E41: Good. I'm glad you would say that. That's a good question; no one has ever asked me that before. Any other questions? (Clients both shake their heads). So, umm, how did you meet?

D26: Uh, I was doing a show and she was, she was not, she was kind of in the middle, but not, just because. . . . Sometimes when you're on stage you can't see the whole crowd. So she was right at that line of blind set and she was the only person not laughing (E: Um hmm). And so, um, it . . . it . . . it bothered me, like, like everyone else was laughing and she's not, so afterward I, you know, I went up to her and I was like, you know, "Why were you not laughing?" and (turning to Celeste) Why weren't you laughing?

C20: Well I, you didn't need my laughter.

D27: I didn't need her laughter. That, that was what hooked me in.

E42: So that's what . . . that's what hooked you in.

D28: Yeah. It was like this giant . . . it was this giant, like, I was . . . I was like, I, she became like this project where I'm going to make her laugh (E: Right) out loud. And I'm 10 years in, and I'm still . . . still working on that.

E43: And you noticed her up on the stage (D: Uh hmm) and that, that stood out to you. When did you first notice him?

C21: Well, before the show he was, I kind of saw him milling around. He wasn't talking too much with the audience or anything, but I kind of, I noticed him. I was like, "Oh, it's one, it's one of the performers."

E44: Uh, what stood out to you about him? Like, I assume there were many performers moving around. Why did this one stand out to you?

C22: I'm partial to brunettes.

E45: So, does that mean you thought he was good looking?

C23: Good looking, yes.

E46: You thought he was a good looking guy. And, um how did you guys, I mean you saw him from a distance; you saw her from a distance, how did you end up meeting and talking?

D29: Well, I just, I ran, right after the show I ran right to her. I mean it was like, you know, "Why? What's wrong? Are you deaf? (Therapist laughs) You know, did you not see everyone else?" I was kind of . . . kind of . . . it wasn't mean or anything, but I was, I was really like perturbed, you know, and she, she did the whole, "Well, you didn't need me. Everyone else was laughing." I was like, "Yeah, why not you?" But then, then it, there was definitely, there was definitely chemistry there. And then I was, I was like, "Well can I, can I take you out to dinner and, you know . . . I want to make you laugh."

E47: She accepted, I'm guessing?

D30: Yeah, it was, I felt though that she kind of accepted just to shut me up, (E: Umm) you know. But it was a real number. It wasn't like 555-2134. So it was, it was real and so uh. . . .

E48: And you mentioned there was a chemistry there, how did you know?

D31: Umm, pheromones? (They all laugh)

E49: How could you tell the pheromones were present?

D32: Because...

C24: I blushed.

D33: Um, I felt my stomach was in knots and it was, it was neat because it was like something I hadn't felt since high school (E: Wow). You know, that whole, that whole... it's not newness thing, but I felt like a 13-year-old boy in high school. And it was... and it was... also it was like, you know there's groupies and everything, and you know, you're up there and you're making people laugh, it's, it's easy to get peoples' attention. This was somebody who wasn't giving me attention. And this was something I had to work for. And so I think this was ... maybe this was nervousness and like, my God, she's ... she's beautiful and I'm, she's not ... she's not throwing herself at me, you know, I'm going to have to work at this, and it feels exciting.

E50: Hmm, and when did you notice the chemistry? Did you notice the same chemistry in this, in this time?

C25: It wasn't, like when he came up to me, it's wasn't immediate when he came up to me, but somewhere along the conversation when he was grilling me, "Why didn't you laugh?" and pursuing me. And I'm skeptical, or was, you know, but there was a little, you know flutter. I was like, "Okay. Alright."

E51: Is that unusual for you to experience a flutter?

C26: Oh, yeah.

E52: So, you, you received that as a good sign. There must be something going on between me and this brunette guy (C: Yeah) that was attractive to you.

C27: Right, right. He was very forward, (E: OK) but not offensive.

E53: Right yeah. And um, when you guys went on this date, when you went to dinner, do you remember where you went?

D34: Um, yeah, it was, it was Albert Ace... Albert Ace; a nice steak restaurant. And uh, it's a ... it's kind of shitty on my part because it's a very expensive restaurant, and I know the maître d, and so I got a really good discount (E: Awesome). Also, it was kind of misleading to take her there, OK, and that was done on purpose. That was definitely done on purpose.

E54: Trying to win her over a little.

D35: Just, yeah and uh ...

C28: You did kind of set an expectation.

D36: Yeah, I would have been better off taking her to a Carl's Jr. You know with my 10% coupon card than Albert Ace, but uh ...

E55: Right. How soon after the initial meeting did the date take place?

D37: Um, I, I was very; I wanted like, as soon as possible. But, since I perform most weekends, I had to wait until the following, the following Wednesday.

E56: OK. And at what point did it hit, hit you that um, this initial meeting and this connection, this chemistry feeling, the butterflies, Dave that you experienced and the fluttering, Celeste that you experienced; at what point did you realize that it wasn't just that? Like, that it was 'I have a potential future with this person.' At what point did that . . .

C29: I, for fear of sounding foolish, it was probably after the salad.

E57: It was after the salad.

C30: Yeah.

D28: It was really good salad (they all laugh).

E58: It sounds like you took her to the perfect place.

D29: They have a really good salad dressing there and uh; for me, honestly, it was that night, because I couldn't stop thinking about her.

E59: And, how did you, when, when, after the salad, and you noticed, 'wow, this might be something,' do you remember how you let him know that you were having this feeling that it might be something?

C31: Oh, I didn't . . . I didn't let him know right away. I kept that close. I was like, 'OK, don't tell all your secrets right at once.'

E60: Right at once.

C32: Umm, so I did, I was kind of aloof on purpose, kind of . . . you know. So it was, it was probably like the third or fourth date, around then that I kind of let him in. Like let him know, 'Oh right, you got me.' You know.

E61: Right.

D30: I, I mean, I got a sense, just for the simple fact that she said yes for the second date (E: Good point). There's this barrier, but she is allowing me to continue punching the barrier. So, so that's a good sign.

E62: That's a very good sign.

D31: Yeah.

E63: And, how did you let her know that you saw more than just this woman that I couldn't make laugh at first?

D32: I . . . I . . . I poured it on hard. I mean I was just like a mix CD. That was . . . the first . . . first date; it was so high school, but that's what was kind of cool about it though; it was just the whole high school feeling. I . . . I just felt like I . . . like each song had a description about why this song was for her. You know, even though I know . . . it was, it was such a weird thing, too, because, I gave her the mix CD first, but I wouldn't give her the descriptions of the songs yet, because I didn't, because that's way too stalkerish. And I let her have the mixed CD first. I even told her there were explanations for it. She was like, 'Let me see them.' I was like, 'Wait, because I don't want to scare you.' You know. She was like, 'What is it? Are you having my head cut off in one of them?' I was like, 'No.' it was funny though, because on the fourth date, when she finally let her guard down is when I gave her the descriptions. And it was horrible handwriting by the way, but uh, she read them and said, 'Oh my God, that's beautiful and I'm so happy you didn't give this to me on the first date because I would have left.'

C33: That's true.

E64: And, did you enjoy the CD (C: I did) when he gave it to you?

C34: I really did. Um, yeah.

E65: Do you still have it? Is it a CD you still own?

C35: Yeah, I do as a matter of fact. I do still have it.

E66: Uh, how long did this high school feeling last? For you it started the night we met (D: Yeah), for you it started the night we went out to dinner. How long were you guys able to keep this high school feeling lasting?

D33: 'Til we moved in.

E67: And how much time did, how much time was that?

D34: We gave it like a year before we did the whole "move-in" thing.

E68: An uh, Celeste, what did Dave do during that year that contributed to the relationship growing in that high school way?

C36: He, well he made me laugh, finally.

E69: He figured out how to do it?

C37: That was important. Um, he, I don't know. He made me feel safe. He made me feel desired. He made me feel important. Um, and, he was affectionate, physically affectionate. And um...

E70: Are you the type of girl who enjoys that?

C38: Yeah. I mean it wasn't like handsy!

E71: No, that's not what I mean.

C39: I mean we could walk together and he could put his arm around me, or around my waist.

E72: Right. And that meant something to you.

C40: Yeah hold me close. And he kept doing, he didn't stop.

E73: Right, right. Dave, what about you? What did Celeste do to contribute to this high school feeling growing?

D35: Um, she made me feel like I was her protector. Like, she made me feel like that I was; this sounds misogynistic in a way, but like I was there for her. Like I was her guardian. It made, it kind of made me feel proud. You know, she felt, like I felt that she felt safe around me.

E74: How did she do that? How did she make you feel that way; do you ... do you remember? I know we're going back.

D36: Yeah, it was just, the whole body language thing. You know, just that, and also she vocalized it. You know, that was cool. It just, It made you feel like a man. Like, 'I'm man, she woman.' Ugg ugg.

C41: Ugg.

D37: So um that was, that was cool. And again it was the whole, it felt like, you know, I was a football player and she was a cheerleader you know. So that was neat.

C42: That was very high school. It was.

E75: Yeah.

D38: I actually got a letter jacket.

At this point I am interested in learning more specifics about the couple with the same goal of using this content to make the following questions more specific. However, the shift that has taken place is that now the details are about the relationship. The key is to ask about the good times the couple has experienced. This requires clinicians to believe in the couple and operate with the assumption that all couples, even the most troubled, have a successful past. To this point in every session, the clinicians work to prepare for the preferred future description. Notice that at this point in the session I have not asked about the problem, and the couple has not shared any details about it. This is not uncommon, as sometimes the problem that led the couple to therapy may make the individuals feel shameful, and consequently the couple may not want to share those details.

E76: That she would wear for you? Umm, I have an unusual question to ask the two of you. Suppose tonight while you are asleep a miracle happens that wipes away all of the problems that caused you to contact me. And instead of those problems, the high school feeling was brought back, where you felt like her protector and you felt safe, and those high school kind of butterfly feelings were back, and that high school fluttery feeling was back. Just like that (snaps fingers) this miracle occurs overnight, as you were asleep. But, because you're asleep you can't know that it happened. You know, I mean, how could you, you were sleeping? When you woke up the next morning, what would be your very first clue that something was different, that this feeling was back?

Notice the "miracle question" was constructed with the couple's details in mind and thus was no longer a technique. Instead, it was a co-constructed part of the session. This is what leads to the description of the couple's preferred future, and the majority of the remaining time in the session will be spent answering this question.

C43: We'd be spooning instead of on the edge of each, you know the other side of the bed.

E77: Umm. And what time would you wake up?

C44: Uh, we would sleep in. It wouldn't be, but, there would be daylight, but it would be like 8:30 in the morning or something, nine o'clock.

E78: And if you woke up at 8:30 and noticed that you were spooning, that would be the first thing you become aware of that something was different. Dave, what about you? What would you notice?

D39: Umm, she'd kiss me to wake me up.

E79: Where would she kiss you?

D40: On the lips.

E80: And um, how would you respond to this kiss from her to let her know that you recognize it?

D41: I would do my favorite kiss to her, which would be on her neck.

E81: And uh, how would you respond to this Celeste, to let him know that you had noticed this difference?

C45: I would probably wrap my arms around him, kiss him fully on the lips, pull him close.

E82: Hmm, and would this be an unusual way (D: Yes) for the two of you to start our, to start your morning? (Both clients nod their heads). Um, how would you let him know that this unusual start to the morning, you thought was good? You were pleased by it?

D42: She'd make me breakfast.

E83: We'll get to that in a second.

C46: Well, I wouldn't, I wouldn't stop. I would be responding.

E84: And, that would be a clue to him?

C47: I think so, yeah. Well, you know, I used to kiss him right behind the ear, like real soft, you know. He liked that. He knows exactly what that means. (E: Oh). That's, yeah.

D43: Sex time.

E85: Would that be an unusual ...

D44: Yes.

E86: And, and would you be pleased to have her ... (D:Yes) doing that thing, and have it be sex time?

D45: Yes

E87: And how strange would that be to start the morning off ... (D: Very strange.) very intimately, very sexually?

D46: Very strange.

E88: What would the two of you do next?

D47: Umm ...

C48: Bask in the afterglow.

D48: Eat.

C49: Eat.

E89: And what would you eat?

D49: I would cook breakfast. That would be, that's, that was one of the things that we would do back in the day.

E90: Dave, on a day like this where a miracle has taken place and caused you to have such an unusual start to the day, what would you cook?

D50: Umm, I am allergic to eggs. I can't have eggs, but she loves eggs. So I would cook her, bake her an omelette. Make her an omelette.

E91: OK.

C50: And then I would stab him in the neck with an EpiPen. (All laugh) No, I'm just kidding.

E92: You'd have to revive him.

D51: Yeah I would make her something that . . .I mean, because, because of my allergies I do all of the cooking. And, but she doesn't eat the stuff that I'm allergic to (chicken, eggs, and shellfish), and so I would make her something that she usually couldn't eat.

E93: Hmm, would you be pleased that he had done that? That he made you something that . . .

C51: Yeah, that would be very generous.

E94: Okay, and where's Zoe at this time?

D52: She's probably eating glue. (They all laugh)

C52: At the grandparents.

E95: At the grandparents.

C53: She would have to be for us to sleep until 8:30.

D53: Yeah. (T: Good point). There's no sleeping until 8:30 with her.

E96: Good point.

D54: (Banging on his own legs) "Get up."

E97: "Move around. Stop me from eating glue." (Clients nod) And, after breakfast, what would the two of you notice that would tell you that these feelings were persisting?

D55: We wouldn't be fighting.

E98: What do you think you would be doing instead?

C54: I like to sit on the couch with his arm around me, just . . .

E99: Would you be pleased to have this happening?

C55: Yeah. Just sit and be quiet and be together. We need that.

E100: And what would you be doing as you are sitting on the couch, quiet, being together, holding each other?

C56: Not a damn thing. Just enjoying each other's touch . . . feel against each other.

E101: And without Dave saying anything, how would you know he was enjoying this touch? You know what I mean? Sometimes we're just sitting on the couch and it's like, "We've got to hurry up and get up and do something." You know, you can feel that. Like how would you know that Dave was like . . . without him saying anything, how would you know that he was like, just enjoying being in your presence with his arm around you, enjoying your touch?

C57: Because, he would . . .he would just lightly, with his hand, kind of rub my shoulder. Slowly! Not like, (rubbing her arm quickly) "Okay, let's go, get up." You know, it would be like, just, "This is my girl and I like it."

E102: Right, and uh, how would you know that she was also enjoying that we're just sitting together and touching?

D56: She wouldn't . . .she would . . . there's this . . .God, it's been years. There's this sigh she does; this when I would touch her, this ahhh.

E103: What does that sigh mean to you?

D57: "I'm yours, and you're mine."

E104: And would you be pleased to receive that sign? (Dave nods his head.) Umm, how long would this moment last?

D58: How long does Zoe got at Mima and Mipa's? I don't know.

E105: On a miracle day, how long would you guys sit there?

D59: Till it was sexy time again.

C58: We could probably do that for 30 to 45 minutes.

D60: I mean my arm would go numb, so there would have to be some repositioning.

E106: How different would it be to sit in that moment for 30 to 45 minutes for the two of you?

C59: We don't do anything for 30 to 45 minutes (D: Yeah) at a time right now.

E107: So, this would be unusual.

D61: Yes.

E108: OK. What would you do next? What else would occur that would cause you to know that these feelings were back?

D62: I would like to go and . . . this sound, as stupid as this is, I would like to go to a movie. Not a kids' movie. You know, not *Madagascar 12*. I would like to go to an adult movie, maybe even with subtitles. Maybe at the Angelica, get some red wine and some Ju-Ju-Be's, and not have, I guess, have that, I would like to date her again. I would like to take her out on a date again.

E109: Hmm . . .and is this the type of activity that you would enjoy as well?

C60: Yes!

E110: And if the two of you, as you were getting dressed to go on this event, what would be different? How would you know that "I'm getting dressed with this feeling that hasn't been present in a while?"

C61: Oh, we'd be flirting, while getting dressed.

E111: While getting dressed.

C62: Together. Instead of, "Alright, you go, you get dressed. Alright it's my turn. Let's go, hut, hut, hut, hut, hut." We would take our time. And, we would kiss a little bit, and hang out, and be in the same space without discomfort. Without tension. Without urgency to . . .

E112: When the tension, urgency and discomfort is gone, what feeling would you use to describe what's there?

C63: Simpatico. Kind of . . . anticipation.

E113: Um hmm. And what's your way of flirting. How would you, as you guys are getting dressed in the same space, with this simpatico, anticipatory feeling, what would be your way of flirting with Dave?

D63: She'd put her ring back on.

E114: That would be part of what you might wear that night.

C64: Yeah.

E115: Dave, would you notice that? How would you respond?

D64: The asshole in me would be like, "Well, it's about damn time." (E: Yeah) But I wouldn't want to ruin the moment.

E116: But on a miracle day, yeah.

D65: On a miracle day I would say, how beautiful it made her look.

E117: How different would that be for you to hear?

D66: Very different.

E118: Celeste?

C65: That would be, that would extremely different. That would be very different.

E119: And uh, after you guys are dressed, and in the car and heading to the movie theater, how would you know that this miracle was continuing? For the two of you, the miracle had kind of followed you into the car?

C66: We would, I would sing loudly and off key, so we would turn the music way up. We sing together, sing stupid songs. Maybe we'd play that mixed CD.

E120: And would that be unusual for you guys to play that CD as you're driving to the movie theater, kind of singing together?

C67: Yeah, we haven't felt like that.

E121: That would be a good feeling. (C nods) Okay Dave, what about you? How would you notice that you're in the car . . . ?

D67: I wouldn't, I wouldn't turn on NPR. I wouldn't do that. Um, yeah we might do the singing, singing thing. Um, I, I actually know the words to *Breakfast at Tiffany's*, so uh, I'd actually do a lot better on that one.

E122: Can you sing it on key?

D68: No. If on key means in the key of L. But, yeah, I could, I could see that. I could see, you know, it'd be, it'd be, umm yeah. I wouldn't be road-raging. I would probably get in the right- hand lane. Just drive slowly and not mind if people were passing me or tailgating me. I have an issue with that. That makes her nervous. Um, we probably would have left on time um, because, most of the times if we're going together places, we don't leave on time, and uh, sometimes I think that's her doing something passive-aggressively toward me, but that is beside the point. You didn't ask that question.

E123: No, I didn't.

D69: Um, no you didn't; I'm sorry.

E124: It's OK.

D70: But umm, yeah. It'd be . . . yeah it would be nice.

E125: And how would you convey to her that you thought this was nice. This was good. Like normally, you might have judged the behavior; like you said the asshole in you would make you think that there was passive-aggressive . . . (D: um hmm) or um, "finally the ring is on." How would you address this behavior on this day, and let her know I think this is very nice.

D71: I would hold her hand, while we drove.

E126: Would that be unusual to hold her hand?

D72: Yes.

E127: And Celeste, when you got to the movie theater, how would people sitting next to you know that they're sitting next to a couple that has that feeling?

c68: 'Cause we wouldn't notice other people; we would only notice each other.

E128: And as a result of only noticing each other, what would the two of you look like?

c69: Relaxed, not a furrowed brow . . . eye contact, holding hands.

E129: Even as you watch the movie; holding hands?

c70: Calm . . . maybe a little twinkle in the eye.

E130: Right. And Dave, what do you think other people around you would notice that would give them a clue that whoever this couple is, they must be quite in love?

D73: I would probably do um, something that I remember that she loves, that is the, uh . . .put my hands behind her head and brush her hair out.

E131: As you watch the movie?

D74: Yeah. It's very . . . it's weird, it's a very calming effect on her and me. And, um, it's nice that she has long, straight hair, 'cause it wouldn't get caught.

E132: Makes it easier.

D75: Makes it easier. Yeah, that was, that was always . . .uh, a nice thing.

E133: Um, what would you do after the movie?

D76: After the movie . . . it's dinner time.

E134: And where would you go to eat?

D77: I would try to find one of my friends that works in a nice restaurant to get a discount. Um, but huh . . . we love like . . . we both like P.F. Chang's. We're both big fans of that so . . . It's the one place I can go, It's the one Chinese restaurant I can go and order fried rice without eggs, so that's a bonus for me. But uh, yeah.

E135: And what would be different about this dinner that would cause you to know that something's happening differently between the two of us?

D78: We'd be talking.

E136: What would you be talking about?

D79: How horrible the foreign film was that we went to. How we should have known it was bad because it was French, but we went anyway. We'd probably be talking about how awesome the day is. Because we would probably be both freaked out that we were having this amazing day.

E137: Having this amazing day.

D80: And, why don't we do this every day.

E138: Celeste, what do you think you would be doing during this talk to let him know that this good feeling was still continuing with you?

C71: Um, I'd be sitting close to him. Kind of like at the movies; I'd lean in to him. Um, we'd be talking instead of looking around, or people watching. Um, I'd sit close enough to him that like, our thighs were touching.

E139: Do you enjoy that?

C72: Yeah (nodding head)

E140: Is that a good sign, the server would notice that this couple must be really feeling good because they are sitting that close to each other?

C73: Yeah, yeah. And talking, and not under our breath, but having a conversation that only the two of us can hear.

E141: Right, um, and after dinner what do we have plans to do?

C74: Walk. After all that Chinese food . . . walk.

E142: On a miracle day, where would you guys like to walk?

C75: Celestial Park.

E143: Celestial Park.

C76: Yes.

E144: Yeah, and um as you walked around this park, what would be different? Like, how would you know that this feeling was still present for us?

C77: He'd put his arm around my waist, pull me close. We'd walk together and, probably not talk.

E145: And how would you respond to this arm around you? How would you let him know that you were pleased, you were receptive, you were in the space you wanted to be, you felt safe, how would he know that?

C78: I would probably sigh again. (E: Um hmm) That little sigh.

E146: And if this little sigh were to occur this time Dave, walking around Celestial Park, what would that mean to you?

D81: That would mean she was very happy.

E147: And how would you feel about yourself as a . . .as a man?

D82: Very proud.

E148: And how do you think you would clue her in to the fact that you felt very proud?

D83: I'd kiss her. Stop, kiss.

E149: Uh, how would this night end? How would you like this night to end?

D84: Um, one of the things we never do anymore, I'd love for us to go home and um, take a shower together. I'd like that very much. And not because we've been out all day and stinky. You know, but um, that's one of the things we used to do early, early on.

E150: So that's a good sign.

D85: Yeah.

E151: And at what time would we go get Zoe? How long is Zoe going to be at . . .

D86: She's going to stay the night at grandma's and grandpa's.

c79: It'd be great to have 36 hours, just 36 hours.

E152: And you've told me how Dave and Celeste would have their very best wake up; how would they at their very best go to sleep?

c80: Still wet from the shower. And naked.

D87: And spooning.

E153: You'd start the day, you end the day how you started it.

D88: Yeah.

E154: As the two of you were laying there naked, wet, and spooning, as you look back over the day, what would your thoughts be as you were dozing off and falling asleep?

D89: Why don't we do this every day?

E155: What about you Celeste, what would your thoughts be?

c81: I'd probably think about Zoe. Just a little. How this is how she came to us. And how, what an awesome feeling it is to have that, that connection. And how it turned into something so beautiful.

E156: Um, wow. Thank you guys for answering all of my questions. I actually could ask you some more questions, but we're running out of time. So um, I'm going to take a break for a moment and um, come back and give you guys some feedback. Is that OK? OK.

BREAK

E157: Thank you guys for uh, being patient. And um, I want to tell you a few things that I noticed as we were having our conversation. And uh, Dave if it is OK, I would like to start with Celeste. But uh, Celeste, the first thing that I noticed is um, you seem to be a very caring person. Um, it's very obvious to me that this relationship and your feelings for Dave are very genuine and very real. And you have a very loving way about yourself. You said several times throughout that conversation how important touch was to you, specifically his touch. And I remember you remarking about the softness of the touch. And you seem very genuine; like there's a genuine way about you. Like uh, you're not going to laugh unless you were moved to laugh, and you're not going to spoon unless you're moved to spoon. And I think that's such an amazing way for you to go about things. Um, Dave, you seem very perceptive. Like of all of the people in the audience you, she stood out to you. Like you noticed her. And uh, outgoing, like uh, that one person, you had to uh, go out and like meet. You could have done anything, but you decided to meet her. And um, you have a protective way, and you do it in a very accurate way. Like, the very things she needed you to do, you were able to do, without her telling you that she needed you to do them. Several times you would say things like, um, in the car I'd hold her hand. I would look at her and say, "would you like that?" and she would say, "yes, I would,

I would like that." Like you have this way of knowing how to comfort her with this safety feeling, which I think is good. And, you're very connected to her like, several times throughout this day you were, like the connection between the two of you would be growing several times throughout the day and I thought that was extraordinary about the two of you. Um, so I just have one last question and um, I'd like to ask you to do something if you could. So if 10 is like that every single day, and Zoe gets to be raised by that couple, and zero is, we're as far away from that as we could possibly be, where would you say you are today, when you came in here?

D90: Four.

E158: Celeste, what would you say?

C82: Yeah, I'd say three.

E159: Okay. What I'd like to ask you to do is, all of the signs that we've just discussed and that you would notice that would cause you think, "we've moved up from a four to like a 4.5." If you get real ambitious, start looking for clues of five, but no higher than that. And as you notice them I would like to ask you guys to discuss what you're, what you're noticing, what clues the two of you are noticing that causes you to know that we've moved up from a four, or in your case a three, to a 3.5. And again, if you get really ambitious look for signs of five, but nothing higher than that. If you get really ambitious look for signs of four, but nothing higher than that. Sound OK?

C83: Yeah.

E160: So, how'd we do? Did you find our chat useful to you?

C84: Yes.

E161: What are you going to take away from our talk?

D91: Um, I'm going to try to be more physical. I'm going to try to be more, um, audible. I'm going to try to talk to her more.

E162: Wonderful! Celeste, what about you, what are you going to take away from our chat today?

C85: I'd like to try to uh, try for the two of us to be part of the same orbit, instead of two independent orbits. Trying to find that overlap again, and that connect.

E163: Wonderful. Thank you guys very much.

As the session ended it was very clear that change had occured. The couple was warm, close, and affectionate. This occured without the nature of the problem being discussed, or even mentioned.

I know you may be thinking this was an easy couple and that this approach can't work with those "hard" couples. Let me assure you, it can. In fact, this could have easily been a hard couple had I used other language choices in the session. For example, in the beginning of the session Dave was quite frustrated when he mentioned Celeste not wearing her ring. It was also clear that Celeste was distant and potentially closed off. However, by not amplifying those emotions and instead building a conversation on the couple's hopes, even though the hope was hard to find at first, the session went in a very different direction.

I hope in reading this chapter you can understand that hope is always more important than the trauma symptoms or traumatic event. I know this is still a groundbreaking idea, but it is the essence of the solution-focused approach from the beginning.

10 Post-traumatic Stress Disorder and the Military

■ CALYN CROW

The military's reason for existing is to prepare individuals for combat and survival in a war. To discuss the military's mission, core beliefs and culture, in conjunction with mental health, almost seems like an oxymoron; yet it is absolutely possible that both can be accomplished. It is possible to create a balance between a rigid and structured mission of survival that requires a specific and definitive skill set with a mentality that promotes emotional and mental well-being, also requiring a specific kind of skill set. This is precisely why I spend much of my time working to engage military personnel and their families both in the United States and overseas. They deserve, as we all do, a solid understanding of how both can be true. This is a community of people who I am fond of and who are close to my heart. Providing services to individuals and families in the military has been greatly rewarding.

It has also been challenging at times—this is likely why I am so fond of military people. Generally speaking, people in the military are not a touchy-feely group of individuals. That is not to say that they are without emotion. In fact, my experience working in this culture and with all branches of the military proves quite the contrary. By and large, they are a dedicated and connected group of people. I find the military community to be a very strong, caring, passionate, virtuous, loyal, committed, and honorable group of men and women. They refer to themselves as a family and take their jobs very seriously. Their job is not just a job, it is a way of life. They do their best to take care of one another and those around them.

The military has always been comprised mostly of men. Being in the military has traditionally been viewed as a male role, a role built on masculinity. According to the Defense Manpower Data Center, as of January 31, 2015 (Chalabi, 2015), there were approximately 1.4 million individuals serving in the United States Armed Forces. A little over 200,000 of these individuals were women. This means that 0.4% of the U.S. population were active duty military personnel. The Department of Veterans Affairs (VA) used this data from the Department of Defense, the U.S. Census Bureau, the Internal Revenue Service, and the Social Security Administration to estimate that as of 2014, there were approximately 22 million military veterans in the United States. If we total these figures, 7.3% of all Americans have served in the military at some point in their lives. According to the Pew Research Center in an article entitled, "The Military-Civilian Gap: Fewer Family Connections" (http://www.pewsocialtrends.org/2011/11/23/the-military-civilian-gap-fewer-family-connections/), most Americans had family members who once served or were currently serving in the armed forces. The article goes on to say that 57% of those aged 30 to 49 say they have an immediate family member who served in the military. Among those aged 18 to 29, the share is only one third. Almost half of military veterans have a parent who served, compared with 41% among the general public. A lot of people who have chosen to go into the military have also grown up with parents and/or grandparents who were in the military.

■ MILITARY CULTURE AND MENTAL HEALTH

The military culture has not historically embraced or taught the importance of mental health and/or the emotional well-being of their soldiers and their families. This is not unique since American society in general has not historically done a good job teaching children how to acknowledge, manage, and communicate their emotions. A lot of children are not taught the skills needed to manage their emotions in a healthy way. Young boys in particular seem to be taught that it is not proper to have or express emotions. They are taught that it is not manly to cry, when in fact it is a healthy and normal way to release frustration, anger, sadness, and joy. Boys and young men are taught that if they do express emotion then they are weak or a sissy. The military culture is an extension of these beliefs and consistently reinforces these myths. It is no wonder that individuals struggle to seek help at the first signs of a problem. I have seen how difficult it can be for servicemen and women to acknowledge that there is an issue, let alone open up and talk about it with someone. A lot of people have never talked about their military experiences and decline to do so even after they return to civilian life.

I have experienced firsthand military doctors and clinicians being more concerned about malingering (when a serviceman is fabricating symptoms in an effort to evade duty) than an individual's reported mental health concerns. I have witnessed individuals in need of mental health treatment not receive adequate care or the necessary services. It's almost as if they are an inconvenience. Thankfully, there has been a shift in the military mindset in more recent years, with more effort and resources going toward mental health services and an emphasis on the soldier's mental and emotional well-being. Most people who I have worked with have had a deep appreciation for this support. I have received numerous challenge coins (a small coin bearing an organizations' insignia or emblem, given out as a token of appreciation) over the years in appreciation of my support to a specific group in the military.

■ PTSD AND SOLDIERS

Going into combat with all of your men and women healthy in all aspects (e.g., mentally, emotionally, physically, and spiritually) puts you at an advantage. Many have used the analogy of *you are only as strong as your weakest link*, whether this is in a family, work group, community, culture, or society. The overall health of the group matters and potentially changes your overall position and chances of success.

As described in chapter 2, PTSD is listed as a new category in the *DSM-5* called Trauma and Stressor-Related Disorders (TSRD), which all have the common characteristic of exposure to a traumatic event or otherwise adverse environmental event. According to the National Institute of PTSD, PTSD can occur after a person has been through a traumatic event. Men and women in the military who have experienced trauma prior to having joined the military may or may not experience PTSD later as a result of a traumatic event occurring while in the military. People who are not in the military also experience PTSD as a result of a trauma. No one is immune to PTSD. Being diagnosed with PTSD is not a sign of weakness. Box 10.1 shows the criteria required for the diagnosis of PTSD. An individual must exhibit all of these criteria. This criteria comes from *DSM-5*.

When I talk to others about working with the military, the first thing people generally say is, "Oh you do PTSD work?" The answer to this question is, "Well . . . yes and no." As cited by a Quick Series (n.d.), "Many children and most adults (nearly 90%) have at least one intense traumatic event in their lifetime, not everyone develops PTSD." The reference goes on to say that of the general population, approximately 5% of men and 10% of women are diagnosed with PTSD. It states that "rates are higher in specific sub-populations depending on the type and intensity of the trauma." Victims of natural disaster, abuse, sexual assault, accidents, torture, urban firefighters and police officers, combat veterans and individuals experiencing other serious events may experience increased rates of PTSD. The National Institute of Mental Health (2016) cites that not everyone who has experienced a trauma develops symptoms of PTSD, and not everyone diagnosed with PTSD has experienced a traumatic event.

According to the National Center for PTSD (http://www.ptsd.va.gov/public/PTSD-overview/basics/how-common-is-ptsd.asp), women are twice as likely to experience PTSD than men, and genetics may play a role in an individual's chance of developing symptoms. Experiencing a trauma in and of itself does not mean that a person meets the criteria for PTSD. In fact, most people will not develop the disorder. The National Center for PTSD reports that "about 7 or 8 out of every 100 people (7–8% of the population) will have PTSD at some point throughout their lives. About 8 million adults have PTSD during a given year and this is only a small portion of those who have gone through a trauma."

BOX 10.1 ■ PTSD Criteria

Criterion A (one required): The person was exposed to: death, threatened death, actual or threatened serious injury, or actual or threatened sexual violence, in the following way(s):

- direct exposure
- witnessing the trauma
- learning that a relative or close friend was exposed to a trauma
- indirect exposure to aversive details of the trauma, usually in the course of professional duties (e.g., first responders, medics)

Criterion B (one required): The traumatic event is persistently reexperienced, in the following way(s):

- intrusive thoughts
- nightmares
- flashbacks
- emotional distress after exposure to traumatic reminders
- physical reactivity after exposure to traumatic reminders

Criterion C (one required): Avoidance of trauma-related stimuli after the trauma, in the following way(s):

- trauma-related thoughts or feelings
- trauma-related reminders

Criterion D (two required): Negative thoughts or feelings that began or worsened after the trauma, in the following way(s):

- inability to recall key features of the trauma
- overly negative thoughts and assumptions about oneself or the world
- exaggerated blame of self or others for causing the trauma
- negative affect
- decreased interest in activities
- feeling isolated
- difficulty experiencing positive affect

Criterion E (two required): Trauma-related arousal and reactivity that began or worsened after the trauma, in the following way(s):

- irritability or aggression
- risky or destructive behavior
- hypervigilance
- heightened startle reaction
- difficulty concentrating
- difficulty sleeping

Criterion F (required): Symptoms last for more than a month.

Criterion G (required): Symptoms create distress or functional impairment (e.g., social, occupational).

Criterion H (required): Symptoms are not due to medication, substance use, or other illness.

According to the American Psychiatric Association (2013), PTSD is a disorder in which an individual may experience a criterion of symptoms. People may experience symptoms such as: flashbacks (flashing memories or replays of a traumatic event), nightmares, wanting to avoid large or crowded places/events, hypervigilance, and/or significant mood fluctuations. Symptoms also increase to the point that it begins to interfere and negatively affect one's day-to-day functioning, in such ways as impaired interpersonal relationships among family, friends, or coworkers; negative effect on one's ability to perform at work or in school; impact on accomplishing goals, tasks, and responsibilities; and decreased ability to take care of personal hygiene.

■ MILITARY COMBAT AND PTSD

In the military, individuals are exposed to varying types of combat situations. One gentleman who I worked with experienced bullets flying past his head, was exposed to explosives, and things being blown up on a regular basis. For him this was a regular occurrence that became his new normal. He reported that he and his battle buddies walked around dazed and unaffected by these types of situations, however, these types of events can lead to PTSD. According to a *Psychology Today* publication in 2012, Julian Ford writes, "There is no preparation for the extreme danger and deadly encounters of war. Even the strongest person can be completely impervious to the traumatic shock and stressful aftermath. Symptoms of post-traumatic stress are almost universal in the wake of life-threatening military incidents. Lasting problems with PTSD, anger, depression, or addictions can occur for years to at least one in three soldiers."

As cited by the National Center for PTSD (http://www.ptsd.va.gov/public/PTSD-overview/basics/how-common-is-ptsd.asp), "The number of Veterans with PTSD depends on the service era. With Operations Iraqi Freedom (OIF) and Enduring Freedom (EOF), roughly 11-20 out of every 100 Veterans (11-20%) who served in OIF or EOF have PTSD. With the Gulf War (Desert Storm), about 12 out of 100 Gulf War Veterans (12%) have PTSD in a given year. About 15 out of every 100 Vietnam Veterans (15%) were diagnosed with PTSD at the time of the most recent study in the late 1980's, the National Vietnam Veterans Readjustment Study (NVVRS). It is estimated that about 30 out of every 100 (30%) of Vietnam Veterans have had PTSD in their lifetime." There are other factors that can occur in a combat situation that can make an already stressful situation more intense and contribute to PTSD or other mental health problems. These factors can include a person's specific job type in the military, where one is located, the politics surrounding the war, the type of enemy one is up against, the level of support a person may have, and the level of contact one may or may not have back home (National Center for PTSD, 2016). Additionally, "At least one in every three to five women serving in the United States military is sexually assaulted, and most (an estimated 80%) suffer silently without reporting the trauma for fear of the stigma, retaliation, or impediments to their career. Military men also are sexually assaulted, albeit more rarely and almost never officially reported. These women and men are highly likely—50% or more—to develop severe and chronic PTSD and related problems" (Ford, 2012). According to the *Psychology Today* article, among the veterans that utilized the VA, "23 out of 100 woman reported being sexually assaulted, 55 out of 100 woman (55%) and 38 out of 100 men (38%) have experienced sexual harassment while in the military" (Ford, 2012). "There are more male veterans than female veterans. Although military sexual assault is more common in women, more than half of the veterans who have experienced military sexual trauma are men" (Ford, 2012). Despite these numbers, it is important to remember that a lot of people have recovered from PTSD or have reduced symptoms to manageable levels.

■ HOW I CAME TO USE SFBT WITH THIS PARTICULAR POPULATION

I have been working with the military since 2006. For 10 years, I have worked with individuals, spouses, and children from all branches of the military. I have been to various military installations in the United States (Buckley Air Force Base [AFB] in Colorado, Kirtland AFB in New Mexico, Langley AFB in Virginia, Ft. Carson Army Installation/Peterson and Schreiver AFB in Colorado Springs Colorado, Camp Foster Army Installation in Kentucky), overseas (Camp Courtney in Okinawa and Yokosuka Navy Installation in Japan, Osan Air Base in South Korea and Vilsick Army Installation in Germany), as well as several National Guard and Reserve Pre-Deployment, Deployment and Reintegration weekend events for individuals and families.

I first began utilizing SFBT when I was in graduate school where professor Tracy Todd taught the course on SFBT. I was immediately intrigued by the approach. Clients have the tools within to help them find their own answers; if it's not broken, don't fix it; solutions are not necessarily related to the problem. This seemed to resonate with me. I remember Tracy saying things like, "You are not the expert on your clients, and only clients can be the experts on themselves." He would say, "Who do you think you are, to know what is best for someone else?" It was humbling and yet something I, too, agreed with. I am not sure everyone in the class liked this kind of directness; however, it seemed refreshing to me. It seemed respectful of the person in front of you who is experiencing some type of struggle and quite possibly consumed with some type of hurt, shame or guilt, and who is reaching out to a complete stranger. How honored could one be and what greater reward than to empower another with the knowledge that they themselves already possess the tools they need to resolve their concerns but perhaps never even knew they had. It acknowledges an individual as a human being first and one with the ability to decide what is best for them and their family. Not to minimize the clinician's role and what they provide, but this is a gentle reminder of who is really in charge of one's life. I have noticed with this approach that I tend not to have a resistant client; in my experience, it has been quite the opposite. Once an individual realizes and trusts that you are in it for them, they quickly hop on board and I sense this spark of hope in them.

In 2006, I began a position at Buckley Air Force Base with the Department of Defense doing Internal Employee Assistance Program (EAP) work. I was recruited by a former employee from the substance abuse counseling program where I had previously worked; he was formerly on the team and also practiced SFBT. We were excited to be out on our own, yet also in the company of a like-minded person with regard to SFBT. This is when I began working more specifically with the military population. This organization was complex to say the least. It consisted of all branches of the military (Air Force, Navy, Marines, Army, Coast Guard, National Guard, and Reserve), several government civilian agencies, and over 50 defense contracting companies. The workforce was largely made up of men, military, former military, and/or people with a strong military association.

I was a young clinician who desperately needed to be taken seriously if I had any chance with this population. Being a SFBT clinician helped me with this role. I was taught early on in my career to have solid boundaries with clients. I have a direct yet gentle demeanor; however, I was not a touchy-feely type clinician, which I found to be beneficial with this population. Sticking to the principles of SFBT, avoiding problem talk/past problems, focusing on the future, and what is important to the client now was what really worked. I couldn't ask the question, "How does that make you feel?" This population makes fun of that phrase on a regular basis. The purposeful and to-the-point SFBT questions allowed clients to quickly explore what is important to them, what it is they want/need currently and going forward, as well as the ability to go as deep and detailed as needed while systematically incorporating those closest to them. Emotions often arose as a result of these discussions in session. We stayed in the presence of emotion as long as it was needed and in an effort to acknowledge and validate the client's experience. I have never understood people who say that SFBT is all surface and ignores feelings. My experience is quite the contrary even with a military population.

■ CASE EXAMPLE

Tim is a 26-year-old male who is married with no children. He had been in the U.S. Army for a little over five years upon his medical discharge. He was deployed to Afghanistan for approximately one year. He began to experience concerning behaviors approximately one month after his return. He reported going to work and then going out drinking every night, which he believed was normal for him. One evening he and his fiancé were returning home and after having been startled by her, he reported grabbing her by the throat and putting her on the ground. He said that he was on the verge of beating her but also not knowing what was going on. He reported that something clicked in his head and he knew that something wasn't right. He stated that he was still not able to talk himself into getting help. After that event, his fiancé began to lock the bedroom and bathroom doors when Tim went out at night in an effort to avoid what had happened the previous evening.

Tim confided in a couple of friends a few nights following this incident. They insisted he get help and informed him that this type of behavior was not normal and that he probably needed to talk to someone. He reported not taking this seriously and thought that he could handle it. Due to significant concerns, one of the client's friends reported him to his commander in an effort to get him the necessary help. The command leader became involved and ordered the client to get treatment. Initially, he was sent to the VA hospital, and it was recommended that he participate in an inpatient treatment program. The client reports that he felt like he was in a prison and declined to stay there. Tim reported going back to his command leader and telling him that he would take an Article 15 (a non-judicial punishment available to officers that allows them to administratively discipline troops without a court martial) but that he wasn't going back to that hospital. His commander supported him and arranged for him to obtain intensive outpatient treatment through a facility in Highlands Ranch. Tim was diagnosed with PTSD, and his reported symptoms included anxiety, depression, sleep problems, restlessness, stress, guilt feelings, suspicion, worry, irritability, and mood swings.

Tim participated in outpatient treatment for approximately two months and was eventually assigned to see a clinician at Buckley Air Force Base. Without meeting with the client, this clinician recommended he participate in a group program in Colorado Springs for an hour each day starting at seven in the morning. He reports that he spent four hours a day driving to and from this hour-long group meeting. Tim stated how "pissed off" he was about having to do this. He shared that on one particular day while in a group session, he was introducing himself to another gentlemen who accused him of lying about his experiences and didn't acknowledge his time in the military. He was told that he had never been deployed.

He states that the guy on the other side of him began to instigate an argument with this gentleman and the next thing he knew he was caught in the middle of a fistfight. He reports being in between the two and breaking them up. The three of them were called out of the group to talk with the group leader. The client asked if this behavior is normal, and the group leader indicated that it is and that they try to keep it from getting physical; however, they do encourage everyone to say exactly what is on their minds. Tim decided at that point to not go back. He did not believe that getting into fights would help him to better himself. Again, his commander supported him.

Tim was required to go back to the outpatient clinic. He was told he would be meeting with a new clinician. He states that this experience was not helpful either. Tim states that he was regularly "questioned" by the clinician. He reported that the clinician suspected that he was lying. Tim felt frustrated by this and again did not want to go back. Shortly after this, he stated that the clinician planned to sign paperwork for him to go to Korea. Tim felt as though the clinician wanted to get rid of him and didn't want any interaction with him. Tim reported to his commanding officer that he did not want to continue seeing the clinician. He reported that he would go back to Highlands Ranch, despite misgivings. Tim stated that at this time his commander informed him that he only had six months left in the army and that the army was planning to medically retire him. He stated that this was a tough pill to swallow and struggled for the next year as he transitioned out.

Following his discharge, the client obtained a contract position similar to what he was doing in the army. He reported falling back into his old ways and began to drink almost daily again. He reported not doing anything about the concerns and reported having some suicidal thoughts. He reported seeing that his relationship with his wife was on the verge of ending and at that point he decided to get help again, at which time he began accessing solution-focused brief therapy (SFBT) counseling on the recommendation of a good military buddy who had also previously accessed SFBT. On the intake paperwork when asked what he would like to get out of therapy, he reported wanting to "be able to control my emotions and live a somewhat normal life."

■ SESSION 7

CLINICIAN: How are you?

TIM: Not bad. Last week . . . was actually good.

CLINICIAN: What was better?

TIM: I was able to focus on a lot of techniques. Because I knew that we weren't scheduled for a while—it really made me focus on things, do what I had to do in order to better myself. And then Sunday came around, and it all seemed to go out the window.

CLINICIAN: OK, we'll get to Sunday. I am curious though first, what techniques you used up to that point that you felt made a difference?

TIM: After asking what it is that my wife and I can do together, not just what I can focus on.

CLINICIAN: In relation to what?

TIM: How to help us out.

CLINICIAN: OK.

TIM: She was curious what she could do. I didn't really take it as one thing I could do or one thing she could do, but what we can do together.

CLINICIAN: OK, cool.

TIM: We were more open with each other. We were having conversations that would go deeper than what we normally go. I didn't shut myself off.

CLINICIAN: How did you stay open?

TIM: Well, it was like you had said . . . sometimes I have to let that little kid come out, be open to things that have happened already. We just talked. It got off of being serious and kind of got to joking, which I am not the biggest clown out there. At that point, it usually gets uncomfortable for me but I was OK with that. I didn't think that the conversation needed to be completely serious, I felt like we actually got somewhere and I didn't shut off, I didn't.

"What's Better" Question

As my first question I generally go back and forth between asking *what's better* or *what's different* since the last time we met. If it's clear to me before getting started that there may be potential concerns, I stick to *what's different*. It seems more neutral and not so assuming. I do like *what's better* though and notice people pause after being asked this question. They often follow the pause with *oh, what's better*—as if they were not expecting to answer this particular question. Sometimes they look a bit confused, as if they've never considered that something might be better this soon. Or that there is a natural tendency to think the clinician may want to know more. They generally take a minute to think, search back into their week(s) and then naturally begin to rattle off several things they have noticed that have been better.

This "check in" question is important; it often sets the tone for the session. It allows a client to take time to recollect, pay attention, or notice things that may have occurred that would indicate signs of progress since the last time they had been seen. Oftentimes, people coming to therapy (or even people in general) have not been taught to look for successes or evidence that progress is being made. As an SFBT clinician I look for clues that tell me that what we are doing is working, that our time spent together has been effective, and that the client is getting closer to their goal. Acknowledging this progress with the client from the beginning and following up with questions like *how were you able to do this?* allows us to reinforce and highlight what they are doing that appears to be helpful. This question reinforces that progress happens in between sessions and not just while in the therapy session. If someone happens to ask, "What do you mean, what's better? Nothing is better," I abandon the *what's better* question out of respect. Clearly they are letting me know that they don't think anything is better. I will then say instead, "Yea ok, *what's been different?*" This seems to be a bit more neutral and allows a space for anything to be discussed.

CLINICIAN: Can you give me an example of what you did do?

TIM: I went to San Jose for work. I didn't get a chance to talk to my wife a lot. I was talking to friends when she was at work. We'd get done with dinner at the company level and she would already be in bed. One of the classes though that they had out here was about how to have an open mind. A lot of it in my opinion, also coincided with a lot of the stuff that we have talked about in here. I was excited to be able to tell her about that stuff. Normally, I shut off and I try to keep work at work and just be done with it, but I felt like I learned something new and was able to go back to her and talk to her about that stuff. We both opened up. I wasn't completely shutting work off anymore and so now she has an idea of what I do, whereas for the last five years she has had no idea.

CLINICIAN: So, you were able to find something that you could share with her?

TIM: Yes.

CLINICIAN: And you took advantage of that opportunity?

TIM: Yes.

CLINICIAN: Very cool.

TIM: That set the mood for the whole day. She took off Wednesday to pick me up from the airport. It was a stressful day. She had car issues and it was in the shop, while I was gone. I wasn't able to help her out with it, but I felt like because I was able to open up and actually talk to her, it didn't take things to a new level, stress-wise. The stress was minimized. It was the car, I didn't add anything to it and neither did she. We were open with each other.

"What Did You Do Instead" Question

People are quick to talk about what they don't have, who they aren't, what they lack, or what they didn't do. SFBT questions are designed to elicit more information about what a client did instead versus what they didn't accomplish; it opens up a whole new world. It is believed that these are potentially some of the solutions the client is in search of. Shining a light in this direction provides more information in the direction a client is wanting to go.

CLINICIAN: What difference do you think that made for her, that you were more open and shared a little more about your work world?

TIM: I don't know. I mean, I think she knows, I am not saying that I wasn't ever committed. I am, but that is always something she has asked me to do. There were just things, I didn't ever want to talk about.

CLINICIAN: Things that you didn't want to talk about? Things you chose not to talk about?

TIM: Yes.

CLINICIAN: Not a matter of what you couldn't talk about?

TIM: Yes. It wasn't just related to work, it could be anything. If I didn't want to have a conversation, I didn't want to have a conversation. That made things worse. For the last week though, we have been having a lot of conversations. There isn't an awkward silence at dinner anymore.

CLINICIAN: And you think that to her that might mean there is more commitment on your part?

TIM: I think so. We talked in the past about how we wanted to expand our family. The talks have stopped because of things that have come up. That conversation has again come up. This time around, I was more open to it. I was never opposed, I just never gave any input or insight. I could see why she could be upset about that. She might feel that if it did happen, she would be by herself, she would be all alone in it, but now she sees I am contributing to this relationship and wanting a bigger role.

CLINICIAN: That's cool!

TIM: It felt good.

CLINICIAN: What difference does it make for you, to be more open to have your wife feel you are more committed? That's kind of a loaded word too . . . committed to what? You talk about maybe expanding your family. That's some big stuff. Maybe there is more to that commitment, too, that you are talking about?

TIM: I wouldn't say that for me, it doesn't just stop with my wife. My adoptive mom and I have had some lengthy conversations lately that have actually been good. Whereas before, we'd be ten minutes into our conversation and I would immediately be pissed off. I could go days without talking to her. It was Thursday and we were on the phone for an hour, just talking. That is something that hasn't been done since I was very young. With friends, and my conversations with them, I am talking to them without trying to hold anything back or beat around the bush with my answers and questions. My wife and I, there is more commitment. I don't want her to feel like she is alone in this. I think by me opening up a little bit, I can get rid of some of that feeling. I definitely still have more work to do but I think it is a good start.

CLINICIAN: Sounds like it shows a different level of engagement in the relationship?

TIM: Yes.

CLINICIAN: I am curious too, did you not know that before?

TIM: I wouldn't say that I didn't know it. For me, it was more or less a thing, I didn't care. I am showing my commitment in other ways and if you're not picking that up, that is your problem. I was being selfish and not meeting her needs. In looking at it, it is not a very big need. At work, I can't stand if someone only gives me a part of something. I can't do my job. I don't know why I would expect my wife to feel like she is doing her part in the relationship, if I can't provide her with the knowledge.

"What Difference Does It Make" Questions

This type of question allows for a more systemic exploration of the importance to what someone is doing. It takes the conversation deeper in terms of one's purpose, as well as the effect it may have on them or others closest to them. It creates an opportunity to begin incorporating a client's system. It is a reminder of why a person is doing what they are doing.

CLINICIAN: So how are you different? It seems like something in you switched.

TIM: Yes, and it really felt good to be able to do that. Not that there was a weight lifted off my chest. I don't feel like I am hiding anything anymore . . . not that I ever was, I don't have secrets. She knows what I know. It doesn't take much more effort to give a full detailed answer versus a short answer.

CLINICIAN: Seems like you are going out of your way to be more open. You said something a minute ago and that is that you didn't really care before. Do you care now?

TIM: I do care. I see the difference it has made. Not just with her or my mom, or my friends, but within myself.

CLINICIAN: So in your conversation with your adopted mom and being on the phone for an hour, is it that you are not getting angry anymore when you are in the conversation with her, or is stuff still coming up, you are just managing it differently?

TIM: I'd say it is a combination of both. She would say things, you know, with a loaded point. She says things that she knows will make me mad and that I am going to get irritated. Then, I am the bad person when I don't want to talk anymore. I'll go days without talking to her. I can see that the same thing happens with my wife. If I don't talk to her or I don't respond to things, you don't know what to say, you don't know what to ask. It is unfair for me to get upset, looking back at things. As much effort as I have been putting into getting mad or allowing myself to get mad, it is less effort to tell them.

CLINICIAN: Even with her, being more open is kind of resolving some of this other stuff that has been happening.

TIM: Yes. We haven't had a terrible relationship but it has been rocky. There are things that come up and we don't talk about because I just get mad . . . now we were able to talk about some of those things. She didn't get mad, and I didn't get mad. We would try and talk over one another, but she wasn't hanging up on me, and I didn't hang up on her. It didn't even get to the level that it normally got to.

CLINICIAN: Why do you think that is?

TIM: I didn't allow myself to.

CLINICIAN: What did you do instead?

TIM: I had to take some deep breaths. She would ask, "Why the pause, it sounds like you're hyperventilating." Normally, I wouldn't have said anything except, I need to go, but because I did take the pause, I didn't allow myself to give that reaction. I was able to explain to her what was going on. She never would have known before. I would explain to her why I was taking a deep breath. If I could identify then what the trigger was, which I hope my mom and I get to that level. I don't get to see her, she lives in Missouri, the only communication we have is over the phone.

CLINICIAN: So, you are staying with it. Even when you are experiencing some intense emotion you aren't shutting down, you aren't running away, you are staying with it. You're explaining to them what is going on.

■ SESSION 8

CLINICIAN: Let's start off with what is better since the last time I have seen you?

TIM: I don't know, I think a lot.

CLINICIAN: Like what?

TIM: I took off a week from work and went hunting. That did a lot for me. I was able to get away. I was able to clear my mind and not have to deal with anything. It felt great. I felt great, came back and things with my wife have been awesome. I haven't had any thoughts of suicide or anything remotely close to that. I feel like I have been on an up.

CLINICIAN: How long has it been since you haven't had those types of thoughts?

TIM: The last one was just before we talked the last time we met. So, it's been like a month and a half or two months.

CLINICIAN: Ok. What made you decide to go hunting?

TIM: It's something I grew up doing. I always enjoyed it. In the summer we did it. Even though it wasn't always a success in getting anything. I definitely felt like getting out there, getting away from the city and have no phones. I had no interaction with anybody. It was nice.

CLINICIAN: So what difference did it make?

TIM: It gave me a lot of time to think. A lot of time sitting out there in the woods with nature. I was able to reflect on a lot of things . . . my past, and like you said, letting the little boy come out. You know, hunting is supposed to be quiet, but sometimes I couldn't help but talk to myself and kind of laugh at a situation that may not have been funny when it happened; but looking back on it, with it being out of my control it was kind of funny. It was a time to clear my mind.

CLINICIAN: Did you go by yourself?

TIM: I went with two friends.

CLINICIAN: OK. You were concerned about being around weapons again, weren't you? There was a time after your deployment that this was an issue?

TIM: I was. It was more or less the sound of the weapon firing. Not having any control. Not being around it. Being out there I wasn't tested because we didn't hear any gunshots.

CLINICIAN: Oh, OK. Hadn't you gone with friends to the range since being back?

TIM: I have been to the range a couple times.

CLINICIAN: And you kind of worked through it?

TIM: I still get really anxious. Not to the point where it is debilitating. I do get worked up and kind of nervous. If there are too many people, I will leave. If there is roughly five people, I am conscious of what is going on, I can separate myself and get as far away as I can. It tends to help, but I don't know if that is the right answer.

CLINICIAN: So this hunting trip wasn't really much of a concern for you prior to going?

TIM: It was.

CLINICIAN: It was, ok.

TIM: Because of the sound of the gunshot when you are out in the woods.

CLINICIAN: You decided to go anyway?

TIM: Yep.

CLINICIAN: That is what I am a little curious about. How were you able to push through the worry, anxiety or those thoughts and not let it stop you from going? That seems like a big deal?

TIM: It's what we talked about. I don't want to allow things to get me worked up or make me anxious. I don't want them to run my life. I want to get past that. I know I have to expose myself to some of it, in order for me to experience those things and to tell myself, hey, it's really not that bad. You are not in that game anymore. This is the United States. It's different over here.

CLINICIAN: Was going on the hunting trip, again another situation that you put yourself in where you managed your thoughts and it continues to help you get closer to your goal?

TIM: Yes, on the drive up there, I was nervous. It was a 3 hour drive and another buddy was driving with me. We could talk and I was not saying anything for a while. I just kind of thought about it. I was getting a little nervous and a little anxious. He'd ask why are you being so quiet, why did you shut up? I explained to him, what I was feeling and what I was thinking. He gave me more reassurance. It's not the area where you were. I don't know what it was like, I didn't serve, and I wasn't over. You don't have to worry about that out here. I'm here if you need someone to talk to or confide in, we can do it. If we get out there and it is too anxious for you, we can go back to camp.

It was nice to have that friend in that supporting role that made things it a little bit easier.

CLINICIAN: So you chose to open up to him and talk to him about how you were feeling? And this is something you have been working on?

TIM: Yes.

CLINICIAN: Sounds like he was supportive and even gave you options, too? It's always good to have options when you are getting anxious about something.

TIM: Yeah.

CLINICIAN: Sometimes when we get anxious, we lose our perspective and forget we have options.

TIM: It's easy to become narrow minded very quickly. That trip opened up a lot for me.

CLINICIAN: Like what?

TIM: I was able to talk to a friend. I was able to express myself. That is something I have had trouble with. I came back and told my wife that I wanted to do something. I don't know what I want to do, I want to test myself. She asked me what I wanted to do. She started naming stuff; I didn't want to do any of that. I sat at work that day . . . we have a classified section and somebody posted that they were selling tickets to the Nuggets game tonight, so without talking to my wife, I bought them. I will put myself in this situation, we'll see how this goes. I was a little hesitant, a little nervous, but I think we will have more enjoyment than anything. Taking that step feels like a little bit of a relief. I haven't been to a sporting event or something in a large crowd like that since I came back.

CLINICIAN: Really?

TIM: It's been three years.

CLINICIAN: What? I know one of the big things for your wife is going to concerts. That is something we talked about last time. Something you were struggling with. This is kind of something similar to that, huh?

TIM: Yeah, I then may be able to go to concerts with her after this. We have tried small concerts 100 to 200. That tends to get a little overwhelming for me. I noticed that before those, I wasn't in the greatest place. After coming back from this trip, being able to open up to people and talk to them. Knowing that I have a bigger support system other than my mom and my wife, I am willing to try something else.

CLINICIAN: Have you gone to the basketball game yet?

TIM: No, it is tonight.

CLINICIAN: Ooohhh, fun! When did you decide to buy the tickets?

TIM: I saw them, it was kind of a spur of the moment thing, I saw them posted. I ran to my vehicle and looked to see where the seats were. The deal was too good to pass up. I bought them and then I told the wife afterward.

CLINICIAN: And she was ok with that?

TIM: Um . . . kind of (chuckle).

CLINICIAN: Are you taking her?

TIM: I am. She wasn't OK with the money.

CLINICIAN: What was she OK with?

TIM: The fact that I was willing to do this, that I didn't question myself and I'm not allowing myself to talk myself out of it. The tickets are bought now. We have them, it's kind of hard to back out. Whereas before with the concert, I'd tell her that I would go and when the time comes to buy the tickets, I don't want to go.

CLINICIAN: What is different about you this time? It sounds like the doubt is not there . . . the questioning . . . what is there instead?

TIM: I don't know. I mean after that hunting, trip I feel relieved. I feel like a new person per se. The weight has been lifted and I am ready to open up doors in my life that I've closed out for the last couple of years.

CLINICIAN: Very cool, congratulations!

TIM: Thank you.

CLINICIAN: That's exciting.

TIM: It is.

CLINICIAN: So what are your best hopes for today, what do you need from today?

TIM: I guess more tools and techniques. I have started journaling a little bit. I have talked to my wife. I have opened up my support system to more than just my wife and my mom. I now involve friends that are with us, not on a daily basis but who have some type of interaction with us. I've let that little boy out. More techniques, so that way if I get to a point that if one of those isn't working, I have another option.

CLINICIAN: Well, I know the last time you were here, it seemed like everything was going really well and then you had that incident with your wife. You mentioned it feeling like it set you back?

TIM: Yes.

CLINICIAN: How did you continue to move forward after we met from there?

TIM: I went home and I talked to my wife about it. I was able to let her know that she was not the one I was mad at. I was frustrated at the situation, not her. Once I was able to do that, I was able to talk to my mom and sister and get the rest of the story. I had a calmer mindset, and once that happened, I realized that I was in the wrong for jumping to the conclusion. It did nothing but make the situation worse. I continued to let my emotions get the best of me, which affected everybody. From there, I tried not to keep my emotions locked up. I didn't allow them to jump out. I try to gather as much information as I can, before I do anything.

CLINICIAN: Is that something that is different?

TIM: Very much so. After coming back from deployment I wore my emotions on my sleeves. When something happened, I ignored it. Now I try and rein them in a little bit. It is difficult and can be tiresome, but the feeling at the end is a better feeling.

CLINICIAN: Have you had anything come up since the last time I saw you, where you put that into play?

TIM: My adopted mom and this election (chuckle). For me, it was the lesser of two evils. She was adamant that the family go one way, and I refused. I am pretty sure the next step was for her to disown me, but I didn't allow myself to get worked up. I have no control over who she votes for and how she feels. That is not something that I can control. Besides, I refused to let it get the best of me. Even though emotions were definitely involved in the conversations and things would get a little tense, I wasn't going to let that happen.

CLINICIAN: What did you do differently?

TIM: It was my approach. There was a particular conversation where things got a little heated. We started talking over each other, it continued to escalate. I asked my mom, "What are we solving by this?" You are not getting anything out of this, I am not getting anything out of this. Why are we fighting over it?

CLINICIAN: You were the one that stopped, put the brakes on the conversation?

TIM: I could feel all the physical . . .

CLINICIAN: What did you notice?

TIM: My heart was racing, I was very fidgety, I was sweating, and my hands were tensing up.

CLINICIAN: And so you were very much aware of that?

TIM: Yeah. I knew if I let that go on anymore, it would just end up bad. I don't know if she didn't hear me at first or ignored it. She continued on. I became a little more adamant the next time. A little more stern in my voice. I asked her, "What are we getting out of this?" It is not something to fight over. It's not something to ruin our relationship over. It's four years.

CLINICIAN: What was her response to you getting a little more adamant, setting more of a limit?

TIM: She came back to tell me that was the most intelligent thing I said during the entire conversation (both laughing).

CLINICIAN: Was what?

TIM: That we are not getting anything out of this, us fighting over this was pointless.

CLINICIAN: Wow!

TIM: Me being a smart ass said, "That is the most intelligent thing you have said during this entire conversation." (laughing more).

CLINICIAN: It turned into a joke. How cool though that, she gave you credit for stopping this unproductive cycle that she was just as much caught up in.

TIM: After that, we talked, we got off the politics. I told her why I did it. She said, I never would have thought of that. She said, I didn't know you were getting to that point.

CLINICIAN: How did you do that?

TIM: Just stopped the conversation, stopped talking about the politics. I told her it wasn't my intention, my intentions were not to get worked up, heated, or start an argument with her. Sometimes my emotions get the best of me. It's a snowball effect. I continue to roll, and if I don't stop it when I recognize it, terrible things happen. I told her that I felt like it was a success for me to realize I was having physical symptoms of my emotions rising. I felt like this was a huge win for me to stop things there. She apologized over and over for getting me worked up. I ended up telling her 'thank you' because I learned something about myself. I know that I can do it now, and I recognize more symptoms of myself getting worked up. I can, when I need to pump the breaks. I tried to take everything that was semi-negative and looked to see what was positive about it.

CLINICIAN: Let's review all of these skills and tools and techniques that you have. What would you start with?

TIM: Let's start with communication. I feel that is the biggest one. I have noticed, definitely with my wife, when I talk to her and when we open up, it leads to more and more. It's not just what I was thinking, something else comes up, something else comes up, something else comes up . . . and not all bad, and some are good. It is giving me the ability to recognize different things. Those feelings, emotions, and thoughts that I am holding in. I don't have that option anymore. Once I start talking to her, the conversation goes more in depth. If something is to make it past that, the door is not opened. I guess the next step is for me to recognize it when it starts. Either the physical things that are happening with my body or I need to recognize my thought process is changing, or my mood, my demeanor.

CLINICIAN: What do you start to notice physically?

TIM: I feel drained, I am tired all the time, my body feels heavy, and I'm carrying extra weight around. If I don't realize that, I become more fidgety, I start to tap my heel, bounce my knee, my palms will get real sweaty. I always talk with my hands. I don't ever notice myself sitting there tapping my knee, or my hands getting real sweaty unless I am starting to get worked up. My emotions are starting to get the best of me.

CLINICIAN: You mentioned your heart racing. I want to make sure you know, it's OK for you to feel these things, that's natural. Those emotions are natural. That is all humanness, and that's specific to you and what gets you going. The key is being aware of when it is happening.

TIM: I have come to the realization that it is natural. I also have come to the realization that when you put those together, things tend to get worse.

CLINICIAN: When you put what together?

TIM: All those physical things, my heart racing, tapping my feet, becoming more fidgety. I notice that the next step is, I become real annoyed or real agitated. From there I usually start to get mad. If I can start to notice those symptoms, I can stop things before I get annoyed and agitated.

CLINICIAN: Yes.

TIM: I don't end up mad. The biggest thing helping me with those has been breathing. People have been saying that to me for years. It sounds silly, but it really has worked, just breathe. I notice I can't just sit on the couch and do it, I have to get up and walk around. Go for a walk with the dogs, play with my dogs, interact.

CLINICIAN: That has been a big one for you, being with the dogs?

TIM: It's been huge for me. I don't know if I have noticed it in the past. It seems now it's kind of subliminal, that's my comfort zone, is my dogs. I would take them everywhere if I could.

CLINICIAN: You mentioned journaling, how has that been helpful?

TIM: Was it last weekend? Yeah, last weekend my wife went out of town. She went out to Arizona to help my little sister plan her wedding. I didn't have an option to talk to anybody; I talked to my dogs, but I don't get any feedback. I wrote things down and it allowed me to talk to my wife when she got back. Nothing was super important, nothing crazy, but there were a couple of things that kind of stuck with me, that I would like to get off my chest and that's one way of doing it.

CLINICIAN: Very good tool!

TIM: It has been. I don't know if I would do it every day, but if I know I am going to be away from my support system for a while then it is probably something I would utilize.

CLINICIAN: If your wife was in here, what would she say that she has noticed about you, in terms of what you do differently to manage?

TIM: Probably my communication. Being more open and receptive to things, not shutting the door because of past experiences. Like tonight, she was super excited when I told her about the game. Not because she wanted to go see the Nuggets but because it was me getting out, being willing to do something with her other than the small things we do.

CLINICIAN: What difference do you think that's going to make?

TIM: It will definitely better our relationship. I feel like I definitely closed the door with our relationship, I kept promising her that I would go to things like concerts or sporting events and then wouldn't go. She would have to go with someone else or we'd have to sell the tickets. I feel like I can open that door with her again. There are other things in our relationship that don't matter, but she has her feelings and thoughts and those do matter.

CLINICIAN: Let me ask you this, on a scale of one to 10 with 10 being that you are 100% confident that you are going to be able to go to the basketball game tonight and nothing within your control is going to stop you from going . . . and one is the complete opposite, where would you rate yourself?

TIM: I know I am going. Talking about it, I am starting to feel anxious. I can feel my heartbeat increase. I told myself all week that I was going. I am not backing out of this one.

CLINICIAN: Ok, is that different? You telling yourself you are going, that you aren't going to back out?

TIM: It is. I usually find myself trying to find an excuse to get out of it. Instead of confronting the real issue.

CLINICIAN: Which is?

TIM: Being uncomfortable, not liking people. If I don't force myself into a situation, where I am going to have to interact with people, I don't. If I don't have to be around people I don't know, then I don't get past it.

■ SUMMARY

During my last session with the client (11th session), it seemed important for him to tell me how different his experience was with this type of therapy. He reported that being here had been a completely different type of care compared to the four or five other types of care he had received. He stated that at Highlands Ranch they wanted him to "self-reflect" and do things "by the book." At Fort Carson, one just "boxed it out." He stated that at the clinic "it didn't seem like anyone really cared." He stated that here, "I've never been told I was wrong." He said that it is about the fact that

> stuff is going to happen, and it's what you do from here. It's really helped me a lot. There is an understanding that there is going to be a bump in the road, and it's not about avoiding the bump. It's, OK, the bump has happened, now what do you do? I have the resources. I am not going to drive with a flat tire, I am going to stop and fix it. A lot of it's on me to continue and I need to keep that mentality. I didn't realize that. Everything is not terrible. One incident does not make my life, it's not going to rewrite history for me. I can most certainly take things from here and adjust my lifestyle if need be or I can deal with it as it comes. I'd rather deal with it as it comes.

I often tell clients that what you focus on gets bigger. I notice people in general are programmed to focus on what is not working and the continuous problems we all face. The problems we have are life problems. These will not likely disappear. It becomes a matter of how we address the ups and downs that life has in store for us. As a clinician, I have a choice to make with regard to the path I take with clients. Utilizing SFBT questions and interventions not only helps a client to define what it is they want instead of the problem or where they want to go—they are on a path of discovery. You model this concept of focusing on what is working and teach them to notice signs of progress. You teach them to evaluate what helps them get closer to their goals and what they want. You teach skills that clients naturally begin to pick up on during your work together. This enables them to trust their own guide from within, the tools they have, and the ability to apply these skills to any situation going forward.

■ REFERENCES

American Psychiatric Association. (2013). Diagnostic and statistical manual of mental disorders. (5th ed.). Arlington, VA: American Psychiatric Publishing.

Chalabi, Mona (2015. March 19). What percentage of Americans have served in the military? Retrieved from https://fivethirtyeight.com/datalab/what-percentage-of-americans-have-served-in-the-military/.

Ford, Julian (2012, November 11). Recovering from military trauma. Retrieved from https://www.psychologytoday.com/blog/hijacked-your.../recovering-military-trauma.

Friedman, M. J. (n.d.). PTSD history and overview. Retrieved from https://ptsd.va.gov/professional/PTSD-overview/ptsd-overview.asp.

Gradus, J. L. (n.d.). Epidemiology of PTSD. Retrieved from http://www.ptsd.va.gov/professional/continuing_ed/epidemiology.asp.

National Center for PTSD (n.d.). How common is PTSD? Retrieved from http://www.ptsd.va.gov/public/PTSD-overview/basics/how-common-is-ptsd.asp.

National Institute of Mental Health (2016, February). Post-traumatic stress disorder. Retrieved from https://www.nimh.nih.gov/health/topics/post-traumatic-stress-disorder-ptsd/index.shtml

Pew Research Center. (n.d.). The military-civilian gap: Fewer family connections. Retrieved from http://www.pewsocialtrends.org/2011/11/23/the-military-civilian-gap-fewer-family-connections/.

Post-traumatic Stress Disorder (n.d). Retrieved December 30, 2017 from http://quickseries.com/index.php?prodcode=02-0179-001-01.

11 Child Sexual Abuse

■ DAWN CROSSWHITE AND JOHNNY S. KIM

■ CHILD SEXUAL ABUSE OVERVIEW AND CONCEPTS

This chapter focuses on sexual abuse, its negative impact, and how SFBT can be used with clients who have experienced this trauma. Child sexual abuse (CSA) has been defined in various ways within the medical, scientific, clinical, and legal professions and this can vary in the United States on a state-by-state basis and also by country. A recent definition from Whitelock, Lamb, and Rentfrow (2013) that encapsulates many aspects of child sexual abuse is:

> In essence, CSA involves pressuring, manipulating, or coercing people under 18 years of age to engage to engage in sexual activities with older people even though the children are psychologically and developmentally unable to consent to or understand the behavior (p. 351).

Thus, this definition of CSA involves specific sexual behaviors between a child or adolescent and a significantly older person as one of the key defining components. Most places define a child as being under 17 years of age and an older person as someone five or more years older than the child (Holguin & Hansen, 2003).

One complicating factor in identifying sexual abuse come from laws around age of consent for sexual activity. There is less of an agreement around the age for sexual consent (when a person can legally consent to sex) or age for sexual maturity and laws vary not only across countries but also change over time. For example, Spain raised the age of consent for marriage and sexual activity from 13 to 16 years of age in 2009 while it is still 14 in Germany and Austria (Burgen, 2013). In the United States, the age of consent for sexual activity varies by state and currently ranges from 16 to 18 years of age. This is an increase from the 1800s when the age of consent in the United States was 10 or 12 years of age, with Hawaii being the last state to raise the age of consent from 14 to 16 in 2001 (Volokh, 2015).

There is also a wide range of sexual situations that children may experience when abused, but most definitions use specific sexual behaviors between a child or adolescent and a significantly older person as a defining criterion. The term "sexual activities" refers to various behaviors that seek to sexually stimulate a child or adolescent (Holguin & Hansen, 2003). The range of activities includes intense sexually abusive contact with the sexual portions of the child's body such as genitals, anus, or breasts by the adult or the child touching the sexual portion of the adult's body. Contact sexual abuse can involve penetration (penile or object) of the vagina, mouth, or anus as well as nonpenetration acts such as kissing and fondling. On the other end of the range is noncontact sexual abuse, which includes genital exposure, voyeurism, showing/making pornography with children involved (Finkelhor, 1994; Holguin & Hansen, 2003).

Another important criterion for CSA is an abusive condition. This typically occurs when there is a power imbalance in the relationship, which creates a violation around the notion of consensuality. The abuser typically uses threats, force, intimidation, or manipulation against the child to obtain sexual activity (Collin-Vezina, Daigneault, & Hebert, 2013). Other defining characteristics of an abusive condition involves the adult having a significant age or maturity advantage over the child, being in a position of authority or caregiver role; or using trickery or force to carry out the illicit activities against the child (Finkelhor, 1994).

When a child or adolescent is sexually abused by a family member, the abuse is considered intrafamilial CSA, while a non-family member is considered extrafamilial CSA (Holguin & Hansen, 2003). For intrafamilial CSA, the perpetrator is someone from the child's family, such as parents, stepparents, aunts, uncles, cousins, and siblings. The family members usually reside with the child, although this is not always the case. For extrafamilial CSA, the perpetrator is someone outside of the family such as a teacher, coach, friend, or stranger (Fischer & McDonald, 1998).

■ PREVALENCE RATES FOR CHILD SEXUAL ABUSE

Over the years, many studies have tried to estimate the prevalence rates for child sexual abuse internationally. A study by Pereda and colleagues (2009) examined child sexual abuse over a 12-year span across 28 different countries and found prevalence rates have remained fairly constant, with CSA rates for men below 10% and for women between 10% and 20%. A more recent systematic review on the prevalence of child sexual abuse by Barth and colleagues (2013) examined 55 studies between 2002 and 2009 across 24 countries. Results from this study found prevalence rates ranged from 8% to 31% for girls and 3% to 17% for boys. While several systematic review studies report consistent findings on the prevalence of child sexual abuse internationally, caution is warranted in drawing firm conclusions. Limitations around these studies include the under-reporting of child sexual abuse cases, differing definitions and criteria on child sexual abuse, and reliance on self-reported data (Pereda et al., 2009).

Research studies have found there are differences in terms of prevalence and negative impacts on children based on whether the perpetrator was intrafamilial or extrfamilial, although the evidence is not always clear (Fischer & McDonald, 1998). For example, different studies found different conclusions about the seriousness of the child sexual abuse. An earlier study by Russell (1983) found extrafamilial abusers were involved in more intense sexual abuse contact of the sexual portions of the child's body such as genitals, anus, or breasts than intrafamilial abuse. However, a study by Erickson, Walbek, and Seeley (1988) discovered that intrafamilial abuse occurred more often and in many instances gradually progressed from touching to penetration. A later study by Gomez-Schwartz and colleagues (1990) found similar rates of intense sexual abuse between intrafamilial and extrafamilial abuse cases.

Fischer and McDonald (1998) cite several research studies that noted differences between intrafamilial and extrafamilial abuse; their study found consistent results around gender and age differences as well as duration of abuse. Previous research studies have found that girls are more often victims of intrafamilial abuse while boys were more likely to be abused by extrafamilial perpetrators. Studies have also consistently found that younger children (e.g., preschoolers) experience more intrafamilial abuse while older children (e.g., older than five years) experience more extrafamilial abuse. Finally, research studies have found intrafamilial abuse was longer in duration than extrafamilial abuse, possibly due to the greater accessibility to the child victim.

A more recent study by Finkelhor and colleagues (2014) reported lifetime prevalence of child sexual abuse and sexual assault in late adolescents for both boys and girls by family member, acquaintance (anyone not categorized by respondent as a stranger or family member) and stranger. Their study found that 17-year-old girls had lifetime rates of sexual abuse of 5.5% by a family member, 19.6% by an acquaintance, and 3% by a stranger. Their study also found 17-year-old boys had lower lifetime rates of sexual abuse of 0.6% by a family member, 3.1% by an acquaintance, and 1.4% by a stranger.

■ IMPACT OF CHILD SEXUAL ABUSE

A large body of research has found that people who experience child sexual abuse have an increased risk for long-term physical health problems. Compared to nonvictimized peers, CSA individuals are more likely to experience and seek treatment for health problems such as gastrointestinal ailments, chronic pelvic pain, general pain (Irish, Kobayashi, & Delahanty, 2010). Researchers are also considering the impact of child sexual abuse as a predictor for major health problems later in life such as gynecologic or reproductive health problems, cardiopulmonary symptoms, and diabetes (Collin-Vezina, Daigneault, & Hebert, 2013).

In addition to health-related problems, victims of CSA also experience psychological, emotional, and social functioning problems and often have a negative view of their own health (Whitelock, Lamb, & Rentfrow, 2013). Research has found that victims of child sexual abuse are more than three times as likely than non-child sexual abuse individuals to have contact with public mental health services (Cutajar et al., 2010). Victims of child sexual abuse have higher risks of mental health problems such as depression, anxiety, PTSD, borderline personality disorder, low self-esteem, and paranoid ideation. Relatedly, victims of CSA are significantly at risk for behavioral problems such as self-harm, substance misuse, sexual dysfunction, engagement in high-risk sexual behaviors (i.e., unprotected sex, prostitution, multiple partners) and interpersonal problems (Maniglio, 2009). The trauma victims experience with sexual abuse is believed to distort the victim's self-concept and lead them to feeling stigmatized. Additionally, victims experience betrayal from trusted adults and feelings of powerlessness about the abusive situation (Collin-Vezina, Daigneault, & Hebert, 2013).

Many caregivers and family members of the victims are also negatively impacted following disclosure, even if the disclosure is significantly delayed. It is typical for family members to experience psychological and emotional distress such as shock, disbelief, shame, and self-blame when CSA is disclosed or discovered (van Toledo & Seymour, 2013). A study by Hill (2001) found that women experienced powerful feelings of guilt and failure as a mother to protect their children. Many women also expressed anger toward their male partners who were the perpetrators as well as the criminal justice system in the same study. Besides the psychological distress experienced, many caregivers experienced loss of economic stability if the father was the perpetrator of the abuse. Conflict with other family members due to denial from the family perpetrator is also common and adds to the stress and isolation of the mothers (van Toledo & Seymour, 2013).

■ PRACTICAL APPLICATION OF SFBT AND SEXUAL ABUSE/ASSAULT

Because of the supportive and accepting aspect of the model, SFBT is a powerful counseling approach to use with clients who have been sexually abused. Providing a supportive, nonjudgmental response to victims of child sexual abuse often leads to better outcomes. This is particularly important with initial disclosure of CSA when many caregivers may react with disbelief, especially when involving a family member (van Toledo & Seymour, 2013). Providing support and counseling to caregivers and family members of the victims are also necessary since many are ill-equipped to handle the mental and emotional impacts.

Most non-offending caregivers typically receive psychoeducation, group support counseling, and individual counseling. The focus of intervention for the victim, family members, and friends typically centers around strategies for coping with their own stresses, normalizing various feelings and behaviors, reducing anxiety and depression, modifying negative thoughts and behaviors, and enhancing support systems (van Toledo & Seymour, 2013). SFBT provides another useful approach to helping victims of child sexual abuse as well as their family and friends who are impacted by this traumatic event.

Most Important SF Questions You Ask in Session?

One of the most useful questions clinicians can ask is the *difference question* that was utilized in the case example described below. Asking a client, "How would life be different if you no longer had to carry the secret you are holding?" can be extremely powerful both as a homework assignment or in shifting the client's focus away from guilt or shame. By asking this question, the clinician gives a client the chance to process the secret and not holding on to it in a completely different way than they may have experienced in the past. It also allows the client to utilize their strength and confidence to explore other possibilities that may have gone untapped.

There are other important questions to ask when the sexual abuse involves family members. The SFBT approach is especially powerful in this situation because it's non-pathologizing and forces the clinician to keep in check their own prejudices and beliefs (McConkey, 1992). Often times, victims of sexual abuse feel betrayed and powerless, so asking solution-building questions about the client's resiliency can be impactful.

One way this can be accomplished is by asking the miracle question. The miracle question can be useful to shift the focus away from these feelings of powerlessness and betrayal by getting the client to talk about what they want or need. For example, "Suppose a miracle happened tonight while you were asleep, and all these feelings of anger and helplessness disappeared, what changes would you see in yourself that you don't see now? What will you be doing when you're less angry or more confident?" This phrasing of the miracle question allows the client to think about their future behaviors rather than dwelling on their feelings about the past sexual abuse in a way that is non-judgmental. When clients are able to spend time thinking about and talking about their future, they become less critical of themselves and foresee a different relationship with family members (McConkey, 1992).

Other questions McConkey (1992) recommend include those that focus on empowerment and gender issues that might come up in adult survivors of sexual abuse. Some additional questions SFBT clinicians might consider include:

- How will you know when you've resolved the past for yourself?
- What does your family believe regarding how men should behave?
- How do these beliefs affect your relationship with men now?
- How do you think your beliefs about woman's role influenced your decision to disclose your past abuse now?

These are just some examples clinicians can use to explore ways to give power to their client, especially female clients, around their past sexual abuse.

Sexual Abuse Session Utilizing SFBT

Below is a real case example to illustrate ways to use the SFBT approach with a client who had experienced sexual abuse. The client for this case example is a 15-year-old adolescent female named Mary (her name was changed). She is currently living in a foster home obtained through the child welfare system. Mary had been removed from her home three years previously after a case of physical abuse by Mary's mother was discovered. During the investigation, it was suspected that Mary was sexually abused by a family friend but not confirmed because Mary did not make a formal outcry. Mary, however, talked about a secret to the caseworker and the therapist and showed signs of being sexually abused such as sleep disturbances, reported nightmares, appearing distracted at unusual times, refusing to eat, feeling bad about her body, and exhibiting sexualized behaviors. More recently Mary has taken to self-harm and has become disruptive in the foster home and at school. She has also been bringing up "the secret" more and more with her clinician.

Mary was referred to the solution-focused clinician by another caseworker in hopes that she would begin to process the trauma brought on by mom's abusive behavior and the removal from the home. In addition, the referring caseworker felt that Mary needed to "learn new ways of coping besides self-harming behaviors." Mary has seen many different therapists, but nothing seemed to work. The caseworker felt a more strength-based, solution-focused approach might benefit Mary more than the other counseling approaches she has tried.

This case example starts with the third session. In the previous session, Mary began to vacillate on whether she wanted to discuss "the secret." Because one of Mary's strengths is writing, she agreed to write a letter for her homework at the end of the second session. The question of the letter was, "How would life be different if you no longer had to carry the secret you are holding?"

Counseling Session #3

    CLINICIAN: Hello, Mary, it's good to see you today! So tell me, what's been better since the last time we met?

MARY: Today was a good day, nothing to complain about.

CLINICIAN: That's great. What made it a good day for you?

MARY: Well, I got to see my boyfriend and I went to all my classes.

CLINICIAN: That's wonderful! I know you've been struggling with going to your classes, what was different today that you decided to go to all of them?

MARY: Well, to be honest with you, the homework assignment from last week.

CLINICIAN: The homework assignment from our session last week?

MARY: Yeah. I started writing the letter to myself and just began to realize that secrets don't make friends, and it's keeping me from making friends with myself.

CLINICIAN: Nice! I have such a great appreciation for your ability to put things together and allow for the insights to flow. So insightful!

MARY: Thanks, but I think it is because you believe in me and let me know it. My mom never believed me, and it hurt. I was so pissed she never believed in me or believed me that I just said, fuck it! I'm not worth it, anyway.

CLINICIAN: Oh, you're so worthy and deserve all of your greatness. But, can we go back a bit? (Mary nodded yes) You said, "She never believed in me or believed me." Can you say a little more about what it was that your mom never believed you about?

(At this time, Mary became silent and tearful. Rather than rush in with another question, I let Mary sit in the stillness and gave her space to talk when she was ready. After several minutes, she began her disclosure of her sexual abuse.)

MARY: Ummmmm (scratching her chin), this is so hard. I know you'll believe me, but will anyone else? (speaking almost to herself).

CLINICIAN: (I smiled and nodded in encouragement for her to continue.)

MARY: You see when I was really little, maybe three, I had a babysitter who was a boy. He put my brother in the closet and began touching me in my private area. I didn't know what was going on, but I was scared. I asked how come he put my brother in the closet, and he said, 'So we can have fun—just us. I think that is what he said. I don't know. This is so hard.

(Mary began to cry and curl up in the chair.)

CLINICIAN: I can only imagine how hard this is for you, Mary. You are doing a great job.

(a few more minutes of silence and crying)

MARY: (With raised tone) It is hard because I was just a little girl and he kept touching me! It happened a lot, every time he babysat us. I hate that fucker! I hate him and my mom! I tried to tell her when it happened and again a few years ago, before I was taken.

CLINICIAN: Taken?

MARY: Yeah, taken from my home by social services. I tried to tell her. You know what she said? She just said, "No, it didn't. You are just mistaken."

(again, raised tone, as if she were speaking to her mother)

MARY: It did, too! He crawled into my little sister's crib with me. Yes, it did! Can I tell you something else? (looking at me)

CLINICIAN: (I nodded in encouragement and let her guide the session.)

MARY: I've never told anyone this because I figured no one would ever believe me, since *she* didn't believe me the first time. Her [mom's] best friend's sons also molested me one time. There were three of them and one of their friends. I was like six, I think. (Mary let out a big sigh and cried a little more.) I'm done.

CLINICIAN: (I gave Mary a few minutes of stillness so she could regain her composure.)

CLINICIAN: Sounds like you were such a brave little girl, despite not being believed by your mom. How did you find the courage to keep moving forward every day?

MARY: (thinking for a minute) I don't know. I never thought of it that way, being brave and having courage. I just kept waking up in the mornings and doing what I had to do.

CLINICIAN: Not everyone would have been able to wake up in the morning and do what they had to do. You are the kind of person who can, though. Tell me more about how you were able to do so because I think that takes lots of strength.

MARY: I don't know. I mean, like I said in the letter (last week's homework) I want to be my own friend. I know that I want to be somebody, like a writer or forensic scientist. I know that I make problems for myself, like when I don't go to classes or don't do my homework. I don't know why I do that.

CLINICIAN: Those are some exciting goals. Out of curiosity, in your opinion, what would be a very small step you could do to reach your goals?

MARY: (laughing) Going to class every day and doing the work would be helpful.

CLINICIAN: (laughing) Yes, it would be very helpful. Everyday seems a bit daunting, is there a smaller step you can take?

MARY: I don't know. I either have to or I don't.

CLINICIAN: OK. Can we look at it in a different way? How has change usually taken place in your life?

MARY: When I have a goal I really care about, I write it down and then I think of two ways I can pull them off. Like one time, I wanted to go to this weekend church camp but I kept getting in trouble at the foster home I was living in at the time. So, every day for two weeks I made sure my room was clean and if I wanted to yell or not do what I was told, I would remind myself that I wanted to go to camp.

CLINICIAN: That's awesome! You have a great way to achieve your goals. Let me ask you, on a scale of one to ten where ten means your goal has been achieved and one is you have not tried- where are you now at going to class and doing your school work?

MARY: (huge sigh) I don't know, maybe a four.

CLINICIAN: What does that number stand for?

MARY: I'm still angry at my mom, and I'm not sure I'm ready to do better.

CLINICIAN: Fair enough. What would it look like to move up to a five on the scale?

MARY: (laughing) I would call my best friend and talk to her.

CLINICIAN: If she were sitting here right now, what has she said in the past that has helped you feel a little bit better?

MARY: She makes me laugh and is encouraging. Like, I would tell her what you and I talked about. I wouldn't go into detail though, and she would just listen, tell me a joke and give me a hug. (Mary starts laughing.)

CLINICIAN: That sounds comforting, no wonder you call her. You're laughing.

MARY: Yeah, her jokes are funny. She always has me laughing. That might make me move up to a six.

CLINICIAN: Wow, a six! How can those good feelings help you the rest of your day?

MARY: Well, I guess if I start thinking about what we talked about and I start feeling upset, I could remember how my best friend makes me laugh, and that will make me at least smile. I'd just call her.

CLINICIAN: Wonderful! A combination of the two would really help you?

MARY: Yeah.

CLINICIAN: Good. As we begin to wind down our time together, I wanted to let you know how honored I am that you trust me with your experience. More importantly, I'm proud of you for trusting yourself to tell me what happened to you when you were really little.

MARY: Thanks. Once I started talking it was a little easier than I thought it would be. Thanks for listening and believing me.

CLINICIAN: You're welcome. So, since you have such an amazing way to achieve your goals, what improvement would you like to tell me about next time we meet?

MARY: (laughing) I don't know, maybe that I went to school without missing any classes for three days straight.

CLINICIAN: Fantastic! I look forward to hearing all about your success. Feel free to let me know if you need anything before then.

MARY: Thanks, I will. Bye!

■ CASE REFLECTION

One of the key issues that arise for victims of sexual abuse is having a trusting relationship so that the victim can openly share and discuss their sexual abuse experience. In the case example above, the client struggled with this being believed through her previous experience with her mom. When the client stated that "she never believed in me or believed me," the solution-focused clinician allowed the client to discuss this topic by asking her to say a little more about what it was that her mom never believed about Mary. This also allowed the solution-focused clinician to let Mary know the clinician had heard her concerns that mom did not believe her which, in turn, let Mary know that she did not need to remain silent.

Solution-focused brief therapy can also be empowering to a client who was a victim of sexual abuse. The clinician helped Mary to feel empowered by asking her how she found the courage to keep moving forward every day. This question allowed Mary to begin to shift her thinking about the situation from being a victim that people don't believe to being a courageous survivor. The clinician reinforces this concept by asking for details of how she has been brave and able to move forward after the sexual abuse. This question involved positive character interpretation, which builds the client up and allows them to see they have strengths that help them move forward in life.

The solution-focused clinician shifts the conversation towards developing goals for Mary so that she can identify and set behavioral tasks to work on after the session. The clinician begins this process by asking how change usually takes place in Mary's life. This question addresses Mary's competencies, again so that she can see that she has strengths that help her move forward. It also helped the clinician move into using the scaling question. The clinician concludes the session by asking, "What improvements would you like to tell me about next time we meet?" This question allows the clinician and Mary to co-construct goals for next time that Mary feels are important to work on after the counseling session. The homework question also helps Mary to work in a positive way toward change in-between sessions that is in line with the SFBT approach.

After this third session with the SFBT clinician, Mary showed up for another appointment a week later. The clinician began that follow up session by reviewing the past homework. In the follow-up session, Mary came in somewhat more confident and more at ease than previous sessions. When asked about what was different this week, Mary was able to identify that being able to talk about her "secret," being believed and thinking about being told she was courageous allowed her see that there "may not be anything wrong with me." Mary reported that her nightmares had decreased, and she also read a poem she had written, noting it was her "happiest poem" ever. She stated that although she did not make it to all her classes, she had completed all her school work. At the end of the session, the homework Mary chose was to pay attention to her nightmares and write about them, so that a discussion could take place the following week.

Due to the clinician being a mandated reporter, a report about the abuse had to be made to child welfare. At the initial session, while going over the clinician's disclosure statement, Mary was informed about mandated reporting and the three areas that would "break the rule of confidentiality," one of them being someone causing harm to the client. Therefore, Mary knew beforehand that a report would be made. However, a discussion took place between Mary and the clinician so that there were no further secrets. Mary stated that the conversation made her feel respected and stronger "even if no charges will be brought against the guy." Mary could not remember the boy's name, so it is unlikely that charges would be brought against him.

■ SUMMARY

The impact of sexual abuse has lasting negative impact on the victim and the victim's family. The case example in this chapter demonstrated how SFBT can be used to help discuss their sexual abuse experience in a way that is empowering to client and supportive. As the case example above illustrates, having a trusting relationship with the solution-focused clinician is critical so that the victim can openly disclose and process their sexual abuse experience that is non-judgmental. SFBT can be a very empowering process for victims of child sexual abuse that allows them to feel supported yet discover ways they have survived and strengths they have to move forward in their lives.

■ REFERENCES

Barth, J., Bermetz, L., Heim, E., Trelle, S., & Tonia, T. (2013). The current prevalence of child sexual abuse worldwide: A systematic review and meta-analysis. *International Journal of Public Health, 58*, 469–483.

Burgen, S. (2013). Spain raises age of consent from 13 to 16. Retrieved from https://www.theguardian.com/world/2013/sep/04/spain-raises-age-of-consent.

Collin-Vezina, D., Daigneault, I., & Hebert, M. (2013). Lessons learned from child sexual abuse research: Prevalence, outcomes, and preventative strategies. *Child & Adolescent Psychiatry & Mental Health, 7*, 22.

Cutajar, M. C., Mullen, P. E., Ogloff, J. R. P., Thomas, S. D., Wells, D. L., & Spataro, J. (2010). Psychopathology in a large cohort of sexually abused children followed up to 43 years. *Child Abuse & Neglect, 34*, 813–822. doi: 10.1016/j.chiabu.2010.04.004.

Erickson, W. D., Walbek, N. H., & Seeley, R. K. (1988). Behavior patterns of child molesters. *Archives of Sexual Behavior, 17*, 77–86.

Finkelhor, D. (1994). Current information on the scope and nature of child sexual abuse. *Sexual Abuse of Children, 4*(2), 31–53.

Finkelhor, D., Shattuck, A., Turner, H. A., & Hamby, S. L. (2014). The lifetime prevalence of child sexual abuse and sexual assault assessed in late adolescence. *Journal of Adolescent Health, 55,* 329–333. doi:10.1016/j.jadohealth.2013.12.026.

Fischer, D. G., & McDonald, W. L. (1998). Characteristics of intrafamilial and extrafamilial child sexual abuse. *Child Abuse & Neglect, 22*(9), 915–929.

Gomez-Schwartz, B., Horowitz, J. M., & Cardarelli, A. P. (1990). *Child sexual abuse: The initial effects.* Newbury Park, CA: SAGE.

Hill, A. (2001). 'No-one else could understand': Women's experiences of a support group run by and for mothers of sexually abused children. *British Journal of Social Work, 31,* 385–397.

Holguin, G., & Hansen, D.J. (2003). The 'sexually abused child': Potential mechanism of adverse influences of such a label. *Aggression and Violent Behavior, 8,* 645–670. doi: 10.1016/ S1359-1789(02)00101-5.

Irish, L., Kobayashi, I., & Delahanty, D.L. (2010). Long-term physical health consequences of childhood sexual abuse: A meta-analytic review. *Journal of Pediatric Psychology, 35,* 450–461.

Maniglio, R. (2009). The impact of child sexual abuse on health: A systematic review of reviews. *Clinical Psychology Review, 29,* 647–657.

McConkey, N. (1992). Working with adults to overcome the effects of sexual abuse: Integrating solution-focused therapy, systems thinking, and gender issues. *Journal of Strategic and Systemic Therapies, 11,* 4–19.

Pereda, N., Guilera, G., Forns, M., & Gomez-Benito, J. (2009). The international epidemiology of child sexual abuse: A continuation of Finkelhor (19994). *Child Abuse & Neglect, 33,* 331–342.

Russell, D.E. (1983). The incidence and prevalence of intrafamilial and extrafamilial sexual abuse of female children. *Child Abuse & Neglect, 7,* 133–146.

Van Toledo, A., & Seymour, F. (2013). Interventions for caregivers of children who disclose sexual abuse: A review. *Clinical Psychology Review, 33,* 772–781. doi: 10.1016/ j.cpr.2013.05.006.

Volokh, E. (2015). Statutory rape laws and ages of consent in the U.S. Retrieved on from https://www.washingtonpost.com/news/volokh-conspiracy/wp/2015/05/01/ statutory-rape-laws-in-the-u-s/?utm_term=.e8a9b59f4e54.

Whitelock, C. F., Lamb, M. E., & Rentfrow, P. J. (2013). Overcoming trauma: Psychological and demographic characteristics of child sexual abuse survivors in adulthood. *Clinical Psychological Science, 1,* 351–362. doi:10.1177/2167702613480136.

12 Childhood Trauma

■ JOHNNY S. KIM, JACQUI VON CZIFFRA-BERGS,
AND STACEY ANNE WILLIAMS

■ ADVERSE CHILDHOOD EXPERIENCES

When dealing with childhood trauma and adverse childhood experiences, SFBT can be implemented as a protective or restorative measure to help children improve their resiliency and ability to adapt to difficult circumstances. Child maltreatment and abuse can result from a myriad of circumstances including (but not limited to) physical or emotional neglect, physical abuse, psychological abuse, sexual abuse, bullying, or individual events that the child finds traumatic. This chapter will look at the prevalence of Adverse Childhood Experiences (ACEs), what happens when incidents are compounded, the societal and economic impacts of childhood trauma, and bullying during childhood. We will explore how the SFBT model can be used to help children to cope and reframe negative thoughts or experiences into positive and growth-oriented ones.

One common approach to measuring childhood adverse experiences is by administering an ACE survey asking if, during a person's childhood, they ever experienced various traumatic events. These questions are an adaptation of a survey used as part of the ACE study by Kaiser Permanente and the Centers for Disease Control and Prevention (CDC) that looked at 17,000 adults in the United States. The ACE study originally focused on identifying the prevalence of 10 categories of stressful, traumatic childhood experiences in a typical middle-class adult population and exploring what long-term effects these experiences had on the individual (Felitti & Anda, 2014). The 10-category ACE study included: psychological abuse by parents, physical abuse by parents, sexual abuse by anyone, emotional neglect, physical neglect, alcohol/drug use in the home, divorce or loss of biological parent, depression or mental illness in home, mother treated violently, and imprisoned household member. These categories are equally divided between two constructs: aspects of child maltreatment and parental or family incapacities (Finkelhor, Shattuck, Turner, & Hamby, 2015). Thus, an ACE score was the summation of each category that an individual experienced and ranged from zero (no incidents or events in any of the categories) to 10 (incident or event in every category).

Results from the ACE study, which was conducted between 1995–1997, found a surprising number of adults reported traumatic life experiences in their childhood and adolescence than originally understood (Felitti et al., 1998). However, the ACE study used a sample of adults who grew up in the 1950s and 1960s, and the questions in the survey were based on individual and societal concerns that may not reflect current childhood adverse experiences. Recognizing this limitation, researchers have recently proposed additional categories to the original ACE scale to expand on the original study and update it for current widely recognized childhood adversities. A study by Finkelhor, Shattuck, Turner, and Hamby (2015) updated the original ACE scale and found four additional categories that helped improve the ACE measure in predicting health outcomes. The revised inventory of ACEs now includes the original 10 categories but also questions around bullying/peer victimization, isolation/peer rejection, exposure to community violence, and low socioeconomic status. As the previous chapter focused on the trauma of sexual abuse, this chapter will focus on the childhood trauma of bullying in particular.

■ ACEs AND NEGATIVE HEALTH OUTCOMES

Why measure an ACE score? Research has found that there are serious consequences to the body's physical health and well-being as well as to the mental health of persons who have experienced traumatic experiences at a young age. This research shows a strong correlation between adverse childhood experiences and increased use of health-care services, poorer academic and memory outcomes, increased likelihood of substance abuse and risky behaviors, depressive disorders, anxiety disorders, and poor long-term health outcomes including diabetes, hypertension, heart disease, and obesity (Habetha et al., 2012; Chartier, Walker, & Naimark, 2010; Anda et al., 2006). The likelihood of having multiple health problems later in life is compounded by the subject reporting multiple ACEs. Chartier and colleagues (2010) note that the odds of having multiple health problems increased by 22% when individuals reported one adverse experience, 48% when individuals reported two, and by 172% for individuals reporting five or six experiences when compared to those with no adverse childhood experiences.

■ SOCIETAL AND ECONOMIC IMPACT OF CHILDHOOD TRAUMA

To get a general idea of the economic consequences of childhood trauma, it would be necessary to get a comprehensive scope of all costs associated with direct *and* indirect consequences of childhood trauma, including immediate medical needs, long-term health conditions (mental, emotional, or physical), child welfare, special education, and costs associated with the criminal justice system, as an example. Estimates from different countries and agencies vary due to their sensitivity and what "costs" they include or exclude. This means that estimates of the true long-term economic impacts vary by what the researchers choose to include as relevant costs and by what factors they forget to consider, choose to exclude, or do not consider relevant enough for inclusion.

For example, one study suggests that the total cost of fatal and nonfatal child maltreatment within the United States during one year was somewhere between $124 billion and $585 billion (Fang, Brown, Florence, & Mercy, 2012). Another study estimated societal costs to approximate $104 billion for one year within the United States. Estimates from Canada reach $15.7 billion in a year, while Australia reports that follow-up for child maltreatment in one year cost between $4 billion and $10.7 billion (Habetha et al., 2012; McCarthy et al., 2016). Without having a comparative analysis across various countries and regions that use the same methodology and the same indicators of loss across economies, it is impossible to get an accurate picture of the full economic impact that childhood trauma and maltreatment has on society today. The National Children's Alliance reported that in 2015, over 300,000 children were served by children's advocacy centers nationwide. They estimate that 702,000 children were victims of maltreatment, abuse, and neglect during the year 2014 (the National Children's Alliance, NCA, is the national association and accrediting body for children's advocacy centers nationwide).

■ BULLYING AS A TRAUMA EXPERIENCE

Although an age-old problem for youth across the globe, bullying gained significant recognition and began to be a focus of empirical research during the 1970s. Reports of suicide and suicide attempts are splashed across the media as a call to action in dealing with the current issue in face-to-face interactions and as a result of the rise of bullying via social media and the Internet (Hymel & Swearer, 2015). At times, bullying has been reported as the cause of serious incidents of retaliatory harm against individuals and against groups that have contributed to the distress and emotional, physical, social, and educational harm of the victims (Horner et al., 2015). High-profile cases, such as the 1998 Columbine massacre in the U.S. state of Colorado, have received both national and international attention and demonstrate the deep need that schools and parents have for dealing with this epidemic, which the Centers for Disease Control and Prevention and the Department of Education have recognized as a public health concern affecting youth (Horner et al., 2015; Hymel & Swearer, 2015). In fact, the effects of bullying on victims have shown to have both immediate effects as well as delayed long-term effects that can last into adulthood, prompting depressive issues, high risk of substance use, and suicidal ideation or attempts (Zhou et al., 2017).

In a 2016 study of 5,784 students in the United States, 27.6% reported at least one incident of bullying within the last year. Of those who reported being bullied, 16.2% reported being bullied either one to two times per week or daily (Vidourek, King, & Merianos, 2016). In a study on bullying and victimization in Chinese children, 15% to 30% of children are reported to experience bullying (Zhou et al., 2017). Youth who have been bullied show negative effects such as avoiding school, truancy, eating disorders, depression, poor self-esteem, suicidal ideation, suicide attempts, anxiety, fear, difficulty concentrating, loss of trust and relationships, and poor academic performance (Horner et al., 2015). If this prevalence of bullying is compounded by the fact that many students have already experienced one or more adverse childhood experiences at home, individuals may benefit from strategic interventions, such as SFBT, which aim to build resiliency.

■ HOW WE REALIZED THAT SFBT WORKED WITH CHILDHOOD TRAUMA

Counseling children and adolescents around traumatic events poses added challenges for any professional clinician. Developmentally, they are different from adults, and other considerations must be factored in counseling sessions. For example, older adolescents often struggle for independence and autonomy and may be reluctant to share any personal thoughts or feelings with parents or caretakers. Additionally, children and adolescents are often brought to counseling by others and thus can be viewed as mandated clients who may be reluctant to meet with clinicians. Children and older adolescents also experience intense emotions due to developmental and hormonal changes and may have a difficult time with emotional regulation (Matulis, Resick, Rosner, & Steil, 2014). Depending on their age and development, children may not possess the skills to talk through traumatic experiences. This can be partly from the fact that they are not developmentally advanced enough to verbalize certain feelings and emotions; or it may be because the impact of the trauma is such that it overwhelms the brain and prevents verbalization and analysis that several other therapy modules require (SAMHSA, 2013).

Fortunately, SFBT is a well-suited therapeutic approach for working with children and adolescents who have experienced traumatic events. Solution-focused clinicians strive to talk at the level of the child and ask questions about coping strategies and what the child did correctly during difficult times. The collaborative and empowering questions clinicians ask help to build self-worth and self-efficacy by reframing traumatic events. Another strength of SFBT is the clinician can avoid retraumatizing the child by staying solution and resilience focused. For many children, talking about trauma (problem-focused) can inadvertently retraumatize a child; however, focusing on the child's best hopes or preferred future, recalling exceptions and amplifying coping and strengths leads to posttraumatic success (Bannink, 2014) and resilience building.

SFBT is a good fit when working with children that have experienced trauma as solution-focused clinicians are more concerned about the child's best hopes or preferred future, finding strengths and positive coping strategies than spending time recalling details about the trauma or traumatic events as this is not necessary for positive therapeutic outcomes. This emphasis on their best hopes and preferred future can make the counseling session more comfortable for children who often don't want to talk with strangers about their problems or worries. Rather than spending several sessions trying to establish rapport before shifting the counseling focus on the traumatic problems, SFBT can begin in the first session to discuss with the child what they want and ways they've been successful in the past with similar problems.

■ CASE STUDY OF SFBT AND THE CHILDHOOD TRAUMA OF BULLYING

Trauma touches the lives of children in much the same way it affects adults (King, 2017), and therefore our application of SFBT still follows the same process. The only difference is that the clinician asks questions in a more playful and simplistic way. This chapter describes the application of SFBT using the solution-focused art gallery (as discussed in Chapter 3) with a nine-year-old girl named Renni (her name has been changed for confidentiality purposes). Renni is experiencing harsh verbal bullying at her school, and as a result of this traumatic experience her grades are getting worse, she is starting to withdraw socially, and has started showing signs of refusal to attend class. Children that are being bullied are far more likely to fear school and perceive being less popular and less accepted (Vidourek, King, & Merianos, 2016). To illustrate the application of SFBT in a session with Renni, we have broken the session up into the solution-focused art gallery to illustrate Renni's best hopes, discover her strengths, create a virtual dress rehearsal for change, and invite her to keep doing what works.

■ THE BEST HOPES ROOM

The most important aspect of SFBT is discovering the client's desired outcome. Just because the client is a child that has experienced something traumatic does not mean the child does not know what they want to change in their lives. However, children who have experienced trauma often answer the desired outcome question with the assumption that the clinician will fix it for them or that others will change their behavior. The best-hopes question is often answered with an external goal. Often the child will answer the best-hopes question by saying things like, "Tell the other children to stop hurting me." This is a valid and reasonable goal that the clinician can work toward after the session. However, this sort of request shifts the focus away from the client and is not within the client's control. Our job as SFBT clinicians is to turn the external goal into an internal goal. As clinicians we need to explore the child's strategy by asking such questions as "Suppose I did go talk to the other children, what difference would that make to you?" This is to help the child determine what the desired outcome (internal goal) will be. Redirecting the focus back to the child's internal goal does not mean the clinician ignores the child's request for assistance but rather explores other strategies the child can use to help deal with traumatic experiences such as bullying. Below is an excerpt of the session held with Renni that helps demonstrate this idea:

CLINICIAN: So, Renni, what would you like to talk about today?

RENNI: Well the children have been bullying me and calling me names. They have been calling me crazy and cuckoo because I do not have the same religion as them, and I do not celebrate Christmas.

CLINICIAN: So the children have been calling you names and this hurts?

RENNI: Yes, very much.

CLINICIAN: Renni, I was just wondering what do you want to get or achieve by talking to me today? What can we do that is helpful?

RENNI: I just want you to go tell those other children to stop bullying me. I just want this all to stop.

CLINICIAN: It sounds Renni as if you have really been thinking about this. And it sounds as if you have already started making plans, like talking to me; because you really want this to stop. And it sounds as if you are really determined to have this all resolved.

RENNI: Yes.

CLINICIAN: And it sounds as if you have been thinking about how to get this to stop.

RENNI: I have, yes.

CLINICIAN: Suppose Renni, suppose I did go to those children and I spoke to them about respecting one another. What would be different for you?

RENNI: Well, I would just feel more free if they were not bullying me, more confident, more brave.

CLINICIAN: Wow, so you would feel more free?

RENNI: Yes.

CLINICIAN: And more confident and more brave?

RENNI: Yes.

■ THE RESOURCE ROOM

Once we know what the heart's desire or desired outcome is, we can move into the resource room to discover the child's strengths and resources during the traumatic event. This is the room where we can also find exceptions, which refer to the times when the child has coped well in the past. In this room, the SFBT clinician selectively listens to any signs of resilience, strength, and success. These resources and strengths might be evident in how the child coped during the trauma or visible in past experiences. In Renni's case, the counselor can talk with the other kids about their bullying behavior, but in the session needs to also focus on what resiliencies Renni brings. The resource room is filled with strengths and beautiful strategies she implemented in a previous scenario.

CLINICIAN: Renni, I am just wondering if you have ever had a time here at school where you have felt free, have felt more confident, and where you have felt brave.

RENNI: Yes, well (pause) when I was singing in the school concert.

CLINICIAN: Wow, tell me a little about that.

RENNI: Well it was a solo, and I had to sing all by myself.

CLINICIAN: Really? Wow, how did you get it right to do that? How did you get it right to stand in front of all those people and sing and be so brave?

RENNI: Well, I just thought to myself I should just pretend that I am singing to my mom like I was when I was practicing.

CLINICIAN: So you spoke to yourself and decided you are going to pretend you are singing to your mom?

RENNI: Yes.

CLINICIAN: And what else did you do to become brave and confident?

RENNI: I thought it was only me, and I sort of put a bubble around myself.

CLINICIAN: You did! That is such a good idea. I would like to find out more about that. So you stood in front of all the people and they were all out there, and you pretended to sing to your mom and put a bubble around yourself. Tell me about that . . . how does that work?

RENNI: Well, the bubble it is around me (playfully motions with her hands that a protective bubble is circling around her), and I am inside and I can pretend I am looking into the mirror and it is just me (smiles).

CLINICIAN: Amazing, so you put a bubble around you, and you can then pretend it is just you? And when you look in the mirror what happens?

RENNI: Well, when I look in the mirror I know it is just me.

CLINICIAN: Wow, so tell me how does the bubble work when you walk in front of all these people on stage?

RENNI: Well I just put my bubble on and think this is my moment, and I am not going to think about what everyone else is saying about me (shakes head). I just put the bubble on and just sing.

CLINICIAN: So you said to yourself I am going to put the bubble on, this is my moment, and I do not care what others say about me and you just do it.

RENNI: (Laughs) yes.

CLINICIAN: And it worked?

RENNI: Yes (giggles).

■ THE PREFERRED FUTURE ROOM

Once the strengths and resources of the child have been identified and amplified, it is important to create a virtual dress rehearsal of the preferred future in a playful way. Playing out scenes where the desired outcome *has already been* achieved creates an experience where the child is resilient, already coping, and where things are already different.

CLINICIAN: Renni, I want to do a little scaling question with you, and this is how it works. I am going to draw it on this piece of paper in pink; you like pink don't you?

RENNI: Yes.

CLINICIAN: We are going to draw a zero and at the other end of the line a 10. And at the zero, we are going to put feeling sad, hurt, and bullied. And at the 10 we are going to put free and brave and covered in a bubble. Renni, I am just wondering before you came to chat with me, where were you on this scale?

RENNI: I was definitely zero.

CLINICIAN: And Renni where are you now? I haven't spoken to the children yet but where are you now?

RENNI: I think I am at about a six.

CLINICIAN: A six! Wow! So you have moved from a zero to a six even before we spoke to the class?

RENNI: Yes.

CLINICIAN: Wow! What helped you move from a zero to a six?

RENNI: I think just talking to you and you telling me about my bubble.

CLINICIAN: So talking to me has helped and reminding you of your bubble has helped?

RENNI: A lot yes.

CLINICIAN: I want to see your bubble please? Put your bubble on.

RENNI: (pretends to put her bubble around her with her hands)

CLINICIAN: So suppose we pretend that my hands are mean words coming at you OK, is your bubble on (I pretend my hands are words coming towards Renni)?

RENNI: Wait let me get it on (wraps her arms around herself and playfully puts her bubble on).

CLINICIAN: OK, here it comes, "You are cuckoo."

RENNI: (Blocks the words—my hands—with her hands)

CLINICIAN: Wow, you pushed that away very fast. OK here are more, "You are funny and strange because of your . . ."

RENNI: (Blocks the words—my hands—immediately)

CLINICIAN: Wow your bubble really works. I did not even finish my sentence.

RENNI: (Laughs)

CLINICIAN: What is it like having such a powerful bubble?

RENNI: I feel much better. The words aren't getting to me.

CLINICIAN: That's right you are inside your bubble and it is protecting you.

RENNI: (Nods)

CLINICIAN: So Renni, what must you do different at school to move from a six to a seven?

RENNI: I think when the bullies are bullying me, I must just put on my bubble and block it (pretends to put her bubble on again).

CLINICIAN: That's right!

RENNI: I can stop it easily, it is just their mean words. I am the good one.

CLINICIAN: Show me again.

RENNI: (Pretends to put her bubble on)

CLINICIAN: (Making waves with her hands again as if her hands are words) "You are different and wei. . . ."

RENNI: (Blocks the words—my hands—immediately)

CLINICIAN: Wow this bubble works well.

■ THE SUMMARY AND TASK ROOM OR GIFT SHOP

Ending the session with a selective summary of the child's resilience and amazement amplifies the best resilient version of the child. Inviting the child to do more of what works builds and empowers the child and creates a gift of posttraumatic growth.

CLINICIAN: That's right you are the brave one, this is your moment to shine and be the star. I am so proud of you for coming to talk with me today, you are incredibly brave. I am so impressed by your incredible plans and for making a decision that this has to stop. Also, Renni, I am so impressed with the power of your bubble. It is strong and powerful and it works. Renni, I want to invite you to try something for me.

RENNI: Yes, yes I will.

CLINICIAN: I want you in this week to come, to put on your bubble, to keep it on, make sure it is always there and to come back and tell me what is different. OK?

RENNI: OK, I will.

■ SUMMARY

Children are creative and have a natural way of bouncing back and adapting. Treating childhood trauma, and in particular bullying, in a solution-focused way is respectful and takes children's strengths and feisty natures into consideration. Focusing on the strengths and resilient behavior of children helps them see themselves as strong, clever, and able to cope. Playing out the preferred future as if it has already happened builds children to perceive themselves as tough and flexible instead of broken and damaged. Even though SFBT is a model of questions, it can be applied in a playful way to guide children toward the answers within themselves and recognize their clever ideas in dealing with difficult situations. Despite their pasts, these children can still go on to become proud individuals.

■ REFERENCES

Anda, R. F., Felitti, V. J., Bremner, J. D., Walker, J. D., Whitfield, C., Perry, B. D., et al. (2006). The enduring effects of abuse and related adverse experiences in childhood. *European Archives of Psychiatry and Clinical Neuroscience, 256*(3), 174–186. doi:10.1007/s00406-005-0624-4

Bannink, F. (2014). Post-traumatic success. *Post-traumatic success*. New York: W. W. Norton.

Chartier, M. J., Walker, J. R., & Naimark, B. (2010). Separate and cumulative effects of adverse childhood experiences in predicting adult health and health care utilization. *Child Abuse & Neglect, 34*(6), 454–464. doi:10.1016/j.chiabu.2009.09.020.

Fang, X., Brown, D. S., Florence, C. S., & Mercy, J. A. (2012). The economic burden of child maltreatment in the United States and implications for prevention. *Child Abuse & Neglect, 36*(2), 156–165. doi:10.1016/j.chiabu.2011.10.006

Felitti, V. J., & Anda, R. F. (2014). The lifelong effects of adverse childhood experiences. In D. L. Chadwick, A. P. Giardino, R. Alexander, J. D. Thackeray, & D. Esemio-Jenssen (Eds.), *Chadwick's child maltreatment: Sexual abuse and psychological maltreatment* (Vol. 2, 4th ed.). Florissant, MO: STM Learning.

Felitti, V. J., Anda, R. F., Nordenberg, D., Williamson, D. F., Spitz, A. M., Edwards, V., et al. (1998). Relationship of childhood abuse and household dysfunction to many of the leading causes of death in adults: The Adverse Childhood Experiences (ACE) study. *American Journal of Preventive Medicine, 14*, 245–258.

Finkelhor, D., Shattuck, A., Turner, H., & Hamby, S. (2015). A revised inventory of adverse childhood experiences. *Child Abuse & Neglect, 48*, 13–21.

Habetha, S., Bleich, S., Weidenhammer, J., & Fegert, J. (2012). A prevalence-based approach to societal costs occurring in consequence of child abuse and neglect. *Child and Adolescent Psychiatry and Mental Health, 6*(35), 1–10. doi:10.1201/b18768-5.

Horner, S., Asher, Y., & Fireman, G. (2015). The impact and response to electronic bullying and traditional bullying among adolescents. *Computers in Human Behavior, 49*, 288–295. doi:10.1016.j.chb.2015.03.007

Hymel, S., & Swearer, S. (2015). Four decades of research on school bullying: An introduction. *American Psychologist, 70*(4), 293–299. doi:10.1037/a003828

King, P. K. (2017). *Tools for effective therapy with children and families: A solution focused approach*. New York: Routledge

Matulis, S., Resick, P.A., Rosner, R., & Steil, R. (2014). Developmentally adapted cognitive processing therapy for adolescents suffering from posttraumatic stress disorder after childhood sexual or physical abuse: A pilot study. *Clinical Child and Family Psychology Review, 17,* 173–190.

Mccarthy, M. M., Taylor, P., Norman, R. E., Pezzullo, L., Tucci, J., & Goddard, C. (2016). The lifetime economic and social costs of child maltreatment in Australia. *Children and Youth Services Review, 71,* 217–226. doi:10.1016/j.childyouth.2016.11.014.

Substance Abuse and Mental Health Services Administration (SAMHSA). (2013). Tips for talking with and helping children and youth cope after a disaster or traumatic event: A guide for parents, caregivers, and teachers. *HHS Publication No. SMA-12-4732*. Retrieved from http://store.samhsa.gov/shin/content//SMA12-4732/SMA12-4732.pdf.

Vidourek, R. A., King, K. A., & Merianos, A. L. (2016). School bullying and student trauma: Fear and avoidance associated with victimization. *Journal of Prevention & Intervention in the Community, 44*(2), 121–129. doi:10.1080/10852352.2016.1132869.

Zhou, Z-K., Liu, Q-Q., Niu, G-F., Sun, X-J., & Fan, C-Y. (2017). Bullying victimization and depression in Chinese children: A moderated mediation model of resilience and mindfulness. *Personality and individual differences, 104,* 137–142. doi: 10.1016.j.paid.2016.07.040

13 Loss, Grief, and Bereavement

■ CARLA P. SMITH AND
ADAM S. FROERER

■ OVERVIEW AND CONCEPTS

Loss, grief, and bereavement are experiences and processes that transcend time, culture, and identity. While oftentimes a struggle to process, these facts of life bind human experiences together. At the same time, loss and subsequent grief and bereavement are so unpredictable and often life changing that treatment has to look as diverse as the people experiencing these symptoms. Over generations, people have been exposed to death, illness, abuse, genocide, war, abandonment, unexpected family transitions, and other severe loss and trauma that has greatly changed the trajectory of their lives and that of future generations. While you have read (or will read) about some of these phenomena as they relate to trauma, this chapter explores the impact of grief, loss, and bereavement as it pertains to illness and death.

Trauma expands the notion of loss; it includes many experiences such as abuse, maltreatment, exposure to tragic events, war, genocide or ethnic cleansing, among other things. The impact of trauma on the lives of victims can be severe if left untreated. The pain of trauma can cause loss and impairment for victims as they navigate the residual psychosocial symptoms associated with the experience(s). Due to these struggles, victims can have a lifetime of exposure to additional trauma, broken relationships, and failed attempts at positive development across the lifespan. Families exposed to trauma—either collectively or through individuals family members—experience the same breakdowns. For both individuals and families, trauma impacts the mind, body, and spirit in ways that tend to change people's personalities, identities, and connections with others.

Therapeutic treatment for experiences of loss, grief, and bereavement vary depending on client needs and the clinical approach of the helping professional. Clinicians who use SFBT aid clients working through these significant, life-altering struggles by focusing on strengths and resilience and exceptions to the problem in the face of what clients may describe as the most difficult periods in their lives: times that bring problems they are unsure how to handle. We present a case illustration of loss where SFBT is used to help a young client focus on her strengths and building solutions for the future while enduring the illness and death of her mother. First, we explore the concepts of grief, loss, and bereavement, highlighting the experience of death of a parent, and the cultural implications.

■ LOSS, GRIEF, AND BEREAVEMENT

Loss and subsequent grief and bereavement inevitably change the life and trajectory of those who experience them. While there are various types of loss, common threads in experiences of grief after loss can be emotional, psychological, physical, and/or relational in nature. Living with the pain of loss and reconciling grief are difficult but necessary skills for human beings to uncover within themselves. Culture, history, and lived experiences greatly impact these skills and the timing with which they are acquired. Factors such as race, ethnicity, nationality, sexual orientation, and class impact the ways people grieve loss. Recent events such as the black communities' confrontations with the police in the United States, or in the civil war in Syria, highlight how context and sociohistorical factors impact grief.

In the United States in 2015 over four million children received Social Security benefits due to one or both parents being disabled, retired, or deceased (Social Security Administration, 2016). While all of these are types of loss, a large portion of the benefits go to children who have dealt with the death of at least one parent. The purpose of the benefit is to compensate for the expected financial strain on families, particularly children, that occur when a parent dies. Much research, time, and attention have gone toward identifying the risks for children who have lost a parent to death. Loss through death is a significant contributor to the trauma and grief individuals and families experience throughout their lifetime. Even though the United States focuses on the financial strain caused by the death of a parent, psychological stressors are even more significant. Attachment, behavior, trust, and connections in other relationships are just some of the ways individuals' lives are affected when a parent dies.

Even outside of death, loss and grief are inevitably tied to trauma. Traumatic experiences are distressing and cause a great deal of struggle and change in the lives of victims. Similar to loss and grief, the disturbance that trauma causes is subjective and therefore different between individuals; even individuals who experience the same type of trauma or experience it with other people (i.e., in a family system) can have unique responses. Traumatic loss—sudden, violent, or unexpected death/loss—brings about added stressors that complicate grief and the bereavement process; it also brings about a context that impacts the systems involved.

Loss

The term *loss* can encompass a great variety of experiences. Loss, as a general term, refers to the actual (or perceived) experience/process of losing something or someone (Oxford Dictionary, 2016). The literature on the human experience of loss describes specific categories such as acute traumatic loss, unexpected/sudden loss, and ambiguous loss (Boss, 1999). The diversity in the terms and definitions used to describe loss is indicative of the diversity in human experiences. The subjective nature of experiences of loss allows people to define for themselves what constitutes loss in general.

Ambiguous loss is a relatively new idea explored in the literature that expands the more traditional view of what constitutes loss. Ambiguous loss describes loss of someone or something that may still be physically present but is somehow psychologically lost or adversely affected (Boss, 1999). With this type of loss, the traditional rituals people engage in to begin the process of closure (i.e., funerals, death certificates, etc.) are not performed. Ambiguous loss is a type of loss that often goes unnoticed, due to the absence of "proof" of loss and thus a reason to grieve. Boss (2009) explored dementia as a type of ambiguous loss, where family members are not grieving the physical loss of their loved one but rather the loss of who the loved one was before the illness. For children and adults alike, ambiguous loss is a confusing and frustrating experience that can often be ignored by teachers or care providers as having an impact on daily functioning.

As children transition through the life cycle into adulthood, they acquire specific ways to cope with loss that are either helpful or detrimental to their overall well-being in processing loss. Adults tend to act toward loss in ways related to how they were conditioned as children within their environment growing up.

Grief

Grief is most often described as the emotional response to loss; it is the way people grieve that affects their daily lives. The ways an individual processes or "handles" the losses they face describes their grieving process. Similar to different kinds of loss, grief has many different forms. Complicated grief, unresolved grief, unattended grief are just three types of grief that affect people who experience loss differently; it depends on the context of the loss. Illness and/or death of a loved one, especially a parent, can bring on these and other types of grief that are challenging to navigate. Grief in general is already a complicated process, so whether it is a child, adolescent, or adult child of a parent who has died, the impact is significant.

All grief can lead to various psychosocial struggles, including dealing with anxiety, depression, attachment injuries, and relational breakdowns that can progress across the lifespan. Children who experience any type of grief can experience long-term consequences in their future relationships and mental health (McClatchy & Vonk, 2009). The cause of these consequences can begin with struggles to grieve a significant loss in the healthiest manner for that child. Adults also experience relational struggles or changes in sense of self as a result of grief, especially when their parent dies.

In hospice care, a lot of time and attention is given to the process of grief, especially for the family of the patient before and after their death. There are psychosocial teams in many hospice care agencies that are set up to work with the psychological, social, and spiritual impact of the illness, pending death, and actual death. Terminal illness and death disrupts individual and family functioning in such a way that normally harmonious families, for example, can become chaotic when a family member dies. As mental and spiritual health professionals work with families processing terminal illness, family secrets or conflicts that have been festering for years often surface. In these cases, families begin to grieve the loss of information they may not ever find out or the loss of a connection if they do find out particularly troubling facts.

These and other factors complicate the process of grief, but there are ways to attend to the various needs of individuals and families as they transition through the strong emotions of grief. Kübler-Ross's (1969) seminal work on the five stages of grief—denial, anger, bargaining, depression, and acceptance—brought attention to the complexity of grief. As clinicians work with their clients to process the grief they are struggling with, the complexity of the details or history can make clients (and therapists) feel stuck. SFBT instills a hope for a better future that can be created by the client (de Shazer & Dolan, 2007). So, while a client may still transition through the stages of grief, they do not have to be stuck there without knowledge of their strengths or ability to construct a future that rids them of the difficulty of it. The SFBT clinician also lets people process their grief in whatever way is right for them.

The truth is, grief and grieving can be arduous and life altering. It can be painful and distressing for a significant period of time, especially when there is little closure or circumstances that exacerbate the loss. It is the client's system that gets to decide what grief looks like for them. Therapist and client alike are affected by the society around them; however, the dominant discourse does not have to dictate how individuals and families grieve. The task of a solution-focused brief therapist—or any therapist for that matter—is to explore the meaning loss holds for their clients and identify the ways they would like their lives to be in the future (which is inherently influenced by this grief experience). It is through language that clients are able to establish their own control in their grieving process. Loss and subsequent grief both initiate bereavement.

Bereavement

Bereavement is the period of time when grief occurs; people who are grieving are the *bereaved*. Walsh and McGoldrick (2013) highlight the complexity of bereavement for family systems, instead of focusing on individual grief (as much of the literature on loss and grief does). The bereavement period can see emotional, mental, and physical changes that fluctuate from moment to moment and person to person. This fluctuation is easily triggered by objects (people, things, etc.) and moments in everyday life. For example, the (seemingly) simple smell of apple pie baking can trigger a memory and cause an emotional response. Loss does not just signify a person (or pet, ability, health, etc.) no longer being there; there are also moments, hopes, and plans that vanish. The bereavement period is complicated by the experiences of these lost moments. The systemic nature of bereavement creates a chain (or circular) influence that inevitably affects groups of people. A family, for example, is made up of individuals whose bereavement period is unique but that is experienced within the context of others. A daughter may be grieving the loss of her father, but her bereavement period is also affected as she comes into contact with her mother, who has lost her husband.

In hospice care, families are often provided bereavement counseling/care for over one year after the death of their loved one. This service is founded on the notion that there is no set time or process of bereavement and various things may trigger emotional, mental, or physical grief. The expectation is that at least one year of birthdays, holidays, anniversaries and the like will go by while the family is getting this extra support. Family members will also experience things like waking up, eating at a particular restaurant, and walking a certain route without that person.

Bereavement, just like grief, has no predetermined period of time, as people can mourn or experience the effects of loss for years or even a lifetime. SFBT provides a space for individuals and families to create their own meaning and construct a future that does not have to be negatively affected by loss. In the same way, they are able to create a meaningful future that reconciles their loss while highlighting their strengths.

■ USING SFBT IN TREATMENT OF LOSS, GRIEF, AND BEREAVEMENT

SFBT has a focus on language, which allows clients the space to produce their own meaning from the loss(es) they experience. SFBT therapists hold a nonjudgmental stance, do very little interpreting, and much more guiding using the boundaries clients set. Therefore, when it comes to loss, grief, and bereavement, clients are empowered to identify their loss and grief, give it meaning, and establish a view of how they want their bereavement process to unfold. They are also empowered to begin constructing a future that incorporates the loss but also highlights how they have successfully managed the grieving process.

The role of SFBT therapists is to remain change oriented and strengths based. SFBT therapists point to exceptions and previous solutions that clients may not readily be able to see on their own as they grieve (de Shazer & Dolan, 2007) and co-construct a description of themselves that includes details of what their lives will be like when they have successfully navigated this process. Equally importantly, SFBT therapists co-create a space with their clients where those clients can gain insight about their strengths and abilities to change a situation in which they feel they have very little control. Especially in cases of loss, people tend to feel powerless over their grief or the ways these losses will impact their future. SFBT situates the client in the driver's seat, highlights what is working (or what has worked in the past) to loosen the grip of grief, and helps to instill hope for a future the client wants in the face of the reality of loss.

When a client presents for therapy due to loss, grief, or bereavement, the problem is not so much that someone or something is gone but more so the process of grieving and managing that grief associated with this absence. Denial is absolutely a significant aspect of the grieving process that people move in and out of, but the process does not end there. The bereavement process can become problematic if or when people have difficulty deciding how they will move on from loss. Specific interventions such as the miracle question can be most helpful when clients have lost someone or something they cannot recover. Since it would not be realistic for the loss not to have occurred or for grief to miraculously disappear, asking a miracle question can resituate a client's brain to think more about how they would like life to be, given their new reality. Miracle questions "communicate respect for the immensity of the problem, yet at the same time leads to the client coming up with smaller, more manageable goals" (de Shazer & Dolan, 2007, p. 6).

SFBT lends itself well to clinical work with loss, grief, and/or bereavement because when clients construct solutions and identify exceptions they never saw on their own, hope replaces hopelessness. The overwhelming nature of loss, grief, and bereavement understandably blinds people to slight changes they can make to overcome problems. The SFBT therapist's job, then, is to listen for exceptions and validate work that is being done. Therapists that use SFBT can be found in many settings and can work around issues of loss, grief, and bereavement.

■ PRACTICAL APPLICATIONS OF THE SFBT APPROACH WITH LOSS, GRIEF, AND BEREAVEMENT

Just like in clinical work with trauma, issues of loss, grief, and bereavement are seen in many practice settings. Even when clients enter treatment with specific struggles, a brief history will uncover grief—whether reconciled or unreconciled—from loss(es) they have endured. Issues of loss are almost always relevant.

Practice settings such as hospice, palliative, and foster care agencies; substance abuse treatment facilities; and jails/prisons will have the highest volume of loss, grief, and bereavement struggles. At the same time, they can still be seen in hospitals, faith-based facilities, community-based agencies, and private practices as well. No matter the practice setting, SFBT can be applied as clients learn to manage the complexity of loss and grief.

The next section highlights specific questions that can be asked in SFBT sessions, whatever the practice setting may be.

Most Important Questions to Ask in SFBT Sessions

A session will be described below that illustrates using SFBT with clients managing loss and subsequent grief. This session will be structured consistent with the approach described in Chapter 3. This means that two questions (or lines of questions) will be most important during the session: (1) **What are your best hopes from this session?** and (2) the miracle question, as well as the other related questions that follow the initial question. In this specific case the miracle question took this form:

> I have a strange question for you. Suppose tonight a shift occurred and that instantly you were absolutely sure that you could live your own dreams and that you're living your life in a way that will lead you to Rutgers University. Suppose that you are feeling happy and simultaneously you know that you are living your life in a way that honors your mom's life. Suppose that because of this balance you are happy and fulfilled; what would be the very first sign or clue that would tell you that this shift had taken place and that you are now living your dreams and celebrating your mom's life?

The best-hopes question is vital to begin any SFBT session (as outlined in Chapter 3). Without knowing what the client would like as a result of the session, the therapist has no idea what kind of conversation should take place. If the therapist does anything before getting an answer from the client about his or her best hopes, then they are at risk of making assumptions, problem solving, or doing something useless or harmful to the client. Because this approach is all about the specific use of the client's language (without getting the answer to this question), the therapist is stuck and should not do anything else.

Once the "best hopes" approach has been established, the second most important question in any SFBT session is a preferred future question (most typically this comes in the form of the miracle question). The preferred future question should be crafted by the clinician using the client's exact words and should be exclusively about the immediate presence of the client's best hopes. Without the exact best hopes, a clinician cannot ask a sufficient preferred future question. Once the preferred future question has been asked (typically within the first 10 minutes of a session) the remainder of the session is used to get a very detailed description of this preferred future. With these two questions a therapist can conduct a meaningful SFBT session.

■ LOSS AND GRIEF SESSION UTILIZING SFBT

Below is a case that is based on an actual session familiar to both of the authors of this chapter. The client was seen by AF, but other family members were seen by CS. The authors consulted with each other about this case throughout the duration of the therapeutic relationship. The client, Zoe, is a 14-year-old Latina American. Zoe was referred to therapy with AF by her father due to the recent death of her mother, Katia, from bone cancer (three months prior to the first session). Zoe's mother was diagnosed with cancer about one year prior to her death, and her illness progressed quickly during that one-year period. Zoe's parents were transparent about the diagnosis and the progression of Katia's illness throughout the entire year. The family worked to make Katia's final months worthwhile and meaningful. Zoe commented that she often felt conflicted about "putting on a brave face" for her mom, and "feeling really sad that she was going to lose the one person that I thought I was always going to have."

Zoe is the younger sister to an older brother, Miquel (aged 16). Zoe's father, Robert, reported during the intake phone call that Zoe and Miguel are quite competitive with each other and constantly argue about who is right or wrong. The arguments, at times, get so fierce that Dad is unsure about how to intervene. Although the arguing occurred regularly before Mom's diagnosis and death, Dad reported that it seemed like the arguments had escalated since Katia's passing. Robert reported that "losing my wife has been really hard, and I'm trying all I can to help my kids through this difficult time, but the fighting and arguing has just gotten to be too much." Robert went on to mention: "I'm afraid that if Zoe and Miguel don't stop arguing, they will end up not even liking each other. They just lost their mother, I'm afraid they'll end up with no one, if they don't have each other."

Dad reported that although the arguing is tiresome and that he does worry about the long-term effect, he also remarked that the kids are also constantly pushing each other to do their best because of this competitive spirit. Robert commented that Zoe is naturally gifted in academic situations and that she is using that to challenge Miguel and his position. Dad reported that Miguel is hard on himself but also that he is also very capable. Dad reported that Miquel seems to argue and yell at Zoe to demonstrate that he still knows more than her.

Dad also reported that Zoe has struggled with the death of her mother and that he feels that Zoe has "lost her confidant and teammate." Dad reported that he and Miquel, "just naturally get along better" and that he has concerns that Zoe feels "left out and unsupported." Robert said, "I go out of my way to make sure that Zoe feels loved and that she still gets to do the things she likes, but I worry that without Katia's support, Zoe just feels like a third wheel a lot of the time." Dad also reported that he has been making a special effort to talk about Mom and the role she played in the family and how much he misses her, too. Dad commented that he has worked hard to commemorate the significant holidays and Mom's birthday during the past three months. He reports that he has been thoughtful about making sure that both kids know that it is OK to mourn Mom's loss but that he hopes he has also given them the message that "Mom would want us to celebrate her life!"

The session below is the first individual session with Zoe.

CLINICIAN: Hello, Zoe. It's nice to meet you (shaking hands). Can you tell me what your best hopes are from our meeting together today?

(The clinician will always begin the SFBT session with the "best hopes" question. This helps the clinician know what the client would like to get out of the session. Without being directed by the client about the desired outcome from the session, the clinician is not able to do anything else.)

ZOE: Hello, I'm not sure what you mean?

CLINICIAN: What are your hopes about what will occur as a result of our meeting today?

(The clinician repeats the "best hopes" question using different words to clarify for the client. Often clients, especially those managing trauma are not expecting to begin a session by talking about their desired outcomes. They have spent a significant amount of time thinking about or languaging the problem or the effect(s) of the trauma; but usually the client has not given much, if any time, languaging what they would like to be different. It is the job of the clinician helping clients managing trauma to begin languaging their desired outcome and preferred future (what they would like to be different in the future). This task begins with the first question of the session: "What are your best hopes?")

ZOE: Well, I'm not sure . . . I guess that I will start to feel better.

CLINICIAN: If you were able to start to feel better, what difference would that make for you?

ZOE: Well, I guess I wouldn't cry so much. I think you know, but my mom just passed away about three months ago. I've been crying a lot since then . . . well even before that really, and I would like to feel better.

CLINICIAN: Your dad did mention your mother's passing on the phone. I can understand why you've been crying. Can you tell me what you would like to be doing instead of crying so much?

(The clinician could have easily started talking about the mother's passing and the related trauma that has been experienced with this loss. However, it is important to note that the clinician used the client's exact language and invited the client to talk about her preferred/desired outcome instead of outlining the details of the loss and trauma.)

ZOE: Just being happy, I guess. Honoring my mom's life and memory instead of just mourning all of the time.

CLINICIAN: What would it look like if you were honoring your mom's life and memory?

ZOE: I don't think my mom would want me to be crying all of the time. She would push me to get on with life, live my dreams, and keep going. One of the things that she really pushed throughout the year she was sick was that I should keep going, not get down, and push through. I think my mom would be disappointed if she saw me so sad and crying all the time.

CLINICIAN: So, by living *your* dreams, you'll be honoring your mom's life and memory?

ZOE: Yeah, I think so. When I was younger, and while my mom was sick, I thought that I had to do the things that she had done. I thought that because she attended Harvard and Yale that I needed to do that to make her happy. Since she passed away I'm not sure that I really have to do that.

CLINICIAN: If you don't have to do what she did in order to be happy and to honor her memory, what tells you that living your own dreams will also be honoring your mom's life and memory?

(Again, note that the clinician uses the same language the client has already mentioned as part of her best hopes: "happy," "honor her memory," and "living your own dreams." The client is directing the clinician at each step of this session what to pay attention to that is related to the best hopes.)

ZOE: Well, I just figured out that I think I want to go to school at Rutgers University. I think they have a really good English program that I think might be really good. I have been talking to my dad since my mom died, and I think that I can live my dreams and do the things that I really want to do, and that mom will be proud of me, *because* I'm living my dreams. She won't be disappointed that I'm not doing the things that she did, but she'll be happy for me because I'm doing the things that will make me happy. I hadn't really thought about it like that before she died.

CLINICIAN: Zoe, that's really cool. I have a strange question for you. Suppose tonight a shift occurred and that instantly you were absolutely sure that you could live your own dreams and that you were living your life in a way that will lead you to Rutgers University. Suppose that you are feeling happy and simultaneously you know that you are living your life in a way that honors your mom's life. Suppose that because of this balance you are happy and fulfilled; what would be the *very first sign* or clue that would tell you that this shift had taken place and that you are now living your dreams and celebrating your mom's life?"

(It is important to note that this preferred future question is the second most important question of the session. The question is very specific to Zoe and is drawn directly from her best hopes: in fact the "miracle question" is simply the presence of Zoe's best hopes. Because SFBT is a language approach this question could not be asked of anyone else and is a culmination of the co-constructed conversation to this point. The preferred future question is completely void of the trauma and/or trauma symptoms because it is completely made up of the presence of Zoe's best hopes. It is also important to note that the rest of the session will be used to co-construct a detailed description of Zoe's preferred future.)

ZOE: Very first sign?

CLINICIAN: Yeah, the very first sign.

ZOE: I guess that I would feel happy and excited to start the day.

CLINICIAN: What time would it be when you woke up and felt happy and excited?

ZOE: I guess it would be 7:30.

CLINICIAN: What difference would it make to you on this day to wake up at 7:30 and feel happy and excited?

ZOE: Oh, it would make a huge difference. I wouldn't instantly be thinking about mom and how much she suffered. I wouldn't be thinking about how hard things are now that she's gone. It would be really different.

CLINICIAN: If you were happy and excited, what would you be thinking about instead?

(It is important to highlight that the SFBT clinician does not stop the client from talking about whatever she needs to talk about, including the problem. However, it is also important to know that one of the most important questions a SFBT clinician can ask clients to avoid further problem-talk is an "instead" question. Just like this example, after the client talks about the problem (i.e., thinking about difficult issues), the clinician asks what the client would like to be thinking about instead of these problematic things.)

ZOE: I guess that I would want to get out of bed and not just lay there all day long.

CLINICIAN: How different would that be for you, to want to get out of bed?

ZOE: That would be really different; I haven't been feeling like that since Mom died. I really miss her.

CLINICIAN: What would you do next on this day when you are feeling happy and excited to live your dreams?

ZOE: Well, I guess I would get up and get ready for school.

CLINICIAN: What would be different about the way you get ready for school on this day when you are living your dreams and you are at your best?

ZOE: Well, I think that I would be getting ready with determination. I wouldn't be dreading the day. I wouldn't be thinking about what was going to happen at school or if I was going to break down and cry during the day. I think I would just be excited for the day, and I would just be thinking about what I was going to wear and how I was going to do my hair . . . you know, just the normal stuff.

CLINICIAN: Who would be the first person to notice your determination, and your happiness, and your excitement?

ZOE: My dad.

CLINICIAN: What would your dad notice about you that would tell him your happiness and excitement are back and that you are feeling determined?

ZOE: I think he would see me smiling.

CLINICIAN: How would this determined smile be different?

ZOE: It would just be real. I wouldn't be faking it. I would just actually be smiling.

CLINICIAN: How would Dad react when he noticed this determined, real smile?

ZOE: He would be really happy.

CLINICIAN: And what would Dad do, without even saying a word, that would let you know that he had noticed the smile, but that he was happy to see you with this real smile on your face?

ZOE: He would smile back at me.

CLINICIAN: What would be different about the way Dad smiled at you on this morning when you are living your dreams and feeling determined?

ZOE: I don't know . . . I haven't thought about that before.

CLINICIAN: OK, if you take a minute now to think about it, what do you think?

ZOE: I guess his smile would be real, too. He wouldn't look weighed down. I think he would also have that real smile where I can see the dimple on his right cheek.

CLINICIAN: What impact would it have on you if you saw the real smile and dad's dimple again?

ZOE: It would be huge! I think it would help me to feel at peace and know that we were going to be alright.

CLINICIAN: How would seeing Dad's dimple again, and feeling peace help you know that today is a day when you can live your dreams and that you will be honoring your mom?

ZOE: I think I would know that Dad was giving me approval, really giving me approval to do what I know will make me happy.

CLINICIAN: That approval would be nice for you?

ZOE: Yeah, it would be really nice.

CLINICIAN: Would anybody else notice that you are feeling happy and determined, and that you are on the way to living your dreams?

ZOE: I guess Miguel would notice.

CLINICIAN: Miguel is your brother?

ZOE: Yeah.

CLINICIAN: What would Miguel notice about you on this day that would let him know that you are determined to live your dreams?

ZOE: I guess that we weren't fighting.

CLINICIAN: What would you be doing instead?

ZOE: Just being kind . . . you know trying to encourage each other instead of yelling at each other all the time.

CLINICIAN: How would Miguel respond on this day when you went out of your way to be encouraging to him?

ZOE: I think he would be suspicious actually?

CLINICIAN: What would tip him off that he didn't actually need to be suspicious, but that you were actually encouraging him?

ZOE: I think that if it kept going, I mean, if I didn't just do it one time and then stop.

CLINICIAN: Would you be happy to keep encouraging Miguel?

ZOE: Yeah, I don't really like to fight with him all the time, but that's just what we do.

CLINICIAN: So, on this day, when you are encouraging him, you would be happy with that?

ZOE: Yeah, that would be a good thing.

CLINICIAN: I have another hard question for you, on this day if your mom could let you know in some way that she was proud of you for living your own dreams and taking on this day in such a determined way, what would she notice?

ZOE: I think she would notice that I wasn't crying.

CLINICIAN: What would she notice you doing instead of crying?

ZOE: She would see me laughing.

CLINICIAN: Do you think she would be happy to see you laughing?

ZOE: Yeah.

CLINICIAN: Would she know that you were honoring and celebrating her life?

ZOE: Yeah, she really would.

The rest of the session continues in a similar way, the therapist and client continue co-constructing a detailed description of this miracle day. No other interventions or techniques are used. This conversation is viewed as the intervention and the only thing that needs to be done in order to create change. The session ends with a simple question from the therapist, "Zoe, do you mind keeping your eyes out for any of these clues that we talked about today? Can you just take note if you see any of the pieces of this change show up?"

■ CONCLUSION

Struggles with loss, grief, and bereavement can be seen both in and out of therapeutic practice. As a whole, our society is inundated with issues of grief, as daily images of loss flood social media and television. The complexity of these struggles can (and often do) change the life course of people who experience them. While these are life-altering struggles, SFBT can help build solutions where hope is not readily available to clients. The difficulties they suffer can often overwhelm their ability to identify a clear path to reaching their goals. However, a SFBT therapist can help guide them toward reconciling their loss and shifting the impact of grief. Just like with Zoe, miracles can become reality.

■ REFERENCES

Boss, P. (1999). *Ambiguous loss: Learning to live with unresolved grief.* Cambridge, MA: Harvard University Press.

Boss, P. (2009). The trauma and complicated grief of ambiguous loss. *Pastoral Psychology, 59,* 137–145. doi: 10.1007/s11089-0090264-0

de Shazer, S., & Dolan, Y. (2007). *More than miracles: The state of the art of solution-focused brief therapy.* New York: Routledge.

Loss. (2016). In *English Oxford Living Dictionaries Online.* Retrieved from https://en.oxforddictionaries.com/definition/loss.

Kübler-Ross, E. (1969). *On death and dying.* New York: Macmillan.

McClatchy, I. S., & Vonk, M. E. (2009). The prevalence of childhood traumatic grief—A comparison of violent/sudden and expected loss. *OMEGA, 59*(4), 305–323. doi: 10.2190/OM59.4.b

Social Security Administration (SSA). (2016). Beneficiary data: Social Security Administration. Washington, DC: SSA Publication No. 05-10085.

Walsh, F., & McGoldrick, M. (2013). Bereavement: A family life cycle perspective. *Family Science, 4*(1), 20–27. doi: 10.1080/194246220.2013.819228

14

Countering Systemic Retraumatization for Sex-Trafficking Survivors

■ CHRISTOPHER K. BELOUS AND
CARLA P. SMITH

Human trafficking has become a pervasive social issue that deeply impacts individuals, families, communities, and societies. The U.S. Department of State (2010) estimated that between 12 and 27 million adults and children are engaged in some form of slavery. Since an estimated 2.45 million people become victims of either domestic or transnational trafficking each year (Kutnick, Belser, & Danailova-Trainor, 2007), this billion-dollar industry is now the second-largest and fastest-growing criminal industry in the world (U.S. Department of State, 2010). Domestically, 14,500 to 17,500 foreign nationals are trafficked into the United States each year (U.S. Department of State, 2015) and hundreds of thousands of U.S. citizens are forced into labor, sex, or some other kind of slavery annually (Carter & Obadi, 2016).

These statistics show the far-reaching, pervasive nature of human trafficking and its impact on our global social climate. There are various types of human trafficking recognized by the U. S. Department of State (Trafficking in Persons Report, 2015): sex trafficking, child sex trafficking, forced labor, bonded labor/ debt bondage, domestic servitude, forced child labor, and unlawful recruitment and use of child soldiers. The Department of State reports, "'Trafficking in persons,' 'human trafficking,' and 'modern slavery' have been used as umbrella terms for the acts of recruiting, harboring, transporting, providing, or obtaining a person for compelled labor or commercial sex acts through the use of force, fraud, or coercion" (U.S. Department of State, 2015, p. 7). While there are various definitions and forms of trafficking or slavery, we will use the terms *human* and/or *sex trafficking* throughout this chapter, as we highlight the term and meaning of *systemic retraumatization*. We are using the pervasive, widespread, but often covert issue of human trafficking to serve as an example of systemic retraumatization to bring awareness to this issue in various settings.

Since the increase of focus and attention on human trafficking, government agencies, task forces, agencies, and committees have been formed in order to solidify definitions and create legislation around the issue. Governmental agencies, the legal system, law enforcement, counselors, therapists, and social work professionals are all engaging in research that influences the ways issues of human trafficking are uncovered and attended to for the victims/survivors and the perpetrators of this devastating social problem. Even though there is more attention to the global issue of human trafficking, understanding the individual experiences of survivors as they move through different systems after leaving a trafficking situation is still often neglected. Furthermore, much of the resources for managing this crisis are given to legal and law enforcement services, while agencies and organizations that provide clinical treatment are left to raise funds to operate and provide counseling services to these victims (Wellspring Living, 2016). Across the board, more attention should be paid to training helping professionals as they interact with survivors of human trafficking so that the systemic retraumatization these survivors face can be minimized.

Treatment of human/sex trafficking is complicated by the criminal nature of it. For example, similar to victims of physical or sexual abuse, there are many instances where perpetrators were once victims. There are other barriers survivors experience as they encounter various treatment settings. Language, culture, economic/financial survival, and lack of knowledge (such as ability to access social services, legal rights, and options for living arrangements, etc.) have been identified by some helping professionals as initial barriers that hinder survivors from receiving treatment they desperately need before and after leaving a trafficking situation (Carter & Obadi, 2016). Additional barriers experienced while seeking treatment include: inadequately trained clinicians, difficulty building trust, insufficient emotional and social support, and systemic retraumatization. These are all hurdles survivors have to battle as they attempt to heal the wounds suffered as a result of being trafficked.

The services for survivors of human trafficking focus mainly on crisis intervention (i.e., housing), domestic violence services (such as therapy), and legal advocacy for issues related to immigration or prosecution of traffickers. Medical services, family violence intervention, and community education/outreach are also types of services provided by agencies to meet the needs of survivors. There is a significant need for mental health services that provide trauma-informed, strengths-based treatment. Additionally, other professionals that come into contact with survivors (i.e., police officers, lawyers, physicians) should be exposed to training that will help them also provide their services from a trauma-informed, strengths-based approach. In preliminary discussions with stakeholders, we found lack of financial resources, the need to address crises, lack of adequate training for professionals, and general distrust of helping professionals by victims/survivors to be barriers to integration of mental health services into those services already provided. New counseling approaches that provide survivors of human/sex trafficking with strengths-based clinical treatment such as SFBT are necessary to not only address survivor's extensive trauma but also to help build solutions for a more hopeful future.

The remainder of this chapter will explore the definition and examples of systemic retraumatization, along with the importance of hope building in treatment. We also highlight the use of SFBT and ways of using this model when working with systemic retraumatization; we also provide a case illustration to display its use with an actual client struggling with trauma as a survivor of sex trafficking.

■ SYSTEMIC RETRAUMATIZATION

Survivors of human trafficking encounter various people as they move through "the system" once they escape or are rescued from a trafficking situation. Each person they encounter has the possibility of adding to or taking away from the trauma they have already experienced, even in ways that may seem insignificant. For example, the look on a nurse's face as they administer shots during an evaluation can either retraumatize or soften the experience for a survivor as they remember the traumatizing experiences of being drugged. *Systemic retraumatization* relates to the experience of continued trauma by the various systems survivors encounter after the initial traumatic experience or event. Survivors of rape have often discussed being retraumatized each time they had to recount the story of being raped to the police officer, the intake nurse at the hospital, a detective, a lawyer, and then to a clinician, so on and so forth. By the time clients enter treatment, they may have been retraumatized many times over by having to talk to countless professionals.

Many of these professionals, including clinicians, can look at survivors of human trafficking from a deficit point of view—identifying what is wrong with them first; some may even ask a question similar to, "What are you struggling with?" Police officers, for example, speak to victims of crimes because that is the nature of their job. Lawyers have jobs related to the justice system, which also insinuates something bad has occurred. Mental health clinicians often have an orientation that focuses on what is going wrong rather than what is going right in their clients' lives. It is this focus on the problem that can often be retraumatizing for those who have already experienced a traumatizing event. We believe a strengths-based perspective that is trauma informed is integral to decreasing experiences of retraumatization and increasing hope building. SFBT may only be for those practicing therapy services, but the fundamentals can be taught to other types of professionals who encounter victims of trauma. This shift in the ways professionals work with victims of trauma can possibly increase hope throughout the process, as well as increase feelings of positive self-worth while decreasing shame and contributing to better outcomes as they survive the initial traumatic event. Once professionals can view people for their strengths and their goodness—not their problems—seeds of hope can be planted.

■ IMPORTANCE OF HOPE BUILDING

We acknowledge that human trafficking is just one experience of severe trauma and that most people have experienced some form of trauma in their lives. These traumatic experiences have a way of diminishing—or even eliminating—hope for a future that is better or where the effects of the trauma no longer exists. Unfortunately, clinicians and other professionals have their own trauma stories that negatively affect their hope or ability to help others build hope. For example, a mental health professional who works with inmates is constantly inundated with stories of trauma and negativity by people who may either have life sentences behind bars or be spending much of their lives imprisoned. Vicarious trauma and burnout, along with their own experiences of trauma, may lead clinicians and other professionals to have difficulty identifying strengths, especially over time. Therefore, learning about how to build hope, along with helping professionals with their own hope building, is integral to the treatment of trauma. As we have noted, starting from a strengths-based perspective can lead to hope throughout the complicated journey of treatment.

For survivors of human trafficking, feeling hope is one of the first strengths to be diminished or eliminated by traffickers. This is because traffickers know that hope can lead to someone continuously attempting to find a way out of bondage. Therefore, they tend to do things like tell their victims they have overwhelming debt that will take years to pay off. Traffickers may also say that the victims are engaging in a crime that will get them put in jail if they speak to a police officer: for example, in order to dash any hope the victim may have for getting away or being set free. Traffickers understand that true hope is important in building a solution for change.

Traffickers understand the importance of hope, and helping professionals should first utilize this to counteract the barriers present for success in clinical treatment. SFBT grows from a foundation that everyone already has strengths inside them that can be utilized to build solutions for the better future they envision. Therefore, hope building is an important part of the process for use of SFBT with trauma victims. Focusing on building hope allows both client and clinician to explore what it will take to reach goals versus focusing on the things that have stopped them. To that end, SFBT is a model we believe can provide tremendous success for survivors of human trafficking as they navigate their journey of processing the traumatic experiences they have endured, while being reminded of the strengths that will allow them to build hope for the future they want for themselves.

■ HOW WE CAME TO USE SFBT WITH THIS POPULATION

As discussed above, there is a significant need for strengths-based treatment of trauma from human/sex trafficking. Given the various experiences survivors endure, from initial victimization through crisis intervention and sometimes treatment, clients are often overwhelmed with a low sense of self-worth, shame, and self-blaming thoughts and feelings. The strengths-based approach of SFBT is one that would most definitely allow survivors the space to uncover and be reminded of the value that is within them, while also helping them establish their own journey toward healing.

More specifically, the automatic expectation that *all* clients, even those with extensive involvement in human/sex trafficking situations, have significant strengths is a key SFBT stance. Secondly, providing space for clients to identify their own solutions, with assistance from the SFBT clinician, can empower them to make the small steps necessary to reach them. Highlighting strengths and empowering clients to build their own solutions can lead to a trusting therapeutic alliance, where clients experience their clinician making their desires priority while supporting them along the way.

For these reasons, SFBT as a trauma-informed, strengths-based model can provide hope and change where others believe there is none. The emphasis placed on the exceptions clients showed as they faced tremendous trauma and hardships is momentum generating; this because clients begin to see their own strengths through what they have endured and thus their shame decreases. They begin to look at what they *can* do versus what they are unable to do. In other words, SFBT can help loosen the grip of the traumatic experiences by showing clients what they are able to do first, rather than focusing on what has happened to them.

■ PRACTICAL APPLICATION OF SFBT

SFBT offers hosts of questions, phrases, statements, and treatment protocols that propose appropriate ways to incite resilience for client as part of the therapy process. For survivors of human/sex trafficking, and those who have been retraumatized through the system, discovering hope and resilience is paramount to success. Positivity toward the future, and a complimentary, trusting, and affirmative stance toward the client can lessen the impact of multiple traumatic instances and increase the possibility of positive processing and growth.

In working with survivors, some of the most important questions to ask are ones focusing on the future, on coping skills, and on building a positive outlook. Just as with any therapy approach, it is not all a series of questions to be asked that will lead to a miracle recovery. Sometimes, formulations are given by the clinician or the client that can be just as profound. A more thorough examination of formulations was discussed in Chapter 3. In order to highlight how SFBT questions and components are best used with survivors, we have written the remainder of this chapter as an integrated case study and discussion of techniques and theoretical formulation.

■ IMPORTANT SFBT QUESTIONS

The concept of hope is often central to the positive, future-oriented view of SFBT. In addition, hope is one of the elements of the common factors debate; a discussion about what elements contribute to change in therapy (Miller, Duncan, & Hubble, 1996). Most of what we have found helpful in our work with survivors, particularly those who have been retraumatized by the system, focuses on hope and the building of a positive orientation. Hope-focused and positivity-inspiring questions include coping probes, resilience highlighting through complimenting, and future-oriented discussions. Many other aspects of SFBT can increase hope and positivity as well—all of which are highlighted in our case example below.

■ CASE EXAMPLE

This case example is based on real-world lived experiences, and the words and quotes located herein are an amalgam of multiple clients in order to protect identity. The actual language used by the client(s) and situations they discuss are included, which may be surprising to some readers.

■ FINDING HOPE

A client, named Hope, was referred to us by a local court-appointed attorney, a public defender. The attorney stated on the phone, "She's a peach. She needs help, but won't get it. She acts like she can't trust anyone! . . . It will help her case if she has a diagnosis." After getting her contact information, an initial appointment was set up. The first author was her clinician, but her treatment team consisted of both therapists, the referring attorney, and her assigned case manager with the bureau of investigation. Little was known about Hope before she came in for her intake assessment. Her public defender previously sent over some paperwork that stated she had been a "victim of sex trafficking" and that she had been rescued in the Atlanta area from her pimp—but that she was not allowed to return to her family in New Mexico (where she grew up) because of the impending trial. Her safety could not be assured if she left the city. The following interactions took place during her first session.

CLINICIAN: It's nice to meet you, Hope . . . we spoke on the phone, what was it? A week ago, maybe? What's changed since then?

HOPE: Nothing. Absolutely nothing. I'm still here—the court people are making me stay. I have no idea when the court thing is. It's pissing me off.

CLINICIAN: Really? No one has told you anything? That is ridiculous!

HOPE: I know, right? What am I supposed to do? No one tells me anything.

CLINICIAN: That is really frustrating . . . this is your life, you should be able to at least know what is going on. Have you spoken with anyone about this?

As you can see, a formula-first session task question was asked during the intake, inquiring about how things have changed or have been altered since the initial phone call. However, in this instance, Hope was not able to see any changes in her life. She was focused completely on the negative situation she was in, and was unable to see any positivity. A natural *coping question* followed (dialogue continues from above).

HOPE: Of course not! Who do I have to talk to?

CLINICIAN: That sounds really lonely. How have you managed to make it through each day? Get your work done . . . continue on?

HOPE: I have to. What other choice do I have?

CLINICIAN: Well, you could have given up, but you didn't. You are still here, and you are still working to make your life better. How did you do that?

In this instance, it took a little more prodding than usual—I had to lead her a bit more than usual into finding some of her own resilience and strengths. Treatment with Hope continued for a while after the first session. She was awaiting the trial date for her case and was struggling with being on her own (away from her pimp and not directly connected with her family for support) for the first time in her adult life. She was 27 years old and had spent the last 12 years in a sex-trafficking ring. She was living on the go with her pimp who would regularly send her on international "assignments" with high-paying clientele. She was considered one of the best of her pimp's "girlfriends" and so was afforded many luxuries the other girls weren't—something she no longer received after being rescued.

HOPE: It's just such a fucking mess. This whole thing . . . like seriously. First I had to deal with being a fucking whore all those years, and now I may as well have traded one pimp out for another!

CLINICIAN: What do you mean? "Another pimp . . ."

HOPE: Yeah, for real. Like, my boyfriend would at least take care of me. I feel like I just got fucked.

CLINICIAN: You mean, you're not getting a fair deal now that you're out?

HOPE: Yeah, I'm living in a freakin' hotel . . . there are bugs and shit. I can't even eat what I want, I have to use these stupid voucher things . . .

CLINICIAN: That sounds pretty bad; but it can't be all bad, can it? Is there any part of your life now that is better than before?

Note, a modified *exception question* was used in the conversation above. The clinician was not focusing on a past circumstance but instead on a current condition overall. Hope was very negative about her current living situation, and the goal of the question was to gently nudge her into a more positive way of perceiving her situation.

HOPE: I mean, obviously, I'm not being beaten or having sex with random people all the damn time.
CLINICIAN: Mm hmm ... (nods)
HOPE: I just wish ... I don't know ... I just wish that I still had nice things. Like good food, a decent bed.
CLINICIAN: That sounds tough; you're going through a lot right now. Do you see any kind of light at the end of this? A resolution of some sort? Something to look forward to?

At the end of this segment is some positivity—a *future-oriented question* and statement. Throughout this part, Hope was unable to really see a point to what she was still doing in Atlanta or in therapy in general. She saw this as an extension of the system that was already holding her back and something that was retraumatizing, yet again, for her.

HOPE: I mean, I'm here. I have to be. They told me I have to come see you. I don't want to be here. If it were up to me, I'd be back in New Mexico.
CLINICIAN: I can understand that; you want to be back with your family and friends.
HOPE: I just think this is all ridiculous. Like tape me or whatever, then let me go, you know? I can take care of myself. The last thing I want to do is keep talking about this!
CLINICIAN: Is it really hard, having so many people talk to you about what's happened to you?
HOPE: Oh yeah, can you imagine? Seriously, I have to retell the same stories over and over. Everyone knows. They may as well take out a fucking billboard on the interstate with my damn face, "Look at her, the dumb bitch who fucked anyone with money for some pimp!" [she looks down, sighs, and appears emotional]
CLINICIAN: That's really tough. You feel that way? Like everyone knows your business and that they are all judging you?
HOPE: Wouldn't you?
CLINICIAN: (nods)
HOPE: And now, I need to talk to you about it, too! Another person, another dumb story time. What do you want to know, therapist man?

In this interaction, Hope started to open up a little but also got defensive and upset about having to re-discuss her situation with yet another helping professional. This led the clinician into needing to discuss a *non-pathologizing stance* and to focus not necessarily on the problem but instead to focus on the future.

CLINICIAN: I don't need to know exactly what happened to you, especially if it's not something you want to cover. I'm simply here to help you, that's all.

HOPE: Yeah, and 'cure' me? Help me with all my mental problems? Save the little whore who got herself trapped up in the life?

CLINICIAN: No, I don't see any of that. I see a strong woman who made it through a dangerous and life-altering situation to come out the other side a fighter.

HOPE: Yeah, OK. Sure. (eye roll, she looks down and is fiddling with some tissues in her hands) I mean, of course there is something wrong with me. I'm pretty much a giant piece of trash. That's how they all saw me. But whatever, you know? I mean I did let this happen to me, so I mean there has to be something wrong with me. That's what he always said anyway. It's my fault. There must be something wrong with me to have stayed with him for so long.

CLINICIAN: So that's what he said, not what you believe ... right? Just because he said that doesn't mean it's true. What do you believe about yourself?

HOPE: It must be true.

CLINICIAN: That can't be true. If it were, you would be in a landfill with other trash, right? You aren't trash, never could be. Those thoughts of you being 'trash' were told to you by him, yes? What do you actually think, now that you are out? What do you think you will be ... where will you be in two years? Five years?

HOPE: Well yeah, he told me that. I mean, I don't want to be trash. I think in a few years I'll be working at a regular job, hopefully home with family ...

CLINICIAN: What else? What will you be doing at this job?

HOPE: Well, this is silly, but ... I always wanted to do hair, you know? Like own a salon and like do people's hair. I got really good at it with the other girls ... they always came to me with questions and asked me to make them look good for their dates.

CLINICIAN: Awesome, so you have some significant talent then! That is an art form, really. How would you go about starting down that path?

In this interaction, our conversation shifted from one focused on her problem and the difficulties of her past, to something that would give her reason and purpose—*hope*—for the future. It shifted into discovering her strengths and eliciting more discussion around *complimenting* and *enforcing positive beliefs* about herself. I wanted to end the first session with Hope by trying to highlight her resilience in the face of this situation she has survived and how she is continuing to be traumatized—but still surviving and overcoming it.

CLINICIAN: Hope, I've heard a little bit about what you've been through, and I've worked with people who have come out of horrible situations like this in the past. I know it's a nightmare . . . literally hell on earth. I am wondering, how did you make it through it? How did you survive to sit here today?

HOPE: What do you mean?

CLINICIAN: I mean, you survived this. You were somehow strong enough not to get hurt to badly, or give in and end it, or any other nasty or bad scenario. How did you get here today?

HOPE: Well, I didn't have a choice—you know? I mean, it was either survive or die.

CLINICIAN: Yes, but how did you survive?

HOPE: I mean, I didn't really have a choice . . . I just did. I just knew that this wasn't going to be forever. I mean, there was no way I was going to have to do this that long . . . something was going to happen. Someone would rescue me, or I'd escape or something. Plus, I was always talking to the other girls, and at night, you know, I'd like pray and stuff. And I knew that this wasn't how my life was meant to be forever.

CLINICIAN: Wow, so you knew this wasn't the way it was meant to be.

HOPE: Oh, hell no! I knew it. I knew I'd get out of it.

CLINICIAN: That sounds like you had some pretty decent foresight . . . you knew you wouldn't be there and knew there was a light at the end of the tunnel.

HOPE: Oh yeah, that's all that kept me going.

CLINICIAN: Do you think you still have that perspective? Do you still see the light?

HOPE: Yeah, I mean, I feel like I'm in it now . . . I just have to cross this part to get out of it, you know?

CLINICIAN: Absolutely!

In this first session, several elements were highlighted that allowed the therapist to work with Hope toward a more positive outlook, even though she was experiencing trauma as a sex-trafficking survivor—and retraumatization at the hands of the justice system that was continuing to dictate her life. At the start of the session, she was feeling very down about her predicament and made several statements that had a negative outlook. At the end of the session, we closed out with a *scaling question*—a bit of an unorthodox location for a scaling question, but it helped expand the therapeutic experience beyond the session and instill a greater amount of hope.

CLINICIAN: Hope, I am wondering, when you came in you were feeling pretty down about this whole situation and your future. How are you feeling now, on a scale from zero to 10, 10 being you feel like it's amazing and awesome, and zero being the absolute worst?

HOPE: Well, I mean, I'd have to say like probably a four or five . . . maybe a three? I am not sure.

CLINICIAN: OK, so if you were to do something after our meeting that would make your life better . . . even if it were to only move a tiny bit . . . say from a four to a 4.5, what would that be? What would that look like?

HOPE: I mean. I don't know. I guess I could talk to the lawyer or something. Tell him that I need to know more about what's going on.

CLINICIAN: Would that help? You would feel better about that?

HOPE: Yeah, I mean . . . I would at least feel like I had more information. Maybe even control over what's going on.

CLINICIAN: Wow, even from a simple phone call you could start to feel like you had control over some things in your life?

HOPE: Well, yeah. I think I will do that. That sounds good.

CLINICIAN: That's great, Hope! I hope you do.

That was how the first session with Hope ended. To give you some closure, Hope continued treatment for about three months before her trial date concluded—in which she testified against her former pimp. She was strong and courageous and was able to be part of the team that made sure he went to jail for his crimes. She was able to see herself as a capable woman, and she returned to her family in New Mexico shortly after the trial ended and cleared to leave the city. They welcomed her back, and at last talk—she was enrolling in a cosmetology internship while continuing therapy.

■ SUMMARY

Sex trafficking is a serious social problem that is often exacerbated unintentionally by the law enforcement process. This can retraumatize survivors and lead to even higher rates of unintended consequences such as depression, anxiety, and PTSD symptoms. SFBT is one of the few types of existing therapy that can specifically help victims by focusing on resilience and strengths instead of focusing on the problems.

In addition, as highlighted in the above case study, retraumatization is lessened by the fact that SFBT does not focus intently on the past but instead focusing on the future. As such, clients are not required to revisit and continually rehash the traumatizing situation. Questions that focus on the ability of the client to survive, as well as questions that highlight their abilities to overcome a situation, can lead to a different outlook. Many people who have suffered through a significant trauma think of the past and what happened to them with a significant negative slant. Instead, consider what it would be like if they reformulated those memories with a positive slant? In our work with sex- and human-trafficking survivors, we have seen that a focus on coping skills and survival abilities leads to an increase in a patient's resilience and self-confidence.

■ REFERENCES

Carter, L., & Obadi, L. (2016, May). *An overview of human trafficking and domestic violence.* Presentation at the Mercer University School of Medicine Master of Family Therapy Program Clinic Meeting, Atlanta, GA.

Kutnick, B., Belser, P., & Danailova-Trainor, G. (2007). *Methodologies for global and national estimation of human trafficking victims: Current and future approaches.* Geneva, Switzerland: International Labour Office.

Miller, S. D., Duncan, B. L., & Hubble, M. (Eds.). (1996). *Handbook of solution-focused brief therapy.* San Francisco: Jossey-Bass.

U.S. Department of State. (2010). *Trafficking in persons report: 2010.* Washington, DC: U.S. Government Printing Office.

U.S. Department of State. (2015). *Trafficking in persons report: 2015.* Washington, DC: U.S. Government Printing Office.

Wellspring Living. (2016, April). *Wellspring living networking webinar: Survivors Series: Mitigating challenging behavior of trafficked youth.* Presentation at the Wellspring Living Monthly Seminar Series, Atlanta, GA.

15 Vicarious Resilience

■ ADAM S. FROERER,
JACQUI VON CZIFFRA-BERGS,
JOHNNY S. KIM, AND ELLIOTT E. CONNIE

Much of this book's focus has been on the various types of trauma that clients may experience throughout their lives. In addition, we have devoted a considerable amount of space to discussing SFBT and why this approach is useful. We have attempted to illustrate that SFBT helps to shift the focus and emphasis from the trauma and trauma symptoms to a more helpful preferred future that highlights strengths, resources, and resiliency through a focus on language. We have advocated that SFBT clinicians should not get distracted by the magnitude or details of the client's trauma; rather, they should listen with an attentive ear to see through these problematic details to find who the client really is and who they would like to become despite their traumatic histories.

Obviously the main thrust of this book is about the clients and their amazing abilities that are retained despite some horrific experiences. It makes sense that this book would focus on how clinicians can work to help clients in meaningful ways. However, it is important to take a moment and also think about the impact this work can have on the clinicians themselves. There has been much that has been said about *burnout, compassion fatigue, secondary traumatic stress, empathic stress,* and *vicarious trauma* (Edelkott, Engstrom, Hernandez-Wolfe, & Gangsei, 2016) as a result of working regularly with clients managing trauma experiences. There is a body of literature devoted entirely to the trauma clinicians can experience just from encountering and working with clients who have experienced firsthand trauma. However, there is also a growing body of research that highlights the incredible positive impact this work can have on clinicians, especially when they help clients focus on their strengths, resources, and resilience. Clinicians can become more and more vicariously resilient by working with the successes of their clients (Tassie, 2015).

■ VICARIOUS RESILIENCE

Vicarious resilience may include the following components: (1) being positively affected by the resilience of clients, (2) having an alteration of the clinician's own perspective about their own life, (3) perceiving that the therapy was valuable,

(4) some personal growth or transformation experienced by the clinician, and (5) feelings of gratification or happiness as a result of doing this helping work (Frey, Beesley, Abbott, & Kendrick, 2017). In addition to vicarious resilience, researchers have also begun looking at concepts such as *compassion satisfaction* (feelings of fulfillment with clients; Radey & Figley, 2007, p. 207, quoted in Edelkott, Engston, Hernandez-Wolfe, & Gangsei, 2016, p. 714), and *vicarious posttraumatic growth* (Arnold, Calhoun, Tedeschi, & Cann, 2005, quoted in Edelkott, Engston, Hernandez-Wolfe, & Gangsei, 2016, p. 714) that results in self-perception changes, changes to interpersonal relationships, and changes in life philosophies.

Although there isn't much research available yet on vicarious resilience as it relates to SFBT, we have our own anecdotal evidence that helps us to know that we have become more happy and resilient from working in this way. We believe that other clinicians have also experienced this pleasant by-product of SFBT. Although this might be an unusual approach to addressing the benefits of working from this approach, the rest of this chapter contains examples from each of us about how we have become more resilient because of our solution focused work. We hope that by reading our examples, you will remember some of your own examples of vicarious resilience.

■ ADAM FROERER

I am so lucky to be able to work with students and clinicians (new clinicians all the way to experienced-level clinicians) in a training capacity. I regularly get to teach and train others to use SFBT. Through this work, as well as my own clinical work, I have heard many personal and second-hand trauma stories and experiences. I have worked in juvenile justice centers, pediatric oncology/hematology units, community agencies with underserved populations, and in college counseling centers. I have been exposed to more trauma stories than I ever imagined as I was growing up in such a privileged situation. However, I love this work because I also have been on the receiving end of *many* stories of growth, strength, and resiliency. I count myself very fortunate to be able to do this type of work. I am continuously amazed at the abilities of people and their willingness to push through hardship. I feel my own level of optimism rise, my resiliency to endure improve, and my hope for something better increase each time I hear about the successes of others around me. I am so grateful that I can be in a field where I get to help people focus on what is going well and what they hope for in life. I am buoyed by the greatness of people!

One of the events that has been particularly impactful to me recently came from one of the participants in an online course Elliott and I taught together. At the end of the 16-week course, one of the participants sent Elliott and me an e-mail with her endorsement of the course. She asked if we would be willing to share it with other clinicians who were contemplating taking our course in the future. Although it was very kind of her to write this endorsement, I didn't expect to read what was contained in the endorsement about her personal life. Here is an excerpt from the e-mail:

> I will say up front that I'm bias [sic]. I took Elliott and Adam's SFBT online class. It was the most life changing experience I've had in a very long time. Not only did it change the way I work with clients, it had a profound effect on me personally.
>
> Here's what I mean: On Saturday before Thanksgiving I went to Target [shopping center]. As I was leaving, I was the victim of a failed (thank goodness) terrorist attack. This event lead to PTSD symptoms for the next 24 hours-that is until I thought of Elliott's books and started going through the transcripts and answer [sic] the questions as though he was asking me the SFBT questions. That exercise pulled me back to my normal life.
>
> The next event that occurred in my life, which SFBT has had a profound affect [sic] on, is a stroke. A few weeks ago I had a stroke. (Elliott and Adam are learning this as of this post.) Fortunately I am expected to make a full recovery. Yet, it has affected my short term memory.
>
> Once again, I'm finding that going back through the course materials has greatly boosted my ST memory coming back. I will also say, that while I'm not seeing clients at this time I did speak with a client by phone that was having a crisis. I was amazed at how the SFBT questions came pouring out of my mouth. My client knew nothing of my stroke situation and later reported how much that session helped.
>
> In thinking about this through my foggy mind, the only thing I could think of was that the course had instilled the skills in my long-term memory.
>
> Would I call myself an expert yet, no. But even at a level that isn't anywhere near that of Elliott and Adam, SFBT can change lives. (Both personally and professionally)."

Getting this e-mail was one of the highlights of my professional career. Knowing that SFBT had been so helpful to this individual during two separate traumatic events was inspiring and gave me an added understanding of what this way of thinking can accomplish. It is humbling to know that the work I did could have such an impact on others. I was reminded, yet again, that people are absolutely amazing, and that we can talk to these amazing people and learn from their greatness!

A follow up e-mail from the same participant came to Elliott and me a few months later. Although the news was not good, I was astounded and humbled by the contents of the e-mail yet again. Below is an excerpt from the follow-up e-mail.

> It is probably not every day that you receive an email like this from one of your students and fans. The purpose is to let you know why I can't attend the July event, which I had so looked forward to. I hope I will be able to attend January's.

It is also to ask for moral support, thoughts and prayers . . . here is why: In [sic] February I blacked out one evening while sitting in my comfy chair reading. The next day I started making doctors appointments to get checked out. Then a month later I started having a migraine. This continued for two weeks. My friend insisted I go to an Urgent Care Clinic. I don't know what triggered the doctor there to do a Pet Scan [sic], but upon reviewing the results he immediately called an ambulance and had me transported to the Medical Center.

This particular Medical Center, unbeknownst to me, is one of the top Neurosurgical Centers [sic] in the U.S. The head of the department decided to take on my case himself.

What they had found was a Glioblastoma (GBM for short) Grade 4 Brain Tumor. The doctor was able to get it all and thank goodness it had not yet begun to "spider web" into my brain.

Next Monday I begin radiation and oral chemotherapy.

If you read the prognosis for this type of "very aggressive" brain cancer it is daunting at best.

I see this as an opportunity to use Solution Focus in a way to help not only myself, but others to stay positive and determined in the face of the most difficult time of life.

This is where I'm asking for your help. If you could have any suggestions as to questions I can ask myself should any doubt or negativity creep in, I'd love to hear what you have to say.

So far I've only had one moment of doubt. At that point I asked myself, what can I do, visualize and say to myself in this moment that will let me know that I'm fine in this moment and have a future to look forward to.

The answer was to stay strong to faith, believe in miracles and know this journey can be used to help others. (Helping others in a strong driving force for me. . . .)

I do indeed want to help others through their difficult medical times and I figure the best way to do that is to start with myself.

If it weren't for you two and your brilliant on-line course, I don't think I'd be in a great mental place for this journey. I love you both for what I've learned from you already and just want to learn more.

Thank you for your time and input."

What an amazing e-mail! What an outstanding person! What a boost she was to me and the other people around her. Yes, it was difficult to hear about the ongoing challenges and traumas this woman encountered, but if all we did was focus on the hardship, we would have missed hearing about her positivity, her willingness to help other people, her ability to remember details at a time when she needed to, and her outstanding ability to "pull [herself] back to [her] normal life." This is just one story that has encouraged me to keep using and promoting SFBT. I feel infinitely grateful that people trust me enough to share the most intimate details of their lives with me. More than that, I feel compelled to be a better person because I get to hear so many accounts of people at their best! I want to be my best so that I can help others see themselves at their best. It is an honor to be able to do this work.

■ JACQUI VON CZIFFRA-BERGS

Practicing in one of the most violent societies in the world, my practice often left me feeling disillusioned and burned out. With the continuous exposure to the horror clients experience and the incredible hurt that people go through, I not only started fearing my job but also going outside; and so a rollercoaster ride with my practice began. I would be able to be attentive to the trauma stories for about three years and then feel the need to change careers; then I would go lecture again and get some distance from the trauma.

During one of my lecturing phases I was fortunate enough to travel to the United States, where I attended a workshop by Steve de Shazer, which changed my life forever. Here was a man who listened differently and who asked such unexpected questions. For the first time, I witnessed a client thinking and taking part in his own therapy, and so my journey in and passion for SFBT started. At the same conference, I also attended a workshop by Yvonne Dolan on solution-focused therapy and trauma. Again a light bulb moment exploded in my head and I realized that I had been asking all the wrong questions. Without intending to do so, I had been retraumatizing my clients and myself by highlighting the fear and reflecting only the negative feelings during the trauma. I was allowing the client to leave my office with only half the story being told. Not once had I asked my clients to expand on what they did during (or after) the trauma that they were proud of, or what they wanted from therapy that would be useful to them. Not once had I asked a client how they coped or how they envisioned the future. It never occurred to me to expand on the little aspects of control, bravery, and remarkable strengths people show during or after a trauma; and without intending to do so, I was keeping my clients stuck in the trauma by highlighting only what went wrong. In retrospect I believe I was also keeping myself stuck in a trauma loop of constantly hearing only how people feel and how terrifying life can be.

Realizing that people "bounce back" (Bannink, 2014, p. 19) and are resilient and even grow in the wake of trauma opened a whole new world for me. Becoming part of a journey that rebriefs resilience and celebrates bravery rather than a dance with terror by debriefing what went wrong changed my relationship with my practice and allows me to love my job again. Once I started acknowledging and honoring that clients who have experienced trauma enter a session with hope—a hope to feel better or cope better—I started building on the already existing hope and allowed hope to grow.

Once I started looking with a solution-focused lens and listening with a solution-focused ear to my client's story; amazing things happened to me and my clients. As a solution-focused brief therapist I am continuously amazed at my clients' ability to cope and handle a traumatic experience. Instead of being exhausted after a session with a client that has experienced a trauma, I now feel inspired by my clients. Where once my clients' stories made me fear going outside, I now feel I too can conquer whatever comes my way. No longer do I need to run away from my practice and go lecture at a university, I now look forward to a practice with a "waiting room full of heroes" (Macdonald, 2011, p. 36). Listening to trauma in a different way has made me see how incredible people are, how resilient people can be, and how brave people become.

Working from a solution-focused paradigm has also affected the way in which I deal with traumatic events that I have experienced in my own life. My solution-focused mindset has enabled me to be honest about my own resilience and acknowledge that I, too, have resources and attributes that help me cope and conquer hard times. I have found that it has also had a huge impact on the way I treat my family. I am much more trusting of my children and husband's ability to cope, make a plan, and deal with difficult circumstances. I now believe in their inner strength and their abilities to bounce back. The philosophy and beliefs of SFBT have become my default way of looking at life, and I am truly thankful for this new life and new way of viewing my world.

I truly believe that solution-focused questions have also rewired my brain and allowed new strength-based, positive, and hopeful neural pathways to establish. I do not consider myself to be a naturally positive and optimistic person; however, SFBT has created a wonderful counterbalance in my brain and has allowed me to see my clients, myself, and my family in a more positive and hopeful way. Even though my practice is still filled with trauma referrals, I am no longer disillusioned by people. Instead, I feel proud of people's abilities to handle life, and I now have a "bring it on" approach to my work and to whatever might happen.

■ JOHNNY KIM

After my undergraduate studies, I volunteered for a year in a service program called the Jesuit Volunteers Corps (JVC), which provides an opportunity for men and women to work for social justice in the United States. I was assigned as a case manager for a community mental health agency in Seattle, Washington, and it was this experience that led me to a career in social work. I worked with clients who had severe and persistent mental illness and were unable to work due to their mental illness. It was intense work but so rewarding that I decided to do a second year in Aberdeen, Washington, working in another community mental health agency before continuing on to my master's degree in social work (MSW). After my MSW, I continued to work in challenging and high-burnout jobs such as a low-income housing program where I worked with former homeless individuals, I worked in a hospital emergency room doing psychiatric evaluations, and eventually I took a job as a school social worker at the Art Institute of Seattle. (It was here that in my first week of work a student committed suicide by jumping out of a student housing building.) Across my various social work jobs, I experienced and witnessed job burnout and compassion fatigue due to the crisis nature of this line of work. There were many times throughout my clinical social work career where my colleagues and I discussed the challenges of working with clients who were constantly in crisis and felt hopeless about their future. Fortunately, I took a course in SFBT in Seattle and eventually conducted research on SFBT during my doctoral studies at the University of Texas at Austin, which allowed me to meet Insoo Kim Berg and Steve de Shazer.

Now as I teach and research SFBT, I am learning more about how this therapy approach can serve as a protective factor for clinicians who are working in high-stress and crisis-filled jobs. One of the constant themes I'd hear from my clients who received SFBT counseling as well as from students and clinicians trained in SFBT is how *hopeful* they felt after a session. As Reiter (2010) noted, "Hope is a major factor in therapy and one that therapists can help foster in clients" (p. 133). In contrast, *helplessness* is often experienced when clients are exposed to uncontrollable negative events (Seligman, as cited in Bannink, 2008). Prior to learning SFBT, I also often felt helpless working with some of my clients because I felt like I needed to solve their problems or have an answer for their current problem situation. Similarly, my clients often felt helpless and hopeless at their situation because all we would focus on is their problems in our session. Learning SFBT has taken this feeling of helplessness and hopelessness away not only for my clients but also for me as a social work clinician. This is because SFBT allows the client to define what their best hopes are and how they have been successful in the past. SFBT clinicians work at asking questions that help clients remember their strengths and successes and ways they can achieve their preferred future self where the problem is no longer there. Clients from all over the world are more likely to talk about their best hopes and success than their failures and crisis situations.

Recently an MSW student who took my SFBT course at the University of Denver met with me to discuss graduation plans as he was finishing up his degree. He told me how much he enjoyed using SFBT with his clients and was excited to be moving into his next phase of his social work career. He also shared a story with me about a recent client experience that reminds me of the power of focusing on client's best hopes. My student met a new client who was struggling with depression and clearly upset. As he continued to use SFBT in his session, the client reported that this session felt different than all the other counseling sessions she attended. She reported that she usually couldn't finish a session without breaking down in tears and often had to end sessions early because she just couldn't continue talking about her problems. However, this SFBT session felt different to her, and she managed to do an entire session without breaking down in tears and saying how hopeful she felt. My student told me that he remembered early on in our SFBT class that I had shared stories with them about how clients will report this approach as different and how I had repeated the same words that were coming out of his client's mouth. It gives me hope that years later the same will hold true about the power of SFBT for both the clinician and client.

■ ELLIOTT CONNIE

I wish I could tell you that I have an easy life, but I can't. I know that everyone has their trials and tribulations, and I should not expect to be an exception. However, my journey seems to be littered with more than my fair share of difficulties. For example, I was born on the South Side of Chicago, and all I can remember from those early years is extremely violent fights between my mother and father. At too young an age I knew that it was time to get my little brother and hide in my room until it was safe to come out.

The first glimmer of hope occurred when my parents let my brothers and I know that we would be moving to Boston. I remember being so excited about this move. As a four-year-old I had a silly thought: I assumed that the fighting sort of lived in our home in Chicago. Like it was literally something that habituated the home and took over my parents' behavior. The good news was that a move meant the fighting would be left behind. Even at my current age, I still remember the journey to Boston, I don't think I stopped smiling the whole time. It was as if we were discovering a new world. Sadly, it didn't take long for me to realize the flaw in my thinking. Alas, the fighting had moved with us.

By my teenage years the fighting had been directed toward my brothers and me. By this time my parents had separated and begun divorce proceedings that would not be finalized until I was in graduate school; however, during visitation with my father the violence commenced. I had to develop some habits to protect myself, and unfortunately not all of these habits were positive. For example, I learned to lie. I had to. When your violent father asks, "How is school going?" there is no way you can tell the truth . . . no way. Lying helped me get through.

I also learned to avoid confrontation; instead I tried to please people. Being weak is a much easier way to survive in a hostile environment than being strong, so I was weak. My confidence suffered throughout my teens and well into my college years. I thought of myself as weak, stupid, untruthful. Basically every bad characterization I knew of, I readily accepted about myself. Later in life, I fought to shed these demons and to remove these labels that I had picked up so I could be the person I was destined to be.

Now, as I look back and address the question of how working with people who have experienced a trauma using SFBT affects me, I have a strong response.

Over the years the clients I have seen have helped me far more than I could have ever helped them. Through doing this work I learned that there was nothing wrong with me; I was just responding to the environment I was raised in. That may seem like an obvious realization, but to me it was groundbreaking. It literally changed my life. Over the years I had the pleasure of sitting with clients who have had some of the most atrocious experiences in life, far more than anything I have experienced, and these clients have kept going. They kept dreaming of a brighter day and believing it was possible. When they slipped up, they forgave themselves and carried on. What's more, I would never dream of seeing my clients as anything other than their very best despite challenging circumstances. Then, at some point it hit me. If I could see my clients as doing their best then perhaps I could think of myself as doing my best.

I said that it was an honor to be a psychotherapist and to be able to work with clients in their times of need, and I mean exactly that. In fact, it is one of the greatest privileges of my life and one for which I will never truly be able to express my gratitude. Doing this work has given my trials purpose and given my life meaning. In this book I hope you picked up some ideas on how to use the solution-focused approach with clients who have been through a trauma; but more than that, I hope you were reminded of just how amazing people are. I hope you were able reconnect with your own sense of pride and purpose for this work that we do. I hope that from now on when you see clients you will see their hope, their strength, their resilience, and their capacity to change. Even in moments when the client seems to be hiding their brilliance from you, seemingly on purpose, keep believing in them.

In those inevitable moments when that task gets too daunting, remember your own strength. Remember your own journey. If that is too tough, remember mine. Remember that I spent much of my youth contemplating suicide yet was able to overcome those demons to live a different life. More than anything, remember that I am not special.

■ CONCLUSION

We hope that this book has given you added insights and helped you know that using SFBT with clients managing trauma can be beneficial, but most importantly we hope that this book has reminded you that people are amazing! We hope that as a result of this book you are more likely to look for and find the greatness in each of the clients you encounter. We hope that you are strengthened as you hear about their strength. We hope that you are more resilient because you get to learn about their resilience. We hope that you are more determined than ever to help people who have experienced trauma to begin describing what will be different when their best hopes are present.

■ REFERENCES

Arnold, D., Calhoun, L. G., Tedeschi, R., & Cann, A. (2005). Vicarious posttraumatic growth in psychotherapy. *Journal of Humanistic Psychology, 45*, 239–263.

Bannink, F. (2014). *Post-traumatic success*. New York: W. W. Norton.

Bannink, F. P. (2008). Posttraumatic success: Solution-focused brief therapy. *Brief Treatment and Crisis Intervention, 8*(3), 215–225.

Edelkott, N., Engstrom, D. W., Hernandez-Wolfe, P., & Gangsei, D. (2016). Vicarious resilience: Complexities and variations. *American Journal of Orthopsychiatry, 86*(6), 713–724.

Frey, L. L., Beesley, D., Abbott, D., & Kendrick E. (2017). Vicarious resilience in sexual assault and domestic violence advocates. *Psychological Trauma: Theory, Research, Practice, and Policy, 9*(1), 44–51.

MacDonald, A. (2011). *Solution focused therapy*. London: SAGE.

Radley, M., &Figley, C. (2007). The social psychology of compassion. *Clinical Social Work Journal, 35*, 207–214.

Reiter, M. D. (2010). Hope and expectancy in solution-focused brief therapy. *Journal of Family Psychotherapy, 21*, 132–148.

Seligman, M. E. P. (2002) *Authentic happiness*. New York: Free Press.

Tassie, A. K. (2015). Vicarious resilience from attachment trauma: Reflections of long-term therapy with marginalized young people. *Journal of Social Work Practice, 29*(2), 191–204.

Adam S. Froerer, PhD, LMFT, is the associate program director for the master's of family therapy program and an associate professor of psychiatry and behavioral sciences at Mercer University's School of Medicine. Adam received his master's degree in marriage and family therapy from the University of Oregon and his PhD a in marriage and family therapy from Texas Tech University. Adam is a solution-focused trainer with BRIEF International and a member of the Solution Focused Brief Therapy Association Research Committee.

Jacqui von Cziffra-Bergs, D.Ed Psych, M.Ed Psych, B.Ed, B.Prim Ed, was an associate professor at the University of Johannesburg and still teaches at universities across South Africa on a consultancy basis. She is an educational psychologist from Johannesburg, South Africa, and teaches SFBT to psychologists, social workers, counselors, and teachers. Dr Jacqui runs the Solution Focused Institute of South Africa, which is an organization that aims to teach and promote world-class training in SFBT.

Johnny S. Kim, PhD, MSW, LICSW, is an associate professor at the University of Denver Graduate School of Social Work. Dr. Kim received his master's degree in social work from Boston College, a PhD in social work from the University of Texas at Austin, and was a Council on Social Work Education Minority Clinical Fellow. He is chair of the Solution Focused Brief Therapy Association Research Committee and serves on the editorial boards of *Encyclopedia of Social Work Online, Journal of the Society for Social Work and Reserch,* and *Children & Schools.* He has published over 50 articles in peer reviewed journals, book chapters, and books.

Elliott E. Connie, MA, is a licensed professional counselor who has spent his entire counseling career working with individuals, couples, families, and groups. He founded and oversees the Solution Focused University, an online community that holds multiple training sessions on this approach, including an annual conference, workshops, and seminars. He maintains a full private practice with couples, children, and families. Mr. Connie is the co-editor of *The Art of Solution Focused Therapy* with Linda Metcalf as well as the author of *The Solution Focused Marriage* and *Solution Building in Couples Therapy.* He has also conducted numerous training sessions and has presented widely around the world.

■ INDEX

Page numbers followed by *f*, *t*, and *b* indicate figures, tables, and boxes.